Positive Solitude

Positive Solitude

A Practical Program for Mastering Loneliness and Achieving Self-Fulfillment

Rae André, Ph.D.

HarperPerennial
A Division of HarperCollins*Publishers*

Acknowledgments appear on page ix.

A hardcover edition of this book was published in 1991 by HarperCollins Publishers.

HarperCollins books may be purchased for educational, businesss, or sales promotional use. For information, please call or write: Special Markets Department, HarperCollins Publishers, Inc., 10 East 53rd Street, New York, NY 10022. Telephone: (212) 207-7528; Fax: (212) 207-7222.

First HarperPerennial edition published 1992.

Designed by C. Linda Dingler

The Library of Congress has catalogued the hardcover edition as follows:

André, Rae.
    Positive solitude : a practical program for mastering loneliness and achieving self-fulfill-
ment / Rae André. — 1st ed.
      p. cm.
    Includes bibliographical references and index.
    ISBN 0-06-016522-7 (cloth)
    1. Loneliness. 2. Solitude—Psychological aspects. 3. Self-actualization
(Psychology). I. Title.
BF575.L7A69   1991   90-55524
158'.2—dc20

ISBN 0-06-092256-7 (pbk.)

92 93 94 95 96 CC/HC 10 9 8 7 6 5 4 3 2 1

To my father

Contents

Preface

It is 7:30 P.M. and you are at home alone. You have read the paper and eaten your supper. The early evening programs are lousy. Since you have been alone quite a lot lately and have had some bad feelings about it, you decide to spend some time thinking about your situation. You reach for a book on loneliness. Maybe it will help you to understand the times of boredom and the moments of pain that you experience when you are alone. Perhaps the author will help you to understand your loneliness and to get over it. After a couple of hours, you put the book down. You are disappointed to realize that reading it hasn't helped. Your feelings of loneliness are worse than ever. Now you are depressed because even the experts have little to teach you about solving your problem. Feeling sad and lonely, you reach for something alcoholic and flip on the tube. . . .

Something like this once happened to me. Some years ago, I found myself unexpectedly divorced. Within two months of the divorce, my mother died. A few months later, my best friends decided to move to another city. I had no children. Except for college and for week-long periods of marital separation for career reasons, I had never lived alone. Suddenly, I faced the 7:30 syndrome: Each night, hour upon hour lay ahead of me. "What do you do alone at 7:30 at night when you are tired and there are still three or four waking hours to go?" I asked myself. What does one do about loneliness?

For an answer I turned to my lifelong friends—authors both known and new. I read widely in popular books and academic books, personal accounts and research studies. Usually, in my reading I find solace and new beginnings. Yet, surprisingly, after most encounters with works on loneliness, I emerged somewhat more lonely and depressed than before. I learned from them how widespread the problem of loneliness is, that there has been relatively little research on it, and that little is known about how to "cure" it. In short, I learned a lot of depressing things about being alone.

I knew I had to find something else—something more hopeful. Yet as I read more, I became increasingly frustrated. I started talking back to my books: "How come you people are so down? Why are you so depressing about the fact that someone is alone? What is the big deal here? People have been alone for centuries: There is probably an honorable tradition in being alone, if you would only look for it!" This was my anger talking.

My intellect also had a few words to say. As a psychologist, I asked myself, "What is loneliness, really?" Is it an emotion, something biological like anger or fear? Or is it something cognitive, an interpretation we humans have created to make sense of the circumstance of being alone? I guessed that if we choose to view loneliness as an inevitable emotion or as a sickness caused by the "disease" of being alone, then we will not get far in overcoming it. On the other hand, if the idea of loneliness is mainly our interpretation of events, then, like all such ideas, it is subjective; it should be scrutinized and, most important, it can be changed.

I asked myself one more question: Had I ever, even once, been happy while alone? Think about it, I coached. Had I ever once enjoyed the blue spring sky while walking alone down the street? Ever once enjoyed a piece of music while lying on the couch alone? Ever once enjoyed a good book alone? Of course, I had. And if I had done it once, I could do it again and again. However unhappy I had been at times, there had always been moments of peace and glimmers of joy in my life. These moments might have been triggered by ordinary events— by seeing my cat basking happily in the sun or by noticing the bright sunbeam itself. For an instant I would take pleasure in the event or I would find solace in it. If I could feel positive emotions when I was alone, even for a moment, I thought, why couldn't I build on that experience to feel positive alone for many moments—even for most of my life?

My experience being alone, interpreted through my professional knowledge as a psychologist, has convinced me that, gradually, thought by thought, action by action, we can alleviate the suffering of people who say they are lonely. On the basis of the actual behaviors and experiences of individuals who are willing to describe their pain, we can develop a practical understanding of loneliness. What is even more hopeful, by carefully rethinking the problem of loneliness, we can help ourselves and each other to become well-adjusted, contented human beings who only happen to be alone.

I began to do research on loneliness and solitude when I realized that I wanted on my own bookshelf a practical handbook that would take a positive view of being alone. I needed to know *how to do it,* and I wanted that advice to consult whenever I needed it—whenever I felt that I was falling into the loneliness traps created by my old belief system about being alone, whenever I faced a psychological problem alone. The book that you have in your hands describes such a way of living. It is the way of positive solitude.

I have written this book for people who are currently alone and who feel, for want of a better idea, "lonely." I have written it for people who want to solve this problem of "loneliness." I have also written it for those people who enjoy being alone most of the time but who want to get even more out of their solitude. Positive solitude is not only about solving the problem of loneliness; it is about using solitude as a means to self-fulfillment.

You may wonder whether pursuing solitude is merely ignoring the inevitable problem of loneliness. Is it repressing loneliness on Monday with the implication that it will return to bruise your psyche on Thursday? We will talk about this issue in detail later in the book, but up front, let me assert that I do not think so.

In some sense, we are, all of us, alone. The emotions we feel when we are alone—as when we are in company—are deeply human. Sometimes when we are alone, we experience negative emotions that are directly associated with our aloneness—for example, sadness or fear. Experiencing these emotions is natural. And sometimes when we are alone, we experience negative emotions that are not directly associated with our aloneness—for example, jealousy or hatred. These emotions, too, are natural. But none of these emotions controls your life. If you take charge of your life, you can also experience positive states and emotions when alone. You can experience emotions like elation, contentment, challenge, curiosity, and even love frequently and continuously. Few people will ever eliminate their negative emotions, but you can learn to put them into perspective. You experience negative emotions not because you are alone and not because you are repressing loneliness, but because you are human.

Today one of society's major difficulties is separateness. People are searching for roots and connections. In our longing for connections, we should consider that being part of a couple or part of a family does not solve all life's problems either. Your problems, especially your psychological ones, will not be solved by your friends. Togetherness is not the total answer. Being alone is not the total answer either, of course, but *solitude is much more of an answer than we think it is.*

Why not give positive solitude a chance in your life? You will find yourself in the company of artists, religious figures, writers, political thinkers, and many other wise people who have sought new paths. Of course, there will be things about being alone that you won't prefer. But, then, you would probably prefer to look like a model, too, yet you nevertheless have adjusted to being less than airbrushed perfect. Being alone may not be your preferred way of living right now, but is that any reason to let being alone ruin your life? You can be alone and not feel bad about it. You can be alone and feel happy. With experience, being alone may even become your preferred way of living most of the time.

If there is any single memory on the subject of being alone that most Americans hold in common, it is probably Wordsworth's lines:

> I wandered lonely as a cloud
> That floats on high o'er vales and hills . . .

If you are anything like me, you only vaguely recall the "o'er vales and hills" phrase, and what remains of the poem in your memory is the image of one's poor lonely self wandering miserably over a desolate landscape. But—how human!—this memory fragment is flawed. We tend to forget that Wordsworth's full poem had a different and happier message about being alone. Do you remember the daffodils?

I wandered lonely as a cloud
That floats on high o'er vales and hills,
When all at once I saw a crowd,
A host, of golden daffodils;
Beside the lake, beneath the trees,
Fluttering and dancing in the breeze.

Continuous as the stars that shine
And twinkle on the milky way,
They stretched in never-ending line
Along the margin of a bay:
Ten thousand saw I at a glance,
Tossing their heads in sprightly dance.

The waves beside them danced; but they
Outdid the sparkling waves in glee:
A poet could not but be gay,
In such a jocund company;
I gazed—and gazed—but little thought
What wealth the show to me had brought:

For oft, when on my couch I lie
In vacant or in pensive mood,
They flash upon that inward eye
Which is the bliss of solitude;
And then my heart with pleasure fills,
And dances with the daffodils.[1]

This book is dedicated to all people who, whether by chance or by choice, are alone, and who wish to fill their souls not with remorse, but with flowers.

Notes

1. William Wordsworth, "I Wandered Lonely as a Cloud," *Norton Anthology of English Literature,* Vol. 2 (New York: W. W. Norton & Co., 1962), 115–16.

Introduction

All human beings are vulnerable to the alienation and anxiety so often experienced by a person who is alone. Especially in our rootless American culture, being alone can lead quickly to loneliness. Today one-quarter of all American households consist of one person. Some of us are uncomfortable being alone without really knowing why. Others are ashamed of being alone. Many, perhaps even most, actually fear being alone. Decades ago, sociologist David Riesman labeled us the "lonely crowd": a people proud of our independence while in reality dependent on others to give us our direction.[1] The truth is that as Americans, we cherish our tradition of rugged individualism, but we know little about how to live it.

Our efforts to join with others do not give us solace. We seek love, but we do not find it. We find that our lives remain if not totally empty, then unfulfilled. Sometimes we try to fill the void by learning what amounts to a fashionable helplessness, giving ourselves up to the pursuit of toys, status symbols, and entertainments. At other times, we keep ourselves busy in the pursuit of relationships because we do not know what else to do. We join singles groups, we play the personals ads, and we pay money to matchmakers, all to avoid being alone. Yet the loneliness goes on. In our cities, it has been called an epidemic.

I believe that we have failed to solve the problem of loneliness because for decades we have been asking ourselves the wrong question. Over and over, in hundreds of ways, we have asked ourselves, "How can I find someone?" In the end, we remain incapable of solving the problem of loneliness because we fail to address the crucial fact that ultimately we are alone. We are completely separate from others; we are alone in the face of life. Only when we acknowledge this fact, when we find the courage to consider it fully, can we ask ourselves the right question: How can I make this solitude into a positive force in my life?

Loneliness, failing relationships, and the loss of community are central human problems of our times. I believe that we fail to solve these problems largely because we do not admit or understand that a fundamental element of a centered personality is the ability to be fulfilled alone. Modern writing and thinking about solitude have helped little. Far too much emphasis has been placed on leaving solitude by finding relationships, and far too little has been said about the positive aspects of being alone. Certainly, no one has attempted to develop a practical psychology for being alone.

Too many of us hold the belief that being alone will lead to unhappiness, self-pity, and depression. In short, we believe that being alone leads to loneliness. With so many people living alone, this belief is a major national tragedy. Millions of people *expect* that being alone will cause a major personal crisis, and this expectation becomes a self-fulfilling prophecy. If they don't "find someone," they believe, their personal crisis will continue indefinitely.

This book sets forth a different belief system. I suggest here that our tragic American beliefs about being alone are largely an imaginary hell that we have created for ourselves—that in our modern society, these beliefs are too frightening and too negative. Thoughtful, mature individuals can bypass this negative belief system to develop *positive solitude*—the ability to think positively about being alone and to plan ways to live contentedly alone.

Positive solitude is an antidote to the despair of trying to "find someone." How often have you heard that you should strive to be a whole, fulfilled person because enthusiastic self-confidence is the ultimate come-on? In contrast, positive solitude suggests that being alone can be an end in itself. Problems of connectedness and community and love will be solved only when we take the radical step of really facing ourselves.

Only when we learn how to be alone, to live alone, and even to love alone—when we face our alienation, our vulnerability, our creativity, our uniqueness, our humanity, and our desires—will the problems of finding others and finding community become less urgent. Positive solitude is an intellectual and therapeutic tool that can help us to balance our society's overemphasis on relationships with a healthy emphasis on ourselves. With positive solitude, we discover that relationships, rather than being the goals of our lives, become explorations. Rather than being the ultimate answer, relationships become one interesting question.

Being alone has always been an existential fact of life. Yet though the human condition is to be separate, it is not necessarily to be lonely. In this book you will learn to view separation as a positive, life-giving experience that encourages the creative, the unique, and the powerful in each individual. In the words of author Melodie Beattie (Codependent No More), you will stop being codependent and start experiencing the serenity, peace, and love inherent in personal independence.

Learning positive solitude is a behavioral goal similar to losing weight or adopting an exercise program. While we cannot simply will loneliness away, we can learn to banish the negative feelings that we have when we are alone. We can learn to replace these feelings with positive experiences. We can learn loving attitudes. We can learn to value and explore ourselves. We can learn to love the relationship we build with ourselves.

Because of our mistaken beliefs about loneliness, the skill of positive solitude has been widely ignored. Americans do not think highly of people who are alone. We seldom emphasize the positive side of being alone, but see people who are alone as outsiders and failures. We frequently make negative assumptions about people who are alone. For example, if you or I see an old man dozing on a park bench, we are apt to think, "Look at that lonely old man." We assume that if he is old and alone, the man must feel lonely. We say of a widow that we hope that she will remarry, assuming that she cannot be "truly" happy now that she is alone. Of a bachelor we may ask, "When is Bob going to settle down?" Our assumption is that he will be happier living with someone else than living alone.

A particularly pernicious belief is that the ultimate way to cure loneliness is to find relationships. Alone, it is assumed, people cannot really conquer their loneliness; perhaps they can adjust to it, but they will never be truly happy. If a person has no relationships right now, friends, family members, and even strangers often assume that he or she is unhappy. Worse yet, many of us believe that people must find the *right* relationships to feel whole. One must have a spouse, and children, and intimate friends. One "should" be involved. By this way of thinking, if people are alone and feeling lonely, it is imperative that they find others, such as an "appropriate" mate, to reduce their loneliness.

Positive solitude refutes these beliefs, describing how loneliness can be reduced within yourself, by yourself. The first step to experiencing positive solitude is to believe that it is possible to do so. You can choose to view being alone as inevitably tragic or you can take a new approach: You can choose to view being alone as a positive, enlightening experience that is relaxing, creative, and much more. A point that I will emphasize over and over in this book is that we *choose* our attitude toward being alone and that the attitude that we adopt toward being alone will inevitably alter our experience of being alone.

Writers and thinkers who have shaped our attitudes toward solitude have themselves been affected by our culture's pervasive negativity toward aloneness. Psychological research, for example, focuses almost exclusively on loneliness, which has a negative connotation, rather than on aloneness, which has a neutral connotation. In questionnaires that study being alone, psychologists ask questions like, "How often have you been lonely?" and "What do you do when you feel lonely?" They do not ask "How often are you alone?" and "How do you feel when you are alone?" They do not ask, "How often are you happy when you are alone?" Thus, they do not start from a balanced perspective that would allow the person being questioned to reveal both the positive and the negative sides of solitude. In fact, they are really studying only the negative aspects of aloneness.

Similarly, most research studies are oriented toward solving the "problem" of loneliness rather than toward preventing negative emotions through the creation of a positive self-image. In the outmoded but still strong tradition of psychology as a healing art, many psychologists have wanted to "fix" loneliness—not to help people avoid loneliness in the first place.

These biases are natural, given the fact that researchers are human. Unfortunately, the published results of the research on loneliness add significantly to our culture's falsely negative view of being alone. For instance, one study of loneliness noted that only 1 to 2 percent of the people studied reported never having experienced loneliness and 10 to 30 percent had experienced cycles of pervasive loneliness most of their lives.[2] The researchers did not ask people how often they had experienced happiness when alone. Nor did the researchers ask whether they had experienced cycles of self-confidence and contentment during their lives. Had they done so, perhaps many people would have answered that they actually had experienced happiness when alone. Perhaps many would have said they had experienced self-confidence and contentment!

"Loneliness" is not the problem. It is likely that you will experience positive and negative feelings both when you are alone and when you are with others. Much of the psychological research on loneliness has done little more than prove once again the adage that if you ask the wrong question, you will get the wrong answer.

Writing that focuses on the positive aspects of being alone is scarce. It is this lack of other positive voices that may have contributed to the modern popularity of a writer from another century: Henry David Thoreau. Many people have been deeply touched by Thoreau's *Walden*. Our premier thinker on the spiritual value of solitude, Thoreau lived much of what he preached. "I had three chairs in my house; one for solitude, two for friendship, three for society," he wrote.[3] His magnificent work has led generations to "follow a different drummer," to explore enlightenment and contentment within themselves. As you read this book, you will understand how *Walden* has been an inspiration for my thinking about positive solitude.

In more recent years, several psychotherapists have made significant contributions to this subject. Author and psychotherapist Victor Frankl, a survivor of the Nazi concentration camps, wrote about the emotional experiences of aloneness that he lived and witnessed there. Frankl later developed a therapeutic technique based on his belief that our central task in life is to discover the meaning of our individual lives. This discovery, he believed, is the key to experiencing a life that feels connected to other human beings. What is most important is that one must discover meaning by oneself, alone. Frankl's *logotherapy*—literally *meaning* therapy—has much to offer to people who are learning positive solitude.

Another psychotherapist, Clark E. Moustakas, has made extensive contributions to the thinking on loneliness in his books *Loneliness* and *Loneliness and Love.* Typical of Moustakas's beliefs is this statement:

> Solitude is a return to one's own self when the world has grown cold and meaningless, when life has become filled with people and too much of a response to others. Solitude is as much an intrinsic desire in man as his gregariousness. Hermits, solitary thinkers, independent spirits, recluses, although often stigmatized in the modern world, are healthy expressions of man's dialogue with himself. . . . It is unlike any other experience—not to have to respond to others, not to be stimulated or challenged by others, just to be alone.[4]

Moustakas's writing has sometimes been dismissed as too personal and philosophical—as not dispassionate enough for use by other professionals. Yet his readership has been broad. Many of his ideas echo those of positive solitude.

Extensive studies on sensory deprivation and the reduced environmental stimulation therapy (REST) technique pioneered by psychologist Peter Suedfeld and his associates have also made important contributions to positive solitude.

Apart from these writers, ideas on positive solitude are scattered.[5] Classical essayists Ralph Waldo Emerson and Michel de Montaigne held positive views of it. Poets, such as William Wordsworth, William Butler Yeats, and Rainer Maria Rilke, have looked favorably on being alone. Among contemporary writers, May Sarton, Anthony Storr, and Alice Koller are notable for their thoughtful consideration of being alone.

Yet for every account of positive solitude, there are dozens that bemoan the problems of loneliness. If creative thinking about positive solitude were more widespread, more ideas for taking advantage of time alone would be generated and shared, and loneliness would be allayed. Eventually, people would come to expect positive outcomes from their time alone. Instead of worrying about our loneliness, we would be looking ahead to growth and change. Instead of feeling anxious about relationships, we would be concerned about things like how to improve our personal creativity and how to put more meaning into our lives. These positive issues of personal growth are the kinds of "meta-grumbles"—to use Abraham Maslow's wonderful word—that mature and healthy human beings should be experiencing.

In the past decade, psychologists have taken an increased interest in loneliness. In 1979, the first major research conference on loneliness was held at the University of California at Los Angeles; since then, academics have worked increasingly on issues of loneliness. Though this book was not written primarily for researchers, I hope that by writing it, I will encourage more of them to work on positive solitude. The intellectual underpinnings of positive solitude derive from a rationalist tradition in psychology that emphasizes personal possibilities for psychological and behavioral self-management.[6] These approaches have been widely accepted by both researchers and therapists. Recent approaches in this self-management tradition include social learning theory, rational emotive theory, reinforcement theory, and cognitive behavior modification strategies. In this self-management tradition, the experience of being alone can be treated just like any other set of behaviors and attitudes. It is evaluated in terms of the satisfaction and health it brings to the individual. Self-management approaches adopt the optimistic and usually realistic view that a behavior that is learned is a behavior that can be changed. Since feeling lonely when alone is, as we have seen, a learned behavior, feeling content when alone is a behavior that can be adopted to replace the loneliness.

Some professionals will resist the positive solitude approach. Psychologists and psychiatrists with a strong belief in Freudian psychoanalytic theory often disagree with self-management techniques. Theorists in this tradition may argue that adopting a positive attitude toward being alone is an attempt to rationalize what they believe to be a deep-seated problem of loneliness. In fact, much of the early research on loneliness was done in the psychoanalytic tradition, which accounts for some of our American pessimism about people's ability to avoid loneliness. In contrast, I believe, and thousands of individuals who live happily alone would concur, that loneliness is neither innate nor inevitable.

It is true that many people are miserable alone. Do unconscious traces of their first experience with loneliness—the separation from their mothers—still exist somewhere within them? Perhaps. Yet for most of us, these traces are vestigial, and they probably affect us only slightly more than did the gills that we once sprouted as human embryos. Research in cognitive psychology over thirty years argues strongly that conscious mental processes and behaviors can be changed permanently. Today many psychological problems, from phobias to reduced self-esteem, are being relieved with the cognitive self-management approach. Therapist-authors in this tradition include Albert Ellis and Scott Peck. Writers who work from the same theory include Dale Carnegie and Leo Buscaglia. These authors' reasoned approaches are all based on the tradition of cognitive self-management, and, adapted for their individual styles, their approaches work. The positive solitude approach works in the same way. Though positive solitude cannot be achieved overnight, it definitely can, with time and practice, become a central mode of your psychological and spiritual life.

I want to point out that the psychological approach in this book is very much a product of my education in a Western, rather than an Eastern, culture. I will later describe in detail "the feedback gap" that occurs when a person is lonely, and I will suggest that people can learn to fill this gap well and productively. This is a distinctively active and pragmatic view that is characteristic of Western approaches to psychological problems. As Margaret Mead once pointed out, "The stiff upper lip, the well-known Anglo-Saxon fortitude, requires in the case of Americans replacement of the missing."[7] Over the past century, our Western, American philosophy for dealing with being alone has become ever more pragmatic. The Victorian American felt obliged to spend a long period mourning the loss of a loved one. Today "Americans on the whole disapprove of those who mope or are inconsolable over the memory of a particular place or person. It is no longer fashionable to die of love, to 'carry the torch' for a faithless love, to pine over a deserting husband, or to grieve long for the dead. In modern times the best compliment that the living can pay a deceased spouse is to marry again."[8] Mead pointed out that at a modern funeral it is common for people to hope that the widowed will marry again. In other words, in our modern Western culture, we not only seek to fill the feedback gap, we seek to fill it quickly.

The psychology of self-management is, of course, part of this Western philosophy: Here one *manages* change. Thus, the approach in this book should be a workable model for most Westerners. Non-Western cultures often emphasize other modes of coping with being alone. Some Eastern cultures stress, for example, a person's fate and the transcendence of loneliness through an exploration of that fate's mystical implications. Some of these approaches will be considered here. We should realize that these other modes of dealing with being alone may be appropriate for some individuals even within our culture. In fact, some of the more interesting material that I discovered on positive solitude integrates aspects of both Western and Eastern approaches. There is certainly more to be learned about positive solitude in different cultures. The in-depth study of Eastern approaches to solitude would be a fascinating exploration in its own right.

Given the pervasively negative views of being alone that are held in our society, the ideas of positive solitude will undoubtedly meet some skeptics. It is all very well to say that one can be happy alone, they will argue, but what about sex? What about touching? What about finding meaning in life without family or others nearby to love? What about having people around to laugh with? Positive approaches to these and other concerns about being alone are the core of this book. I will focus here on making positive solitude immediately applicable in your daily life. Based on the practical application of common sense and on sound psychological theories, I will describe new directions for you to explore when you are alone.

This book is only an introduction to being alone. It cannot fully describe the adventures and the problems, the pleasures and excitements, of life alone, but it shows a positive direction in which to travel. Simply, if a person is feeling lonely, this book bears the message that there is another way.

Writing this book has required and encouraged my own positive solitude. At the same time, I have found great satisfaction in the relationships I have made through this work. I would like to acknowledge, most gratefully, the assistance of David P. Boyd, Jim Goldberg, Robert Holder, Afsaneh Nahavandi, Marianne Penney, Diane Simpson, Marian Turner, Amy Wertheim, and several members of my family. I have also met personally many individuals who would prefer not to have their names mentioned here but who, in important conversations, shared their experiences most graciously and openly with me. Their help has deepened the meanings to be found here.

Notes

1. David Riesman, *The Lonely Crowd* (New Haven: Yale University Press, 1950).

2. Vello Sermat, "Some Situational and Personality Correlates of Loneliness," in Joseph Hartog, J. Ralph Audy, and Yehudi Cohen, eds., *The Anatomy of Loneliness* (New York: International Universities Press, 1980), 305.

3. Henry David Thoreau, *Walden* (Boston: Houghton Mifflin Co., 1960), 96.

4. Clark E. Moustakas, *Loneliness and Love* (Englewood Cliffs, N.J.: Prentice-Hall, 1972), 40–41.

5. Joseph Hartog, J. Ralph Audy, and Yehudi Cohen, eds., *The Anatomy of Loneliness* (New York: International Universities Press, 1980).

6. B. F. Skinner, "What Is Wrong with Daily Life in the Western World?" *American Psychologist* (May 1986): 568–74.

7. Margaret Mead, "Loneliness, Autonomy and Interdependence in Cultural Context," in Hartog, Audy, and Cohen, eds., *The Anatomy of Loneliness,* 397.

8. Ibid.

I
Exploring
Positive Solitude

1
Opening
Your Self to Solitude

We have a soul that can be turned
upon itself . . . in solitude be to thyself a throng.
—MICHEL DE MONTAIGNE, "Of Solitude"

Understanding the Feedback Gap

Human beings experience the world as a cycle of expectations and events. To survive and to thrive we all need feedback from our environment. Feedback gives us a feeling of normalcy: When we get the feedback we expect, our notion of how the world works is confirmed. Feedback also gives us the opportunity to learn: When we do not get the feedback we expect, we must figure out why.

Through feedback, we are constantly learning about our environment and adapting our behavior. This is not only a scientific way of viewing the world, but a commonsense view as well. Within this cycle we live our daily lives: we develop expectations about what will happen when we act, and we experience a range of emotions, from affirmation to surprise, when our expectations are either confirmed or quashed.

It is a physiological fact that if we are put into total sensory deprivation, our brains will invent the input that has been taken away from us. Deprived of sensory feedback, we will become disoriented and, within minutes, will begin to hallucinate. Likewise, human beings experience problems when our *social* feedback is disrupted. Social feedback from friends, family members, intimates, and even strangers plays an especially important role in our lives. Our attention to such feedback is only natural because, for thousands of years, being with others has helped human beings to survive.

The feedback cycle influences us every day. A simple illustration of this influence occurred recently when I went traveling for two weeks. I left my loudly affectionate Balinese cat with a friend, and she was not returned to me until one day after I had returned. During that day, I literally missed her. When I was eating breakfast, I expected her to come yowling to me for her food; when I sat at my desk, I expected her to crawl onto my lap; when I walked into the living room, I expected to find her curled up on the couch. You might casually conclude that I was lonely for her. Yet, if one understands the feedback cycle, it could also be said that when I no longer expect her, I will not feel lonely for her. When I do not perceive a feedback gap in my life, in a real sense there won't be one. One day, my cat will actually be gone from my life. Then, even though I may remember her sweet presence at times, I will not be lonely for her. Having learned to be good to myself, I will have filled the feedback gap left by her absence with something else that is meaningful.

When being alone leads to the feeling of loneliness, it is usually because the lonely person is experiencing a feedback gap. Something like this might happen to you if you have recently been divorced or widowed: You arrive home at 5:30 P.M. after a day at work, just as you have arrived home many times before, except this time there is no one there. You meet darkness and silence. Later that evening, you go to bed. There used to be a warm person there, but now the sheets are cold.

Or perhaps you have just moved into your first apartment alone. You sit down to eat your evening meal. Having been brought up in a family that usually ate dinner together and having lived in dorms or apartments with friends ever since, you feel odd eating alone. Maybe you are harried after a long day's work. You are used to having someone to talk things over with. Now there is no one there to soothe you.

This is the portrait of loneliness: actions that don't get reactions, gestures of love or need or hope that receive no confirmation. Whether the feedback you want from others is lost suddenly or gradually, you still expect it. Habitual pleasures have become fond expectations, and when you do not get them, you are disappointed.

When we are newly alone, the feedback cycle that we are accustomed to has been disturbed, and we have to create a fresh program for getting the feedback we want and need. People who say they are lonely are either not getting enough feedback or are getting the wrong kind of feedback. They may erroneously believe that they can fill the feedback gap only by being with others. Or it may simply not have occurred to them that they can fill the feedback gap themselves. They may lack confidence in their ability and creativity. Whatever the reason, they create a vicious circle. Because they believe they cannot fill the feedback gap themselves, they do not try. Because they do not try, they fail, and so they fall into helpless and hopeless loneliness.

Fortunately, there is an alternative. Being alone will become a positive experience when you learn to provide your own feedback, filling the feedback gap on your own initiative with satisfying emotional, intellectual, and physical experiences. There is a meaningful difference between filling the feedback gap in conventional, yet unsatisfying ways and filling it with positive solitude. Through the experience of positive solitude, you learn that you are not really dependent on others for your happiness. When you are not dependent, your prognosis for the likelihood of discovering happiness is good. You understand and experience personal autonomy, peace, and joy. You can banish the specter of loneliness. You can live your life creatively and fully.

Rethinking the Problem of Loneliness

To understand the problem of loneliness, we must realize that life has a way of unexpectedly disrupting our feedback cycle. Few people relish such disruptions. Once our expectations and plans for the future are decided upon, we want to be able to relax, and we even tend to become complacent. Soon we begin to think we are "all set," but, actually, we are only forgetting the truth about life: that change is inevitable.

Drastic disruptions in the feedback cycle take the form of deaths, divorces, and incapacitating illnesses. Other major disruptions also occur: the disruption of the relationship between a husband and a wife when a child is born, the changes that occur when lovers separate, or the changes brought on by retirement. Some of these changes can be expected, and you may be able to plan ahead to fill the feedback gap that will be left by them. When you can plan ahead, the feeling of emptiness that so often accompanies loneliness is lessened and may not even occur. Sometimes disruptions in the feedback cycle cannot be anticipated. These are especially troublesome because you will not be ready to fill the feedback gap that they cause.

Often in life feedback is simply inconstant. After the intensity of a family holiday season, you may experience the January blues: The feedback in your life has become much less intense. During a weekend spent at a therapeutic retreat involving many group activities, you can easily experience a feedback high. Afterwards, it is also typical to experience a significant letdown. You return to the less feedback-rich environment that characterizes your daily life, puzzling a bit over why the high cannot be maintained, maybe even blaming yourself for losing that intensity.

All people experience these variations in the feedback cycle. All of us face disruptions in our connections with the world. If we are to be well-adjusted human beings, we learn to deal with these situations. We learn how to fill the feedback gap. A basic principle of positive solitude is that it is essential to be able to fill the feedback gap by yourself. Whether a feedback gap opens gradually or suddenly, if you can fall back on yourself to fill it, you can live your life with a minimum of disruption and emotional discomfort. In the long term, the more self-reliant and creative you can become in filling the feedback gap, the more stable you will be.

When we do not know how to fill the feedback gap ourselves, we often say that we are lonely. What really is loneliness? After your tiring day at work, you come home to your dark apartment and imagine it would be much nicer if someone were there. When you eat alone and spend your evenings alone, you are often unhappy, and you say to yourself that you must be lonely. When you are physically alone—living alone, perhaps, or spending a great deal of time alone—blaming your unhappiness on the emotional disturbance, the "disease," of loneliness seems to be logical. It is natural for people who are alone to focus on loneliness as a "problem" to be solved. In fact, it is not surprising that many people focus on loneliness as the major emotional problem to be solved when their lives are not going well.

The newest behavioral-science research suggests that this way of thinking is actually a mistake, because interestingly enough, loneliness is not a true emotion. An emotion is "a set of distinct feelings that have observable and consistent physiological reactions." Psychologists have learned, however, that different people experience loneliness differently and that the experience of it is so inconsistent that what it is cannot be clearly identified. Anger, in contrast, is a true emotion. When people are angry, they demonstrate a consistent pattern of responses. Their blood pressure goes up, they get red in the face, they clench their muscles, and they are generally agitated. Fear is another true emotion. Its consistent pattern includes a faster heartbeat, sweating, and dilation of the pupils. Unlike anger and fear, loneliness has no consistent, unique physiological expression. It is not a discrete, identifiable emotional experience.

Loneliness has been described by its sufferers as everything from feelings of emptiness and boredom to the experience of angst and desperation. Some lonely people are primarily depressed. Others are anxious. Some are angry. Others are frightened. Some individuals say that when they are lonely they experience a variety of emotions—anger and fear at some times, depression at others. What, then, is loneliness? It is not itself a problem emotion. *Loneliness is a word that people use to summarize their experience of the problem emotions they feel when they are alone.*

It is necessary to understand the concept of loneliness because the way we think about it is basic to our effectiveness in filling the feedback gap. People blame loneliness and being alone for a wide range of emotional and behavioral problems. What they are really doing is making loneliness the scapegoat for their various inadequacies in the face of filling the feedback gap. In the end, loneliness is best understood as a word that describes people's failure to fill the feedback gap by themselves.

Let us think about what happens when you experience a feedback gap in your life. You separate from a lover, or a family member dies, or you lose a pet. When a feedback gap like this opens up, you usually experience some unhappiness. For we human beings, whose survival has depended on acknowledging and mastering sudden changes in our environment, even mild change causes some emotional upset. This upset is productive because it forces us to adapt— to run to escape being eaten, to show submission before being forcibly subdued. Predictably, unhappiness is especially likely when the feedback gap occurs as a result of broken relationships. Because we are social animals, such breaks in the feedback gap often cause us significant stress. We are likely to experience a broad range of negative emotions, including sadness, anxiety, grief, fear, anger, helplessness, and depression.

There is an additional change in your life when an important relationship ends. You may be able to hide your emotions from your friends and acquaintances. You may even act pretty much as before. But you cannot escape being *seen* alone. Your actual physical aloneness is suddenly like a badge that you always wear—the modern version of Hester Prynne's red "A": Alone. The most visible alteration in your way of living, both to you and to others, is that you are now physically alone. Whereas formerly you visited friends with your spouse, now you visit them alone. Whereas you used to spend Sunday dinners with your partner, now you spend them alone. Friends once considered you part of a couple and would treat you as such; you were part of "Ted and Sally." Now guess who is coming to dinner? Friends are at first likely to say, "Just Ted" or "Just Sally." Only gradually will they accept your aloneness and think of you as an individual, as the whole person "Ted" or "Sally."

Because your physical aloneness is such an obvious outer symptom of the changes in your life, being alone becomes an important issue. Often when you are alone, "loneliness" is the first word that you will think of to describe your unhappiness. "Isn't it obvious?" you think. "I'm unhappy because I am alone." But think again. You may be unhappy because you have not taken responsibility for your life alone. You have not recognized the feedback gap, and you have not yet figured out how to fill your life with security and with meaning and with whatever else it is that you may treasure.

In our society there are many familiar examples of this phenomenon. We have all heard about people like a woman who is so wrapped up in her children that when they go to bed at night she doesn't know what to do with herself; she claims that at night she becomes lonely. We know harried executives whose business schedules are so fragmented and full that outside work they have little energy for themselves or others; executives like themselves, they believe, are high-energy people who must manage time efficiently even at some emotional costs. But when they are asked about the causes of their problems, they attribute them not to fatigue or to time constraints, not to filling the feedback gap with nonsatisfying activities, but to loneliness. "He travels fastest who travels alone," they say, but add "It is lonely at the top."

Every individual who says he or she is lonely actually has a unique set of life problems and disruptive emotions to deal with. In every case in which people say they are lonely, we can see that beneath their description much more is going on emotionally. A lonely widow says: "You get disgusted when you are alone and you have to do everything yourself, especially when you are not well."[1] Clearly, this woman is discouraged and tired because she is not physically well. She feels incompetent to handle "everything" because she lacks certain practical skills. Like many women of her generation, she is accustomed to having her husband handle many of the practicalities in her life. She feels helpless primarily because she is ill, but she has allowed this feeling to permeate other aspects of her life as well. She says she is lonely, but if she were to look deeper, she would see that being alone is only a symptom of her problems—practical problems that include her illness and her deficient skills.

Here is a widower who also has a unique set of problems:

> Once in a while, once in a while if I come home into the night and sit down, and let's say have a glass of beer and read the paper and think for about a half an hour before I go to bed, I get a little sense of despair. It's not necessary because I know that the kids are well looked after all the time and all this, but it's a lonesome feeling.[2]

What is this man's lonesome feeling? Does it come from being alone, or does it originate in the depressant effects of alcohol and the invariably negative evening news? It is probably true that if this man were with another person, that person would buoy his mood. The depressant effect of alcohol might become, at least for a time, a mutual conviviality, and the two might discuss the news and make light of it. But it is the alcohol and the news, not the fact that he is alone, that are the immediate causes of this man's unhappiness. He can change his mood by avoiding depressants and by reading more positive accounts or making the effort to put the negative accounts into perspective. He might even discover happier ways to fill his evenings. The point is that he can solve his own unhappiness, in solitude, by taking responsibility for it.

Here a woman newly separated from her husband is described:

> In the bathroom closet at bedtime she comes across some of his old prescriptions, abandoned in his getaway; how long, she wonders will it be before all traces of his living in this home will be erased? In bed, she delays turning the light off; the darkness is full of nameless fears when one is alone. Finally, she does turn it off, but stays on her side of the bed, as if he were still there; the night presses upon her, the house makes mysterious noises that cause her heart to skip, and she waits for something to happen.[3]

This woman, too, says she is lonely. Actually, she is suffering from several emotional stresses. She has memories that make her feel sad and angry. She is afraid. She does not feel physically or emotionally secure. What can she do? It is true that she would feel more physically secure if her husband were with her. But she could also take steps to secure her home so she would be comfortable in it by herself. Yes, the memories are painful. But is she in pain primarily because she is alone right now or because she has been abandoned and her self-esteem has suffered? Again, being alone is only the most obvious symptom, not the cause, of her suffering. The real cause is her failure to realize and use her own abilities—the ability to make her home more secure, the ability to rid it systematically and deliberately of traces of her husband, the ability to work through her hurt or anger. This woman is letting the feedback gap fill up with her helplessness. She is not taking charge of it and filling it with experiences that she wants.

When you are alone, this vague concept called loneliness feels like an especially apt word to describe your emotional problems. "Isn't it clear that I am feeling lousy?" you protest. "Isn't it clear that I am alone?" Yes, both these facts can be true. What is not true is that one necessarily causes the other.

In our society, loneliness is an encompassing and socially accept-able explanation for our unhappiness in times of emotional stress. We are likely to use it out of habit, without really thinking about it. It is a convenient word to explain our problems. But it is really too conve-nient. It is overused. It is a crutch. The result is that our negative associations about the idea of being alone are strengthened, and our fears about being alone increase. In addition, because the word *loneli-ness* does not adequately convey the range of concrete problems that underlie it, "curing" the problems is made more difficult.

Relying on loneliness as the explanation for your problems can be incredibly dangerous. Because loneliness does not really exist, solving the "problem of loneliness" is truly an impossible task. Be-cause loneliness itself is not clearly identifiable, it seems and truly is unmanageable. No one can put together a puzzle that has no pieces. It is only when you realize that the word *loneliness* merely symbol-izes emotions—emotions that, because they *are* clearly identifiable, are manageable—that the "problem of loneliness" can be solved.

If, following a personal loss, such as the death or divorce of a spouse, you say to yourself that loneliness is the problem, you are going to be handicapped in filling the feedback gap. It is likely that you will tell yourself "I am lonely" when you should say to yourself, "I am sad" and "I am afraid." When you experience a loss, it is more constructive to think, "I have to work through my grief" or "I have to work on my anger" than it is to think, "I have to do something about my loneliness." For most people, loneliness cannot have one cure, but it must have many. Indeed, loneliness itself cannot be "cured" unless the various feelings that suggest it are dealt with.

If your problem truly was "being alone," then loneliness certainly would be frightening. Then it would be realistic for you to feel helpless and depressed because, of all the negative emotions, loneliness would be the only one that you could not alleviate yourself. Fear is an emotion you can conquer by learning and by courage. Anger you can work out or give up. But, by definition, if being alone is the cause of a problem, you have to be with at least one other person to solve it. You require other people's cooperation to fix your loneliness. And typically we cannot control other people.

No wonder loneliness is such a depressing problem! We seldom hear people say that they fear their anger or that they fear sadness. But we often hear people say that they fear loneliness. If loneliness was a true emotion, then it would be the one aspect of our emotional lives in which we would be totally dependent on others to fulfill our needs. It would be the one emotion that was not under our psychological control. All of these issues would be significant—if our problem were really, literally, being alone. Fortunately, it is not.

The problem is how you, the individual, interpret being alone. If you are alone and do not like being alone, if you find that nothing rewarding happens to you while you are alone, then you are likely to feel emotions like anxiety, anger, and depression. If, on the other hand, you accept that being alone is a state of being, not a state of deprivation, if it is merely a fact that people interpret intellectually and emotionally, then you can experience being alone with a full range of emotions, including happy and positive ones. Being alone need not lead to helplessness and hopelessness because learning how to manage your feelings when you are alone can be turned into a realistic challenge.

Discovering Positive Ideas About Solitude

Among human cultures there are wide fluctuations in the human experience of being alone. It is well known that different languages reflect the different environments in which people find themselves, that because of their landscape, the Eskimos, for instance, have dozens of words for *white*. The Eskimos also have several words for *loneliness*. One word signifies being "silent and withdrawn" because of the absence of other people. Another indicates "being or feeling left behind; to miss a person who has gone." Yet another, their most encompassing term, means "to be unhappy because of the absence of other people.

In contrast, in the culture of the Tahitians, there is no word for *loneliness* in the sense of being depressed or sad because of the lack of companionship.[4] The society has been so open for so long that the idea of being alone barely exists.

In some cultures solitude is revered as a path toward spiritual or psychological transcendence. Throughout history, religious innovators in these cultures, such as Moses, Jesus, Mohammed, Zoroaster, and the Buddha, have sought wilderness experiences to discover major visions. As part of a rite of passage into adulthood, tribal cultures in North and South America, Africa, Asia, and Australia have sent adolescents alone into the wilderness to seek wisdom. Individuals who undertake these rites expect to grow beyond their ordinary selves, and often they do have unique experiences. One modern version of this rite in America today is an integral part of self-development training run by the Outward Bound organization. People are deliberately stranded in a remote place, often under primitive conditions. They are left alone to face their own abilities, their own frailties, and their own solitude and they are expected to grow from this experience.

Over the centuries, examining both the positive and negative sides of solitude has been a major theme in German philosophy. Early German writers held the view that solitude provides an opportunity for reflection and for communication with God and with oneself. The Germans even have a word for positive solitude. *Einsamkeit* has historically meant realizing the strength of one's character by actually choosing to spend time alone. In the 1940s social scientists who studied the experience of Einsamkeit in Germans and Americans discovered that the German people saw solitude primarily as a positive phenomenon associated with words like *strong* and *health,* while Americans perceived it as negative and associated with fear. It may be a reflection of the stresses of modern times that when this study was replicated decades later, the Germans had become more like the pessimistic Americans. Today in Germany two interpretations of positive solitude still exist. One is the idea of solitude as a "splendid isolation," considered to be necessary if a person wants to discover new forms of freedom or even new forms of contact with other people. The second is the idea that through being physically isolated, one can search for new positive experiences. The connotations of solitude now also include what we would call loneliness—the feeling of an inner estrangement and alienation—and the idea of losing a loved one or other social contacts.

These comparisons suggest that our personal experience of being alone is culturally conditioned in significant ways. In America even the language we speak overlooks the idea of positive solitude.

Fortunately, because our attitudes toward being alone are conditioned, they can also be relearned. We can come to the realization that the main problem that most people have when alone is not being alone per se, but how they have learned to react to the changes that have taken place in their lives.

When you understand positive solitude, you are not really dependent on others for your happiness. And when you are not dependent, your likelihood of discovering happiness is good.

Remember that the human feedback in our lives is not always positive. In modern societies, although it is unfashionable to say so, people complicate our lives. Co-workers, strangers on the street, and even family members are as likely to increase the stress in our lives as to allay it. People put demands on us daily and often compete with us for scarce resources. Even when people love us and we love them, they sometimes annoy and obstruct us.

Fortunately, the same society that brings us loneliness and excessive togetherness also brings us the affluence that makes separateness possible. When we are no longer dependent on others for our survival or for positive feedback, we can choose to fill the feed-back gap ourselves, providing ourselves with the experience of independence, centering, and love. Freed from the belief that you need others, you can devote your energies to finding happiness and contentment within yourself. You can banish the specter of loneliness.

A growing number of writers, therapists, and researchers agree with this line of reasoning. They believe that if our society can be less negative about being alone and if individuals can think about being alone in the way I have described, then being alone can be a good experience, even a joyful exploration. They believe that for many who now suffer only loneliness, positive solitude is a viable alternative. One such voice is psychotherapist Peter Suedfeld:

> [There] are positive experiences to be savored in solitude. They are both beneficial and pleasant; and although they may not be "healing" in the strict sense—since there is no illness to be healed—they certainly are so in the wider sense. Aloneness in this context fills a need, removes a lack, impels growth. There seems to be no loneliness; rather the individual feels a freedom from distraction, from the usual restrictions imposed by social norms and the need to maintain face, and the benefits of reducing external stimulation to the point where the still, small internal voices can be heard.[5]

Many existentialist psychologists also emphasize positive solitude. They believe that being alone is a central fact of existence and that accepting it is important to human development. Existentialist therapist Rollo May captured the essence of the philosophy when he wrote:

> We all stand on the edge of life, each moment comprising that edge. Before us is only possibility. This means the future is open. . . . Despair, yes. But it is the beginning of human consciousness and all of the joys that opens to us.[6]

Another prominent existentialist who has studied aloneness is the therapist Clark E. Moustakas. Moustakas makes the useful distinction between "loneliness anxiety" and "true loneliness." Loneliness anxiety—what I have called *loneliness* here—distracts you from your mission in life and leads you to seek too much contact with others. True loneliness—what I call simply *being alone*—involves the reality of facing your life experiences alone.

In *Individuality and Encounter,* Moustakas related his personal experience of true loneliness when he had to decide whether to give his consent for his daughter's major heart surgery. The surgery would either restore his daughter to health or result in her death. In the urgency and gravity of the situation, Moustakas felt alone:

> I tried to draw from deep down within myself a single answer.... While no answer came to the problem of surgery, I became aware that at the center of my world was a deep and pervasive feeling of loneliness. With this feeling came the tentative realization that loneliness is a capacity or source in man for new searching, awareness, and inspiration—that when the outside world ceases to have meaning, when support and confirmation are lacking or are not adequate to assuage human suffering, when doubt and uncertainty overwhelm a person, then the individual may contemplate life from the depths of his own self and in nature. For me, this was a discovery that in a crucial and compelling crisis, in spite of comfort and sympathy from others, one can feel utterly and completely alone, that at bottom, the experience of loneliness [aloneness] exists in its own right as a source of power and creativity, as a source of insight and direction, as a requirement of living no matter how much love and affirmation one receives in his work and in his relationships with others.[7]

Among those who believe that being alone can be a positive experience, a common theme is that *a person alone must be able to provide his or her own feedback.* If you live alone in environments that reinforce your fear, tension, and anger, you will be unhappy; if you live alone in environments that reinforce relaxation, creativity, and happiness, you will be content. Suedfeld calls filling the feedback gap finding your "internal voice." Aloneness, he says, fills a "need"; alone, you remove a deficiency by choosing the feedback that encourages growth. Moustakas points out that the outside world may cease to provide meaning, support, and confirmation—that is, it may fail to provide adequate feedback. When it does, he discovered, the "depths of the self" may provide the individual with necessary feedbacks in powerful and creative ways. The small internal voice, the encounter with the depths of your self, and the pleasure of feeling calm and creative—all these expressions have in common the idea of accepting the responsibility of giving positive, consistent feedback to yourself and rejecting the feedback offered by an uncaring and random world. To say "I'd rather be alone" becomes not a defense, but an honorable choice.

Practicing Positive Solitude: A Case Example

We can fill the feedback gap in conventional, unsatisfying ways or we can fill it with positive solitude. These ideas can be seen in everyday terms in the case of Ron Johnson, a single man in his thirties. Ron split up with his wife two years ago after eight years of marriage. Ron says he feels lonely "a fair amount of the time." He has asked a couple of dozen women out since his divorce, but nothing seems to click. Nothing "feels as right" as his marriage did. He and his wife used to be a popular couple in a set of couples with whom he seldom associates now. "Couples drop you. They mostly want to be with other couples," he explains. "I have a few good male friends; we play tennis and go to ball games—that sort of thing. But my social life isn't what it used to be." He smiles derisively. "I'm certainly not the stereotype of the carefree bachelor; I spend a lot of time alone and I watch a lot of TV, sports mostly. Sure, I'm lonely sometimes."

Why is Ron lonely? He is lonely because he has not filled the feedback gap left by his divorce. He "spends time" doing things, of course, but, sadly, he is truly "spending" time rather than enjoying it. He still longs for the rich feedback environment he had when he was married. For example, he mentions the highly satisfactory interpersonal relationships he and his wife had with several other couples. We may also guess that he and his wife had at least some mutual interests. Probably his sexual interests were at least somewhat fulfilled during his marriage. Now most of these ready rewards are no longer available: no lively set of heterosexual relationships, no full-time companionship, no regular sex life. Instead, Ron has his buddies and his sports, his random dates, his television. Clearly, he understands that these activities and relationships are not enough for him, but he doesn't know what to do about it. For example, he wants a relationship with a woman, but he discounts the women he meets and does not work to develop deeper relationships with them. Ron is also dissatisfied, maybe even insecure, because he does not live up to his ideal of the "carefree bachelor."

We can see that Ron is talking himself into his loneliness. For one thing, he is looking back unrealistically. Like most of us, he remembers the good times instead of the whole picture. Idealizing past relationships, such as the family life we experienced in our childhood, is normal. In a similar way, Ron is remembering only the best in his feedback-rich marriage—forgetting that the best of a long-term, well-developed relationship is a tough standard to use in judging a casual date.

For another thing, Ron is unproductively comparing his life with that of others. He has chosen to compare his life with a media stereotype of the swinging single male. He might have compared himself equally as unproductively with his happily married older brother or with the men in the couples that he used to socialize with. Most likely, he would see them as being better off than he is. We all have this tendency to evaluate our lives in contrast with others' instead of concentrating on the positive that we have in our own situation and instead of spending our energies filling the feedback gap.

What might Ron's situation feel like if he had filled the feedback gap effectively? Well, we should not assume that Ron would be dating a dozen different women or that he is about to be married again. Both these "solutions" would be unrealistic and, perhaps, unwise. If Ron was making a healthy adjustment, he would put it this way:

> Since my divorce I have dated a lot of women. A few of these relationships I have pursued, really getting to know the women well and making friends. Some of these relationships have been sexual, and some have not. I have a couple of good male friends that I buddy around with. I am still close to one of the couples that I used to see when I was married. I make it a point to play doubles with them once in a while.
>
> I also spend a lot of time alone. I do the usual things like watch

TV and read and jog. But I've also really gotten into my darkroom lately, and I've joined the local camera club. I'm thinking of doing some professional photography on the side. It's not the same as when I was with my wife. My interests have changed, but I do have more time, and I have time now for the kinds of things that require intense personal involvement.

I'm not the independent bachelor type—the kind that is out every night with a different woman or at a different function. That's just not me. Actually I enjoy staying home much of the time.

Now Ron is not looking back. He recognizes that his life has changed. He is pursuing new interests and new people—both in depth. In one way, he is doing just what the advice-to-the-lovelorn columnist might tell him to do—he has joined a club that he is really interested in, and although meeting people is not his reason for joining, the club may, ironically, be a good place to do so. Ron may or may not meet Ms. Right at the camera club, but the important thing is that it doesn't matter. Ron is realizing who *he* is, what he likes, where he is going. He is putting meaningful feedback back into his life, both from relationships and from his time alone. He has filled the feedback gap productively. When he waxes philosophical about it, he recognizes that his new interests and attitudes are a natural part of changing, of living. He knows that he will continue to change. Sure, his married brother is happy, he says, but so, in his different lifestyle, is he.

When you experience a feedback gap, the word *loneliness* itself is a trap. When you feel what you are tempted to call loneliness, you are probably describing a period in which you are experiencing a variety of different uncomfortable emotions. How you fill the feedback gap determines the emotions you will feel and whether you will conquer your unhappiness. The responsibility for doing so is yours alone. The reward for doing it is to know the positive solitude experience of self-confidence, joy, and independence.

Notes

1. Quoted in Helena Znaniecki Lopata, "Loneliness: Forms and Components," in Robert S. Weiss, ed., *Loneliness: The Experience of Emotional and Social Isolation* (Cambridge, Mass.: MIT Press, 1975), 106.

2. Robert S. Weiss, ed., *Loneliness: The Experience of Emotional and Social Isolation* (Cambridge, Mass.: MIT Press, 1975), 106.

3. Morton M. Hunt, "Alone, Alone, All, All Alone," in Weiss, *Loneliness,* 126.

4. Letitia Anne Peplau, Maria Miceli, and Bruce Morasch, "Loneliness and Self-evaluation," in Letitia Anne Peplau and Daniel Perlman, eds., *Loneliness: A Sourcebook of Current Theory, Research and Therapy* (New York: John Wiley & Sons, 1982), 136–37.

5. Peter Suedfeld, "Aloneness as a Healing Experience," in Peplau and Perlman, eds., *Loneliness: A Sourcebook of Current Theory, Research and Therapy,* 61.

6. Rollo May, *Freedom and Destiny* (New York: W. W. Norton & Co., 1981), 242.

7. Clark E. Moustakas, *Individuality and Encounter* (Cambridge, Mass.: Howard A. Doyle Publishing Co., 1968), 104–5.

2

Avoiding the
Loneliness Traps

One is one's own refuge.
Who else could be the refuge?
—THE BUDDHA

Changing your life from unhappy loneliness to contented and creative solitude may be one of the most challenging things you can accomplish. Positive solitude is a new way of thinking and being. Everywhere you go, you will be influenced and even pressured to seek togetherness and to avoid being alone. Friends will tell you that you are just into a phase. Psychoanalysts may suggest that you are masochistically repressing your need for affiliation. How will you sort out all these ideas?

Even though you may personally decide that you can be happy alone, your explorations toward positive solitude will simply not be reinforced by the people around you. It will be rather like trying to diet in a family that lives for ice cream. There are no popular songs about how great it is to spend the night alone. There are no models of positive solitude on family television. It would be a kinky nightclub indeed that would invite you in to teach you the pleasures of being alone.

Sometimes the pressure on you will occur because people have other agendas in mind. All kinds of singles groups survive by pushing people's loneliness buttons. Dating services make millions of dollars annually. At times the pressure on you will result merely from people's ignorance and habit. Solitude simply does not have a place of honor in our society. What you will encounter on a daily basis are the old attitudes that lead people who are alone to feel lonely, the pressures that will encourage you to seek to be part of a couple or part of a group.

These aspects of American culture that encourage loneliness instead of healthful solitude are the loneliness traps. A loneliness trap is any common influence that reinforces unhappy loneliness instead of positive solitude. These influences are "traps" because you come across them unexpectedly and fall into them accidentally. When you experience a feedback gap in your life, the traps open up all around you. Often the traps are the quick-fix solutions that are most readily available. They are the easy ways and, often, the socially acceptable ways to fill the feedback gap. The trouble with them is that over the long term, they discourage your acquisition of the important skills of positive solitude: learning to decrease problem emotions when you are alone and learning to like being alone.

Some of the most important loneliness traps are our unexamined beliefs about being alone. During our lives, each of us has developed many personal beliefs about being alone. We based our earliest thoughts on the attitudes of our worried parents: "Are you sure you will be all right alone?" "I can't leave you all alone!" As teenagers, we saw our peers ostracized if they spent a lot of time alone. We thought they were weird, loners. Probably, you have not examined these beliefs closely. Often they are so widely repeated in our culture that they seem to be common sense. Upon inspection, it becomes clear that although these beliefs are, indeed, common, they are not particularly practical or sensible.

The "Inevitability" of Loneliness

Loneliness Trap 1 is the erroneous belief that "when I am alone it is inevitable that I will have some periods of loneliness." Examine the cause-effect relationship implied in this statement. "It is *inevitable* that I will have some periods of loneliness" suggests that being alone causes bad feelings. Yet being alone is a characteristic not so different from other characteristics—like being especially tall or having a particular income or living in a certain community. Of course, any characteristic can "cause" us to feel good or bad if we let it. It is not so much the characteristic itself as the interpretation that you put on it that counts. Being alone does not itself cause periods of loneliness (such as bad feelings), any more than being tall causes a person to feel depressed. It is your interpretation and your habitual feeling patterns that cause the bad feelings when you are alone. If you expect being alone to cause sadness, it is likely to do so.

It is almost true that when you are alone, you will have "some periods" of loneliness. More precisely, it is true that when you are alone, you will have some times of unhappiness. All of us have unhappiness in our lives, and these bad times will occur when we are alone, as well as when we are with others. These periods may actually occur more often when you are alone if for no other reason than because when you are with others your mind tends to be preoccupied. When you are alone, there are fewer stimuli competing with your feelings and ideas for your attention, and previously suppressed feelings and ideas are more likely to surface. This situation is actually good because you are in touch with who you are. But bad feelings are inevitable throughout life, not only when you are alone. Often being alone is not itself the cause of such feelings; it is merely the opportunity for them. If you are more unhappy when you are alone, you should carefully examine potential causes other than the mere fact that you are alone.

To anticipate being lonely is indeed frightening. It is less frightening to anticipate depression or anxiety because these are discrete, identifiable emotions that are known to be curable. Problems like depression and anxiety have been studied extensively, and, unlike loneliness, therapists and clients have developed highly successful therapeutic and personal strategies for dealing with them. In fact, most of the usual problems associated with loneliness have been extensively studied and successfully treated. Helplessness, feelings of low self-esteem, and lack of social skills are all related problems that individuals and therapists have worked with successfully for decades. If you persist in the belief that loneliness is your problem, you will not be able to take advantage of the psychological knowledge that exists and you will experience considerable unnecessary anxiety about your ability to change.

When you are alone, it is not inevitable that you will have periods of loneliness. Realizing the true emotions behind the word *loneliness* is essential if you are to fill the feedback gap successfully. Identifying these emotional issues will help you reduce the impact of this erroneous belief.

"Meeting People" as an Answer

Loneliness Trap 2 is the erroneous belief that when you are feeling lonely, you should try to meet more people. This belief is often what drives people to singles bars, and perhaps it has already driven you there. It is the foundation of the singles industry. It is the advice a newly alone person gets most often.

Again, the seduction of this belief, as with all beliefs, is that there is some truth in it. It is true that meeting people will temporarily occupy your mind. Being active in any way is superficially effective simply because it does not allow time for your feelings to surface. The challenge and the risks of socializing, especially with new people and with those of the opposite sex, can be just as preoccupying as, say, writing a complicated computer program. There is some satisfaction in having gone to a singles bar and survived. Meeting others may take your mind off your persistent emotional problems. It provides some temporary rest and relief from these feelings. Meeting others may also give you the opportunity to see how people like you are dealing with similar problems and may provide you with opportunities to enhance your self-esteem.

In these ways, being with others temporarily relieves loneliness, yet it does not solve the emotional problems that still exist. Unless it is done in a context of working directly on these problems, meeting people is unlikely to alleviate the feelings underlying your loneliness.

If your meeting with others is handled unskillfully or if you are unlucky enough to meet the wrong people, encounters can actually increase your feelings of loneliness. When you are unsuccessful in your socializing, meeting others will reduce your self-esteem. Spending a lot of time with people can foster your unhealthy dependence on them. It can fill your time without being satisfying.

So meeting people as a solution to loneliness is likely to be a mixed blessing. The most effective prescription for the alleviation of depression, anxiety, lack of self-esteem, or any of the other underlying emotions of loneliness is not the wholesale administration of the togetherness drug, but, rather, addressing these problems directly and separately. It is only our widespread cultural insistence that togetherness is a cure for loneliness that permits this erroneous belief to go unexamined.

Do People Need People?

Loneliness Trap 3 is the related belief that "people need people." As the popular song lyrics say, "People who need people are the luckiest people in the world." This belief is wrong both logically and scientifically.

Logically, of course, people who *don't* need people may be the luckiest. If you can be happy and self-sufficient alone, who can quarrel with your success? Independence is a worthwhile goal that many people strive for. What could be more logical than to be independently in control of your own happiness?

Social scientists have actually found little evidence to prove that people need people. Only a few psychologists believe that loneliness is a basic motivater, that once people have satisfied their more obvious physiological and biological drives and have secured and are comfortable with the necessities of air, water, and food, they then strive to alleviate loneliness. But there are few data to support their view, and most modern social science research downplays the importance of the need for others. Adults do have some basic needs that must be met before higher needs become of real importance to them.

These are the needs for security, safety, food, and shelter. The higher needs are thought to include, among many others, the need to achieve, the need to have control over one's life, and the need to be with other people. So being with others is certainly not a basic need. And among the higher needs, no one particular need is more important than any other. There is no reason to suppose that in your life the "need for affiliation" will dominate your other needs.

Modern research has even led to a rethinking of the term *need* itself. What social scientists used to call the "need" for affiliation is now called merely "the motivation to affiliation." Many psychologists eschew the theory of psychological needs. While physiological needs can be demonstrated, it is not clear that psychologically we really need any particular satisfactions. Some of us may "like people." Some may like to be by themselves. And some people may like people on some occasions. But contrary to popular belief, the evidence is that, psychologically at least, people do not absolutely need each other.

Pitfalls in American Popular Culture

Loneliness Trap 4 is found every day in American popular culture, which influences our attitudes through music, television, and print and other media. The attitudes of other people who are affected by this culture, in turn, affect us. Because we take it for granted and do not examine its effects, the popular culture influences us profoundly. It holds many pitfalls for the person who is alone.

If you are alone, indiscriminate retreat into entertainment can be detrimental to your well-being. Popular entertainment is especially dangerous if you are newly alone. Entertainment is made so convenient that it may appeal especially to the person who has been recently hurt by a close relationship. Instead of marriage on the rebound, you do media on the rebound. Your sense of personal initiative may have temporarily waned. Your physical energy level is likely to be low. Under these circumstances, it is easy to flip on the television or the radio to fill time.

It is true that under such trying circumstances, some sort of emotional retreat to safer territory makes sense. But for reasons I will describe, popular entertainment does not represent safer emotional territory. If your retreat consists primarily of exposure to the mindless aspects of popular culture, increased loneliness, in the forms of boredom, sadness, and a sense of emptiness, will be the result. Like suddenly taking on a new lover, taking on the media can be risky.

Music is a significant part of this loneliness trap. Listening to music is one of the most popular strategies mentioned by people who are trying to cope with their loneliness. There are no data to indicate whether this strategy is actually successful. However, common sense tells us that often it is not. First, you are often tempted to choose music that suits your mood—quiet, even melancholic music when you are sad or depressed or fast-paced and lively music when your mood is up. The music you chose reinforces your mood, of course, and if you are depressed this choice is clearly counterproductive.

If you are alone and sad, you should probably decide to listen to mood-changing, rather than mood-reinforcing, music, opting for the up-beat rock rather than the moody ballad. Unfortunately, our popular culture dictates that we cannot always choose the most appropriate music. When you turn on the radio, you put yourself at the mercy of the popular mood, the mood of the disc jockey and, especially, of the lyricists. In our culture songs about love and loneliness are ubiquitous. Love is idealized as the way to happiness, and loneliness is portrayed as the opposite of love. Songs that extoll the virtues of positive solitude (the words do not exactly lend themselves to musical rendition!) are rare. When you are looking for such reinforcing music, you will be lucky if you hear songs like the eighties hits "I Am What I Am" and "Walking On Sunshine." You will not hear these upbeat, uplifting tunes on the airwaves on a regular basis. Instead, you are likely to find a lot of mournful and angry lyrics on love and loneliness.

Every recent generation has had its musical renditions of the love-and-loneliness theme. The forties had Irving Berlin's "You're Lonely and I'm Lonely" and Hank Williams's "I'm So Lonesome I Could Cry" (which was revived in the sixties.) The fifties gave us "Lonely Street" and Paul Anka's "Lonely Boy." In the sixties there were "Mister Lonely" (by Gene Allan and Bobby Vinton), "Only the Lonely" (by Roy Orbison and Joe Melson), and "Sergeant Pepper's

Lonely Hearts Club Band" (by John Lennon and Paul McCartney). The seventies brought "Alone Again (Naturally)" (by Gilbert O'Sullivan), "Lonely Night" (by Neil Sedaka), and "Lonely People" (by Dan Peek). In the eighties we heard Bill Oshan's "Love Zone", in which we were advised that we never have to be strangers "out there alone."

Newly separated individuals, especially, should avoid listening to these kinds of lyrics. They only echo and reinforce the sadness of lost love. Song lyrics seldom evoke the positive feelings of freedom, power, and creativity that can be experienced alone. A major theme in popular music—the advice that finding a new love is the best answer for one's unhappiness—is itself a loneliness trap.

At the center of the popular culture is the great seducer, television. The average household watches television more than forty-five hours a week, during which time you will see just about everything except positive solitude. Television naturally emphasizes exciting sights and sounds—action, dialogue, interesting facial expressions, and interpersonal conflict. It seldom delves into the meanings and thoughts behind the images. It emphasizes action over substance. Yet relating to the substance of life—to our personal philosophy, emotions, and intellect—is essential to positive solitude. On television we seldom see a character alone—walking alone along a hillside, for example, or contemplating life alone with a pleasant cup of tea.

Since visible acts, not thoughts, are its medium, television is hampered in its examination of character. Yet it is thoughts—one's own impressions, sensations, analyses, and meanings—that the person alone lives with the most. You will not learn how to manage your ideas better from watching television, and, in fact, you are likely to find that television has distracted you from doing so. Television dramatizes human interaction, not human contemplation.

Casually flipping on the "tube" propels you into a relationship fantasyland. In police dramas you see the police sharing the action on their beat, not one cop's lonely struggle to make sense of the crass world around him. In the soap operas you may encounter a moment of silence, often at the end of a scene, when the camera focuses on an individual's momentary expression of puzzlement or anger, but that is the full extent of the character study. In the rest of the show, you will view little intimacy—and a lot of togetherness.

Of all possible relationships, television emphasizes families. Worse yet, in spite of some recent innovations, it often portrays the traditional family. Even nonfamily shows create fictional family groups that give enormously unrealistic amounts of personal support and empathy to their members. "Hill Street Blues," "M*A*S*H," and "Cheers" are recent popular examples that create incredibly feed-back-rich interpersonal environments. These fairy tales, pleasant as they are, play to the American dream of community and family.

People who are alone are excluded from the fantasyland. Usually, they are not even portrayed. It is as though they do not exist. The erroneous belief that being alone is basically unhealthy and un-worthy is supported by such programs. If you are alone, television programs certainly will not strengthen your belief in positive solitude, and they may actually weaken your positive self-image.

In addition to its deemphasis on meaning and its lauding of togetherness, television is a loneliness trap in yet another way. Many of us believe that television relaxes us, but this is again one of those seductive partial truths. Relative to other activities you might choose, watching television is actually stimulating. It is, in fact, designed to be stimulating. Its fast-paced programming is created to keep you awake and focused for the next high-energy commercial. Viewers are constantly stimulated with engaging sounds and visuals, with sex and violence. Watching television may be more relaxing than driving in rush hour, but that is about the extent of its charms.

If you are alone, do not think of television as a relaxant. It is much more relaxing to read a newspaper at your own pace. It is much more relaxing to take a walk. The ability to find peace is a prime benefit of being alone. Television does not bring you peace, and it may leave you with a high level of stimulation—stimulation that goes unresolved. Most television is a distraction, rather than a fulfillment. Ultimately, it will leave you with a feeling of anxiety and a sense of emptiness.

Escaping this loneliness trap means at least flipping the dial. You cannot expect to find television programs that model positive soli-tude, but neither do you have to subject yourself to the fantasies of togetherness and the commercial stimulation. It may be best to watch other types of programs, such as nature and news programs. Indeed, it may be that some of the recent popularity of these types of programs can be attributed to the fact that today there are more people who are alone to watch them. Intuitively, many people who are alone may have figured out how to choose programs that are more nurturing of their emotional and intellectual well-being.

Finally, you should be careful about filling the feedback gap with certain types of popular reading material. If you are newly alone, you should be sensitive to the fact that what you happen to pick up may significantly affect your mood. As I mentioned earlier, many of the academic and self-help books on the subject of aloneness inadvertently contribute to this loneliness trap. Having taken the view that loneliness is a problem to be solved, they seldom come up with holistic, realistic solutions. Some of the more entertaining types of reading will also be unhelpful now. The romance novel that you found entertaining before may be discouraging. Love poetry will not be uplifting. Search instead for reading that will enhance your interests, your ideas, and your self-actualization alone.

Seductive Groups

Loneliness Trap 5 is falling into feedback-rich environments that fill the feedback gap quickly and fully, but that do not foster self-understanding and self-sufficiency over the long term. The classic example of this trap is the seductive religious cult that makes people feel totally accepted. Such groups work to fill the feedback gap perfectly and fully. They have even been known to enlarge a person's feedback gap deliberately—initially to deprive a person, for example, of adequate nutrition—so they may then fill the feedback gap even more completely with both physical and spiritual "nurturing." This practice puts people under their control, instead of enhancing people's self-control.

Some popular "support" groups are similarly seductive to people in need of feedback. Such feedback-false environments are usually group activities that are organized by nonprofessionals as self-help groups. Some years ago, I attended a session of a widely known personal growth seminar. As I walked into the room of several hundred people, I was greeted warmly by name by several exceptionally attractive "helpers" who had never met me. When I sat down, the people on either side of me greeted me and went out of their way to get to know me. Wow! I thought. This beats your typical cold conference.

Throughout the evening, we were given exercises that encouraged us to reveal our personal lives and to give others strokes for revealing theirs. People got up in front of the group and gave moving testimonials of how this network of supportive folks had helped them through an illness or to get a better job or to meet a mate.

At first introduction, such "families" seem even better than do real families because their members are either trained or socialized to pay intense attention to each other. But the helpers are indeed trained, the participants are indeed socialized, and outside these groups you will rarely find people who act the same way. The attention feels wonderful, but it is short-lived. The friendship networks are not self-sustaining away from the group meetings. People are not encouraged to focus on building networks, let alone psychological self-sufficiency, outside the group—and, of course, to come to the group costs money, often hundreds of dollars per event. The trainers are becoming rich, the participants high but dependent.

Unfortunately, all too often these new groups of "friends" are emotionally and financially exploiting. These so-called self-improvement groups succeed because they fill their clients' feedback gaps. Whatever the actual content of a group's program, the feedback plan is the same. Intimacy is fostered through exercises done in small groups. The types of questions that are asked encourage people to open up to one another, right away, as they never would on their own, for example, on a first or second date. A norm is established that allows strangers to talk freely with each other. You feel more welcome in this kind of group than in more natural settings. You get positive feedback right away that you are okay or creative or smart. Often friendship networks are encouraged outside the formal sessions to keep the feedback gap filled until the next meeting. But the feedback gap is filled only by the meetings and by the networks associated with them. When you stop attending—when you stop paying or working to attend—the feedback stops. You walk away mystified and disappointed. You have spent a lot of money and have learned little about how to fill the feedback gap in real life.

Group therapy, when done poorly, is another example of this type of trap. In bad therapy a client's chronic dependence is reinforced, rather than changed, by the therapist. Typically, a therapist provides a nurturing, supportive atmosphere for any client who is not able to find such emotional satisfactions in the outside world. Group therapy can be especially powerful. Since the client's feedback gap is filled, he or she feels better. A reputable therapist will use this supportive climate to help the client become emotionally secure and independent of the therapy. Yet when the therapist does not promote the clients' independence, often the clients do not understand that they are not getting what they are paying for. They do not realize, especially early on, that they need change instead of contentment, that this change is often uncomfortable, and that it is the therapist's responsibility to foster this change. Unfortunately, clients sometimes stay in therapy for years under these conditions.

Feedback-rich environments attract people who are alone and lonely, especially among the young. In these groups, large amounts of personal attention are given freely. Mutual goals and shared meanings bind people together. Sometimes life in a group is structured around communal activities. If the lives of young people were previously filled primarily with punishment or meaninglessness or neglect, it is not surprising that the groups exert a powerful influence on them. The young people may feel secure and fulfilled in them for the first time in their lives. The feedback gap is constantly filled for them.

Extremely satisfying for some period of time, feedback-rich groups are a particularly binding sort of loneliness trap. They seldom encourage individual understanding of their feedback-intensive nature. "I was alone and then I was filled" says the convert. True, but the convert has had the feedback gap filled by others. The convert has given up self-control. He or she has not experienced the control and satisfaction that self-fulfillment—literally self-filling of the feedback gap—can bring.

To their converts, members of the cults initially seem loving and responsible. It is only later that disillusionment sets in, sometimes initiated by deprogramming experts hired by concerned friends or parents. Eventually, the converts will understand that their entire lives have been structured for them, including most of their beliefs, activities, and relationships. They may figure out that their feedback gap has been completely filled for them, but some instinct tells them that it has not been filled with their true self. Eventually, many people sense their own powerlessness in such groups. They realize that they want to exercise their free choice. With this choice, of course, comes the responsibility for filling the feedback gap with a special plan designed by and for the individual who is alone, and they must find the courage to face this reality.

The Singles Scene

When feelings of loneliness persist, you may decide to "circulate," thus falling into Loneliness Trap 6. You may do so because your friends tell you to or because you believe others are doing it. Whatever the reason, you attempt to "get out more." You plunge into the singles scene, take courses for singles, enroll in sports clubs, join Parents without Partners, sign up for a dating service, and may even attend singles' nights at the grocery store.

For many, the singles scene is emotionally enervating. You may fail to connect with others, and you are likely to interpret this failure as a confirmation of your personal weakness. You believe the failure is your own, certainly not the fault of the system. Yet there is evidence that social systems that are explicitly designed to bring lonely people together often fail.

There are several reasons why the singles scene fosters failures. For one thing, such systems are unnatural, and their members sense it. Often the "real" goal of these events—to meet someone to love—is incompatible with the stated goal of having fun. Many of the events on the singles scene are appropriate for children and adolescents, but adults expect more from a relationship than a good dancer or a volleyball partner. So mature individuals find that many singles events feel superficial. Adults prefer to see potential partners in broader contexts before connecting with them. They consciously or unconsciously devalue the people they meet at groups that are designed as meeting places.

Another problem is that not everyone connects easily at singles events. The wallflower syndrome is not limited to adolescents. At events for adults, it merely becomes a bit more subtle. The adolescent worry, "Will I be asked to dance?" or "Will she want to dance with me?" becomes "Will I connect?" in adulthood. People of any age experience the same responsibility for extending themselves and the same risks of rejection. In adulthood, however, the stakes are higher. The adolescent's stake is a dance or a date; the adult's stake is a lover or a partner. Although the climate of a singles group is generally engineered by its sponsors to be positive, this hail-fellow-well-met atmosphere is only a facade. What is really happening are tension, selection, and rejection: You put yourself on the line.

Psychiatrist Robert Weiss points out that although the singles scene produces dates and involvement, the resulting relationships are shallow and fragile because there is little basis in them for building trust. Someone you meet at a singles event is not likely to share your values and deep interests to a sufficient extent to build a strong relationship. You may have a few extended conversations, but not much beyond that. Someone introduced by friends at least shares important ties with you, while someone met by chance could be from literally anywhere. This, then, is the risk of the singles scene: If each new relationship brings loss or failure, a pattern of demoralizing short-term meetings and relationships develops.

A major factor on the singles scene is the loneliness industry. Entrepreneurs today are making a great deal of money as the administrators of singles activities. Revenues from dating services, to point to only one part of this industry, have grown enormously in recent years. People also make a lot of money running sports clubs, singles promotions, and singles magazines, yet there is scant evidence to support the contention that people can establish intimate relationships through these means. Because of the money to be made, such institutions will be with us for the foreseeable future. While they may be of some value, any of their promises for introducing you to intimate relationships must be approached warily.

These and other loneliness traps surround you every day, in many settings. In the face of these traps and a society that continues to set them for the unwary, achieving positive solitude will be a challenge. Recognizing the loneliness traps is an important step. Only by understanding our cultural conditioning can we stop being feedback junkies and start being feedback managers.

3
Steps to Achieving Positive Solitude

Only he who has an impenetrable center is himself free.
Only he who is alone can claim to be a man.
—PAUL TILLICH, "Loneliness and Solitude"

Instead of filling the feedback gap with entertainments like television and music, instead of attempting to fill it with new people, the alternative is to fill the feedback gap with your self. You do not need to give up entertainment and socializing, but you do need to learn that you can do a great deal to fill the feedback gap with your individual pleasures and interests.

You can learn to provide your own feedback for a satisfying, unique, and joyful life. You can build a positive mental and emotional life around your own thoughts, sensations, and explorations. You can choose environmental feedback that enhances, rather than detracts from, your self-support. All these approaches add up to giving more self-feedback than you have been used to giving and giving more self-feedback than society has taught you to give. Applying these ideas means taking more control of the feedback available to you every day in your life.

You escape the loneliness traps first by recognizing them and then by choosing a different path. When you are alone, perhaps recently disconnected from an important and habitual source of feedback, you will choose not to reconnect with the world in ways that are only habitual and convenient. Instead, you will carefully consider how to fill the feedback gap in personally meaningful and nourishing ways.

Avoiding the loneliness traps and learning a different way of living are skills. You have already been taught how to feel lonely. Now it is time to learn how to be alone.

Positive solitude first requires a full analysis of your personal feedback systems. Researchers have discovered that most people try to cope with loneliness by adopting fairly haphazard strategies. Many do nothing much but sleep, sit and think, cry, or watch television. They feel helpless and sad. They tend to overeat, to take tranquilizers, or to drink or use other drugs. Others try to keep busy. They read books and magazines, they study or work, they exercise or take up a hobby. Some develop the habit of shopping and spending money. Others turn to religion, while still others go on a perpetual search, constantly going to movies, plays, or concerts or taking drives. And some seek out people. They may call friends or visit someone. They go to places where friends are likely to be. They arrange particularly intimate contacts, like being with a close friend or talking to that friend about their feelings.

Most of these typical responses will work only up to a point. Adopting simple solutions can lead to addictive behaviors—addictive drugs, addictive religion, addictive shopping. Certainly, no one response alone will be effective for long. Even pursuing several of them at once is most likely to fill the feedback gap temporarily without really satisfying you. Instead your approach to filling the feedback gap must be systematic. It must lead to a full and balanced way of living, and, in the end, it must put meaning into your life.

Positive solitude must be learned over time, and basically there are three phases you pass through to acquire it. These phases are not discrete and irrevocably sequential. You should think of them as guidelines to the ongoing, complicated process of learning positive solitude. The three phases are awareness, change, and exploration.

In the awareness phase, you recognize your counterproductive conditioning about being alone and you become interested in finding an alternative. Anyone who has read thus far in Part I and who has begun to apply these new ideas in his or her own thinking is well into this phase. In the second, or change phase, you identify your personal feedback gaps and learn how to fill these gaps with thoughts and activities that build your sense of positive solitude. Part II discusses the various places in your life in which feedback gaps are likely to occur and suggests healthful ways to fill your life. In the third phase of your learning, your increasing ability to experience positive solitude develops into a unique personal exploration. You build a philosophy of solitude. In Part III, you will learn how to meet both the challenge of maintaining positive solitude in the face of many pressures to discontinue it and the challenge of seeking new, highly personal ways of being alone.

Phase 1: Awareness

At one time or another, each of us has heard the advice that you should not marry or take up a new partner on the rebound. Friends often give this advice to you when you are newly separated and emotionally vulnerable. They fear you will take on a new partner who is not a good match. They fear that unless you undergo a period of self-examination, you may repeat the same mistakes you made in your first marriage. If truth were told, you would probably agree with them. You know that getting into a new relationship when you are emotionally vulnerable without examining the old, failed one is seldom wise. Yet, this advice we hear and give ourselves is of limited usefulness because it tells us primarily what *not* to do. What we should do *instead* of marrying on the rebound is seldom explained. One paradoxically creative thing to do is to spend time alone, to reflect, and to work on becoming independent while alone. In short, what you should do instead of jumping into a bad relationship is to work toward understanding and practicing positive solitude.

Your awareness of positive solitude can be broadened and deepened in several ways. Of course, you must be constantly sensitive to loneliness traps that distract you from pursuing positive solitude. You should recognize that we set loneliness traps for ourselves through personal habits that go unexamined. Maybe you are addicted to those romantic afternoon soap operas. Maybe you spend too much time playing cutthroat tennis. Every so often you should make an inventory of your habits and decide which are still really meaningful to you. Having a couple of drinks with co-workers before you go home may improve social relations on the job, but doing so every day may simply be a physically unhealthy habit. Reading the sports section cover to cover is an unhealthy habit if it is driving out your actual participation in sports. Habitually socializing with people who you do not particularly care about can reduce your self-esteem and lead to feelings of boredom and loneliness.

At the same time, it is useful to increase your exposure to people who model positive solitude. Often these models can be found through reading. In addition to the authors and books I have already mentioned, Liv Ullmann's book *Changing* and Anne Morrow Lindberg's book *A Gift from the Sea* describe the authors' impressive personal growth through time spent alone. Thomas Merton has written extensively about the spiritual contexts of solitude. Being alone is a frequent theme in Doris Lessing's realist novels, and Le Anne Schreiber has written a powerful book on loss and solitude entitled *Midstream.*

You also can learn a lot from talking with older people. In addition to spending much time alone, older people remember the era before television and even the era before radio. What did they do then, before the media could be used to fill their time? My father remembers as a young man spending hours in the window seat reading books. He recalls waiting at night—"seriously waiting," as he puts it—for his father to come home with the newspaper. He developed definite personal interests, a strong sense of self.

Among your friends there are probably some people who are alone a great deal and who seem to profit from it. Widows and widowers who have coped well may be an especially fine source of such wisdom. Research has pointed out that widows who are successful alone have used themselves, rather than their families, friends, or formal resources like counseling and churches, as their main coping mechanism. They use their inner resources both to define their new situation and to incorporate their good memories into their new lives. Such people can be unique sources of individual wisdom for those of us who are learning positive solitude.

We all need to be sensitive to our use of language. The accident of being a native speaker of English shapes our thoughts in particular ways. Philosopher Paul Tillich wrote that, "the wisdom of our language has sensed . . . two sides of man's being alone. It has created the word 'loneliness' in order to emphasize the pain of being alone. And it has created the word 'solitude' in order to emphasize the glory of being alone. In daily life these words are not always distinguished; but we should do so consistently, thus deepening the understanding of our human predicament."[1] There is much truth in this statement, though I do not believe that today even the word *solitude* itself fully describes the positive aspects of being alone. *Solitude* is really an old-fashioned word. If you say to people "I prefer my solitude," chances are they will be offended, at the least, by the stuffy tone of your remark. Worse, they are likely to misinterpret your remark to mean, "I don't like people."

To come out and say "I lead a solitary life" will connote unhappiness rather than contentment to most people. It is somewhat more socially acceptable to say, "I want to be alone" because usually the receiver of this message will assume that the aloneness you seek will be temporary, and most people will accept such a temporary wish on your part. But asserting that you want to be alone much of the time for the foreseeable future is quite a different matter. This desire is likely to elicit reactions of disbelief or condemnation. Yet, *both* short-term and long-term periods of solitude may be desirable, though our society is not accustomed to accepting both these ways of living.

Ideally, we should create a new set of terms that describe the positive state of being alone. Currently, our language is certainly limited. Most of the words and ideas associated with aloneness are negative: *loneliness, isolation, withdrawal, desolation, reclusion, exile, forlornness, aloofness, unsociability, companionlessness.* Being called a hermit or a monk is hardly flattering. Among the few English words on this topic with positive denotations, there is none that simply describes being alone as a positive thing without the addition of some negative connotations. Even *unique* implies different, and in a social context being different usually means exclusion. *Seclusion* is somewhat positive in that it means a quiet retreat, but the implication of the word in context is usually that this mode of living is temporary: "After his death, she went into seclusion."

Other words simply do not capture the power and joy that can exist in being alone. *Quiet* and *private* are words that connote pleasantness, but they do not capture the creativity and excitement that are possible when you are alone. *Unity, oneness,* and *identity* are also limited terms. *Self-sufficiency, individuality,* and *harmony* are all separate aspects of the positive side of being alone. Positive solitude is more than any one of these aspects. It is a plan that describes an entire process, and it is a view of the world. If you can habitually think "positive" when you think about solitude, you will have come a long way toward combating the social pressure toward loneliness.

Phase 2: Change

Changing your behavior requires a detailed self-examination and an understanding of the direction you wish to take. To some extent, this process is personal. No one can dictate what will be meaningful or pleasurable for another unique human being, especially when that person is alone. The ideas I present in this book should be seen as guidelines and checklists of possibilities to which you should inject your own thoughts, ideas, and beliefs.

Inventory the times when you are alone and feel bored, tired, hostile, or excluded—in general, when you feel lonely. These are times in which the feedback gap might be more profitably filled. The worst times are when the feedback gap opens suddenly or drastically, as when a spouse dies or a divorce occurs. During these times, the gap looms largest. Many aspects of your daily life are affected, and your emotional security is threatened.

Less easy to recognize will be the feedback gap that occurs when you are pressured to become part of a couple or to be together with others: When you are unable or unwilling to join with others, you may feel guilty, excluded, or frustrated.

When you are alone, you may find that you wonder about how to satisfy your sensual desires, build traditions into your life, and find laughter.

Your work, at which you spend so much of your time, is also a likely place to discover feedback gaps. Look especially at relationships with co-workers and bosses and at the feedback you get from the work that you do.

At the same time, you should keep records of your good times. What do you do that fills your life—even momentarily—with joy, peace, or meaning?

Having recognized the feedback gaps, you must figure out ways to fill them with more positive experiences. You must eliminate the painful and definitely harmful ways in which you fill the feedback gaps—such as excessive drinking or drugs—and you must find ways to eliminate the dull and the merely habitual. As you become more expert at filling the feedback gaps with positive feedback, you will discover that the negative feedback will be crowded out of your life.

Filling the feedback gap with positives requires recognizing what you truly like and need. Although this statement may seem obvious, it is not a simple task. In our busy lives, routine often leaves little time for being sensitive to our desires and goals. One way to help yourself out of this dilemma is to take time out to remember what you *used* to like. What were your consistently favorite activities as a child? As an adolescent? As an adult, whenever you have not been preoccupied with work or school or family, what have you chosen to do?

It often helps, too, to retreat to some quiet place, preferably for several days, and to allow yourself simply to feel—to experience how your body feels when you are really rested, to note your physical tensions, to explore the world with your senses. Often in this solitude you will be reminded of what is most important to you.

Books like Richard Bolles's *The Three Boxes of Life* and Sidney Simon's *Values Clarification* provide detailed discussions of and exercises on how to get in touch with your past and with your emotions and how to reestablish your priorities. Psychotherapy can also help you to get in touch with emotional, intellectual, and sensual needs.

In general, you will want to fill the feedback gap with activities and thoughts that are in some combination meaningful, healthful, and pleasurable. The time orientation of these activities may be present, past, or future as long as the activities are not negative. Activities that you are doing now, to fulfill your sensuality or curiosity are obvious feedback-gap fillers. Take hours or a day off just to explore all your senses, as a two-year-old might. Pick up that hobby you meant to explore years ago. Pleasant memories can also be drawn upon to fill the feedback gap, as can hopes or plans for the future. Reflect on what you have accomplished in life and on what you want to accomplish. The pleasure of following traditions is often particularly powerful and meaningful because traditions span the past, present, and future. Observe them and create new ones as an investment in future memories.

Figuring out your feedback gaps, avoiding the loneliness traps, and choosing meaningful, healthful, and pleasurable feedback require patience and some faith. They require patience because all this self-analysis takes time. When you are aiming for positive solitude, you are doing nothing less than reexamining your life—your bad and good feelings, your habits and behaviors, the meaning of life to you. Acceptance of being alone should not be enough; your goals are full enjoyment and control of your solitude. For most of us, being alone and content with that status is truly a mode that must be learned. Although you may be committed to the goal of positive solitude, achieving it will take time. You are getting into psychological and spiritual shape, and it won't happen overnight.

Have faith, because there will be some false starts and failures. You must resolve to keep tinkering with your feedback systems until some positive results are reached, and then you must be willing to build on these results. Anyone will *adjust* to being alone if given enough time, but mere adjustment is not what you seek. You are not looking merely for solitude. Your goal is positive solitude.

In disconnecting from old ways, you may feel uncomfortable for a while. You may find yourself feeling annoyed, or frustrated, or discouraged. It is normal to do so. Change is usually emotionally disruptive. However, instead of bowing to that discomfort and allowing yourself to reconnect through old habits (such as getting coupled again, for instance, when you have recently divorced), find a way to manage the discomfort and to continue to change. Building in personal reinforcement and encouragement for your continued work toward positive solitude may be useful.

Also, self-nurturing is especially important at these times. You should treat your mind and body especially well—eat healthy foods, get enough sleep, and exercise. It is all right to hide out a bit from the cares of the daily world: Come back to it with a renewed experience of your self.

Concentrate on positive and encouraging thoughts about yourself and your efforts. Seeking information on behavioral self-management through reading or therapy may be useful and, in some cases, necessary. Notice little changes—such as any happiness experienced when alone—and take credit for them. When you are under the stress of change, some regression to familiar and comforting ways, often from childhood, is normal and useful. You should always give yourself permission to be less than perfect and to stop trying so hard.

Phase 3: Exploration

The experience of change is often described as the process of unfreezing old behaviors, learning and adapting new behaviors, and then refreezing your behaviors in the new patterns that you have learned. For people who are learning positive solitude, I think this process might better be described as first, unfreezing behavior; second, changing behavior; and then, as in a spring thaw, letting behavior flow, for the third phase of positive solitude is not a phase in which a behavior that has been learned is now simply practiced; it is a creative, fluid phase. When you are ready to enter the third phase, you have a well-developed sense of the loneliness traps, both social and personal, and you have done a great deal of work to fill your own feedback gap with positive solitude. In the exploration stage, the stage in which you have evolved into positive solitude, you are comfortable being alone all or almost all the time. Your life now becomes an exploration of yourself—yourself alone, yourself in context with others, yourself in relation to the spiritual, yourself in relation to art, and so on. The fascinating part about this stage is that only you can determine exactly what your exploration will be. I can only suggest that if you are truly practicing positive solitude, it will be exciting, and you will be in love with yourself and with life.

Of course, the three phases in the development of positive solitude overlap. As you change your behaviors, new awareness will surface. Exploring includes changing. Moreover, though positive solitude is not a temporary way station and its principles should be carried on throughout life, most people will choose to counterpoise positive solitude with some involvement in relationships. You must learn to manage your solitude in the context of society.

In my work as a psychologist, I am frequently reminded of the striking and challenging way M. Scott Peck opened his fine book, *The Road Less Traveled.* "Life is difficult," Peck wrote. "Life is a series of problems. Do we want to moan about them or solve them?"[2] I believe that positive solitude is one important solution to life's problems. But designing a happy life alone is a challenge. Daily feedback does not happen automatically. No child will cry for your attention. No spouse will bustle around the house or suggest going out to a movie. No roommate will be there to talk to. Spontaneous activities initiated by others simply will not be available to fill the hours of your day. People who are alone must take sole responsibility for thinking about, planning, and initiating their daily activities.

Aloneness is real and must be attended to. The feedback gap is real and must be filled. Being alone successfully rarely occurs without a self-conscious effort. Without the desire and ability to reflect on your daily life and on your behavior, old patterns of behavior will prevail.

There are some risks in pursuing positive solitude. Other people may not understand. They may reject or ridicule you. It is even possible that while you are alone you will fail. In his famous essay on solitude, Michel de Montaigne recounted an anecdote about one person's failure to be alone: It had been pointed out to Socrates that a certain man had learned nothing from his many travels, and Socrates replied, "I should think not. He took himself along with him."[3]

Yet the small risk of failure is worth the reward. To be alone, and to be content with that aloneness, is to be powerful. It is to be creative. To discover that you are an interesting person is like receiving a wonderful gift. When you are alone, you own a most precious part of life: You own time. A mental space opens up in your life for your own exploring and learning, your own being and becoming. In this space you may even find wisdom.

Notes

1. Paul Tillich, *"Loneliness and Solitude,"* in Joseph Hartog, J. Ralph Audy, and Yehudi Cohen, eds., *The Anatomy of Loneliness* (New York: International Universities Press, 1980), 549.

2. M. Scott Peck, *The Road Less Travelled* (New York: Simon & Schuster, 1978), 15.

3. Michel de Montaigne, "Of Solitude," *The Complete Essays of Montaigne* (Stanford, Calif.: Stanford University Press, 1948), 176.

II
Living
with Your Self

4
Being Alone in America

What a lovely surprise to discover how unlonely being alone can be.
—ELLEN BURSTYN, actress

What is the difference between people who are alone and lonely and people who are alone and happy?

All people who are alone spend many hours by themselves. After work they find that they have a totally free evening. They wake up on a Saturday morning and see ahead of them days of being alone. They have no one in particular with whom to spend an upcoming vacation. Some people can deal positively with these circumstances, while others find themselves being depressed. Some will look forward to their time alone; they fill their hours with productivity, happiness, and hopefulness. Others anticipate that these times of being alone will be difficult for them. They expect to be unhappy during these times, so they dread them. They will spend their time alone in boredom, in depression, or even in despair.

What is the difference between people whose time alone is

terrible for them and people whose aloneness is satisfying and even joyful? Is it inevitable that some people will dread being alone while others will actually look forward to it?

We can answer these questions by reflecting on the experiences of being alone that occur to most people over their lifetimes. In one way or another, these experiences tend to be negative, especially for Americans, from childhood, adolescence, and adulthood. As a general rule, in our society positive solitude is seldom taught, whereas the dislike of being alone and the "need" to be with others are nurtured early on.

What Children Learn About Being Alone

All normal infants feel strong, even terrifying anxiety when they are separated from their mothers. In many cultures mothers carry their babies with them during the day and rock and sing them to sleep at night. The infants are seldom separated from their mothers, a constant togetherness that continues well into toddlerhood. In the North American culture, in contrast, we have different practices. Eventually, and fairly early, we deliberately leave our children alone in their rooms. Often our well-meaning goal in leaving them alone is to help them learn how to cope with being alone. Though our intentions may be good, the outcome of this standard practice is debatable. The very young and frightened child may not be able to "benefit" from his time alone in the way the parents intend. Usually, he does not have the capacity to spend the time alone in the peaceful or creative exploration the parents hope for. Rather, he may spend his time alone at best in unhappiness and at worst in anger and in fear. If the child learns to be "good" when alone, by which we mean that he does not cry or fuss to be picked up, he is rewarded by being allowed to be with his parents. But being good is not the same as being content. The baby who is left alone may get the idea that being alone is a time merely to be endured, while being with others is a valued reward. As Margaret Mead pointed out, "[the American child] learns to tolerate loneliness in order to enjoy approval the rest of the time. Not for him the search for some place away from the continuous pressure of others' presence, the relief of a closed door, the sanctuary of his own room."[1] American children have learned that being alone is to be avoided. In contrast, in cultures where young children spend less time alone, they do not learn that being alone is to be endured and escaped. Children who have had the nurturing of extensive positive togetherness may be more open to learning that aloneness, too, can be a positive experience. Ironically, because they have not been taught that togetherness is the ultimate reward, later in life they may actually be more open to alternative experiences, including the experience of being alone.

Of course, the effects on later life of these events experienced in infancy are debatable. We can only speculate on them. When babies become toddlers and young children, however, their experiences alone are more obviously formative. This is a crucial time for children to experience being alone—to think their own thoughts; to explore their own creativity; to experience sensations that are uniquely theirs; and, most important, to realize that they can be happy when alone. Early childhood, when time is unstructured by schooling, is an important opportunity for developing a positive attitude toward being alone.

Yet most children today have little opportunity to learn anything resembling the child's version of positive solitude. Increasingly, children's time and minds are filled with external preoccupations: television, extravagant toys, and all the stimulations to be found in day-care environments. Increasingly, education begins at earlier ages, and parents, eager to give their children an educational edge in a competitive world, structure their children's hours with educational play. The children are often urged to engage in social activities as well. Yet in terms of helping them to be emotionally independent human beings, all this activity is unfortunate. As one expert put it, "The love of aloneness cannot grow up amid the confusing turmoil of incoherent sights and sounds. Neither love of men nor love of God can take deep root in a child who does not know aloneness."[2] The result of constant busyness is that children learn to distrust solitary occupations as being wasteful and inefficient, if not actually sinful.[3] Early and precious opportunities to learn how to be alone, probably always somewhat neglected by busy parents, are less nurtured today than ever before. The result, for American children, is the beginning of what comes to be called loneliness.

Even if parents succeed in giving their children enough unstructured time alone, they often communicate to their children that being alone is frightening, unsafe, and socially unacceptable. If the child is very young, the parent will directly communicate the realistic message that "I can't leave you alone." At some level, the child inevitably interprets this message as, "I can't be left alone; I am incapable" (or vulnerable, and so on). Later, as the parent tries to encourage the child to be independent, the parent may unthinkingly say something like, "You're not afraid to be alone, are you?" or "Are you sure you'll be all right alone?" Of this question the child may think, "Am I old enough to be alone or not? Is there something to be frightened of when I am alone?" The parent of a teenager may be reluctant to hint that the child may feel uncomfortable alone and so, instead of addressing the feelings, might say, "But what will you *do* here all alone by yourself?" The teenager may interpret this question as "I can't amuse myself alone." And, of course, throughout childhood and adolescence, parents send a message when they send their children to their rooms alone as a punishment.

Children also hear adults talking about adults who are alone, and much of this talk is negative. "Such a pity; now he'll be left alone," the parents will say of the divorced man. Or "She can't raise those kids alone!" or "She's moving to the city alone!" or "He's traveling alone!" Given our habitual way of talking about being alone, it is not in the least surprising that children may feel bored, insecure, or frightened when they are alone.

Adolescent and Early Adult Experiences

For the teenager, the issue of being alone is highlighted by the emergence of strong peer groups. Now being alone may carry with it the stigma that the person alone appears to have been rejected by the social group. Teenagers may be careful not to be seen alone. If in truth they are not a member of a group, rejection causes powerful feelings. Their self-esteem is threatened. When alone, the teenager is embarrassed not only in front of peers but in front of family members, who expect a child to develop a "normal" pattern of friendships through a social group. Add to this influence the fact that the teenager's media, especially music, emphasize romance and love and their counterparts, lost love and loneliness. Teenagers are certainly not encouraged to build self-esteem through positive solitude! It is no wonder that, reflecting the society around him, the rejected teenager mourns, "I feel lonely, terribly lonely."

American dating patterns that encourage early heterosexual coupling also threaten the development of positive solitude experiences. In recent decades, American young people have moved away from the tradition of building deep friendships with same-sex friends during adolescence. Instead they have dated one on one at ever earlier ages. Yet the former pattern of building same-sex relationships was emotionally useful. It helped the child to learn independence and to gain a sense of self before getting involved with the deep and complicated emotions attached to sex and love. Traditionally, best friends were soul mates. They were friends of the same sex, age, and beliefs. They were friends to band up with against those "others"—parents and society—who did not understand them. These relationships helped the introspective adolescent to develop a truly independent sense of self. This independence came, in part, from sharing thoughts with the same-sex soul mate, who could help the teenager in a nonauthoritarian way to clarify his or her thoughts. The independence came, too, from separating from each other and further developing these thoughts in private. In this way, an adolescent grew emotionally and intellectually independent through the relationship. By emphasizing an active social life and sexuality, today's early heterosexual dating patterns have diminished this period of peer-supported personal adjustment. Today's teenagers define themselves as much in relation to the opposite sex as in relation to their same sex. It is no wonder that the American teenager, with little encouragement or opportunity to develop the sense of self, feels a lack of identity. Later in life, many will report that this lack of meaning in their lives is a central factor in their loneliness.

The fickleness of young love accentuates teenagers' feelings of exclusion, meaninglessness, and loneliness. The drama often unfolds like this: Suddenly in early adolescence, teenagers meet people of the opposite sex who want to spend time with them. This experience is flattering and it gives them new power. Now they can find love outside their families. In addition, they discover the powerful emotions and sensations of sex. Early love affairs are almost always short-lived however, and when they end, the loss of so many wonderful new pleasures can be emotionally devastating for the teenagers. In addition, there is a new kind of peer pressure. Since they are no longer part of a couple, the teenagers' status in their peer group may diminish. What do teenagers learn from these experiences? Having newly experienced love and sex and having been encouraged by their friends, they come away believing that being part of a couple is an ideal state in life. Certainly, to them, being part of a couple seems preferable to its depressing aftermath—being miserable, outcast, and alone.

Unfortunately, turning people away from positive solitude does not end with childhood and adolescence. Even in early adulthood, most Americans have a lifestyle that inhibits periods of being alone. After high school we may go to college and live with roommates. We may go to work and share an apartment with others, or we may continue to live at home with our families. It is not usually until our midtwenties or later that we may actually experience living alone. By this time, though we have lived nearly a quarter of a century, we have seldom experienced being alone for long periods. We may not even have spent a period of a few days by ourselves, let alone a few weeks, months, or years.

Adulthood: Conforming to Prevailing Beliefs

When we reach adulthood, it is not surprising that the beliefs and attitudes of most Americans reflect the negative experiences they have had with solitude. We have developed the attitude that being alone is bad and that it is to be avoided. Few of us have actually been taught how to be alone and like it. Few parents have paid more than lip service to the idea that their children should learn to face and deal with their own boredom, and, on a more philosophical level, with their own solitude. Few parents have actively encouraged their teenagers to stay alone in the house for the weekend (not knowing how to be at home alone, the teenagers would, of course, fill the house with friends). Parents, peers, and the media have all taught us that being alone is disagreeable. Perhaps it is also unhealthy, we think, and even unworthy. Society tells us, in a word, that being alone is the ultimate social disease.

Though as adults we suffer under this conventional wisdom, we seldom challenge it. The thought of going to dinner alone or going on vacation alone is uncomfortable. We tend to blame ourselves for being alone. We believe that we should nudge ourselves to get out more. We may chide ourselves that being happy alone is simply not in the genes. After all, we say to ourselves, anthropologists have informed us that to achieve safety, food, and sex, people have been living in groups since primitive times. Why am I alone?

As a society we also perpetuate myths that support the idea that aloneness leads to loneliness. We continue, for example, to believe in the empty-nest syndrome—the idea that women suffer a great deal of loneliness when their children leave home. The truth is that most women find this period in their lives to be an exciting new beginning. We continue to believe that older people, who do spend more time alone, are also lonelier, even though the research shows that loneliness actually decreases with age.[4]

In the face of such pressures, we should not blame ourselves for our conformity. Frankly, the social risks of doing anything else are large. Often a social stigma is placed on the person who chooses solitude. Such a person is known, not positively, as a "loner"—as an outcast and a deviant as much as an individualist. As the nineteenth-century philosopher and writer Ralph Waldo Emerson sagely put it, "Society, to be sure, does not like this [solitude] very well; it saith, Whoso goes to walk alone, accuses the whole world; he declares all to be unfit to be his companions; it is very uncivil, nay insulting; Society will retaliate."[5]

Choosing Positive Solitude

What is most surprising is that some people are able to avoid all this enforced togetherness. Some pioneering souls actually resist our society's pressure. They refuse to make the search for others, especially for "significant" others, the focus of their lives. Rather, they concentrate on improving their experiences alone. It is not that these people are resigned to being alone. It is that they are seeking a new direction in their lives; they are actively and positively pursuing the pleasures and stabilities of solitude.

Eventually, I believe, many more of us will follow this lead. In spite of social pressures, an increasingly large proportion of single people in this country are living alone by choice. In recent decades, there has been a steady growth in the percentage of households in which people live alone, from 11 percent in 1956, to 16 percent in 1966, to 21 percent in 1976.[6] It is anticipated that the 1987 statistic for American households consisting of one person—24 percent—will grow to between 27 and 37 percent by the year 2000.[7] A major reason for our independence is that in modern times the facts of survival have changed. In Western societies today, we can live quite comfortably and safely alone. Alone we can feed, clothe, house, and amuse ourselves not just adequately but well. Never in the history of the world have so many individuals had so much financial and physical freedom to do with their lives exactly as they please.

Our psychology has not quite caught up with our new freedom. This ability to live alone makes possible what amounts to a social experiment, an experiment with lifestyles in which people explore the psychological and spiritual effects of living alone. All people who live alone today are a part of this enormous and important social experiment. Clearly, few of us have actually been taught by our parents or by society the psychological skills for being alone. For most of us, our experiences in aloneness as teenagers and young adults have usually been inadequate or even harmful. Society continues to give us ample indications that we are on the wrong path. Yet despite this acculturation, many people who are alone persist in staying alone. They give many explanations for their choice.

For one thing, accounts from people who spend even short times alone suggest that their experiences may be special. Sometimes people who are alone experience their environment with great intensity. They are most likely to do so in a relaxed situation that holds no interruptions or distractions, like the following one:

I was utterly alone with the sun and the earth. Lying down on the grass, I spoke in my soul to the earth, the sun, the air, and the distant sea, far beyond sight. . . . With all the intensity of feeling which exalted me, all the intense communion I held with the earth, the sun and sky, the stars hidden by the light, with the ocean,—in no manner can the thrilling depth of these feelings be written,—with these I played as if they were the keys of an instrument. The great sun, burning with light, the strong earth,—dear earth,—the warm sky, the pure air, the thought of ocean, the inexpressible beauty of all filled me with a rapture, an ecstasy. . . . I prayed. . . . The prayer, this soul-emotion, was in itself, not for an object: it was a passion. I hid my face in the grass. I was wholly prostrated, I lost myself in the wrestle, I was rapt and carried away. . . . Had any shepherd accidentally seen me lying on the turf, he would only have thought I was resting a few minutes. I made no outward show. Who could have imagined the whirlwind of passion that was going on in me as I reclined there![8]

Some people make being alone a habit that they intersperse into otherwise socially busy lives. Here is a recent description by a woman who needs to spend significant amounts of time alone:

I was an only child. I've been used to isolation and in fact, I enjoy my own company. I don't mean this egotistically, but I can be very happy with me and a book and something to do. Some people cannot stand themselves, to be alone. I always had to have my own time. My husband soon learned I needed time to be alone, away from him. Even as a child, I took off certain time for myself and time to get caught up with my own thinking. So I never felt I had to be with people. I enjoy my freedom.[9]

Other people have chosen to spend not just moments or hours, but major portions of their lives alone. They suggest that these experiences, too, can be fulfilling as a lifestyle. In 1843 Emerson observed of these people:

They repel influences; they shun general society; they incline to shut themselves in their chamber in the house, to live in the country rather than in the town, and to find their tasks and amusements in solitude.

... This retirement does not proceed from any whim on the part of these separators; but if any one will take pains to talk with them, he will find that this path is chosen both from temperament and from principle; with some unwillingness too, and as a choice of the less of two evils; for these persons are not by nature melancholy, sour and unsocial,—they are not stockish or brute,—but joyous, susceptible, affectionate; they have even more than others a great wish to be loved ... They will own that love seems to them the last and highest gift of nature; that there are persons whom in their hearts they daily thank for existing,—persons whose faces are perhaps unknown to them, but whose fame and spirit have penetrated their solitude,—and for whose sake they wish to exist. ... [These] are degrees on the scale of human happiness to which they have ascended; and it is a fidelity to this sentiment which has made common association distasteful to them. They wish a just and even fellowship, or none. ... They say to themselves, It is better to be alone than in bad company. ... They feel that they are never so fit for friendship as when they have quit mankind and taken themselves to friend.[10]

A notable contemporary seeker of positive solitude is May Sarton. In her book *Journal of a Solitude,* Sarton described a year in which she was ending a love affair and finding what she called her "real life." She wrote, "I begin to have intimations, now, of a return to some deep self that has been too absorbed and too battered to function for a long time. That self tells me that I was meant to live alone, meant to write the poems for others. ... Friends, even passionate love, are not my real life unless there is time alone in which to explore and to discover what is happening or has happened."[11]

Even a brief introduction to positive solitude may lead to major changes in one's lifestyle. A famous example is the experience called the Solo, which is offered within the international wilderness training school Outward Bound. The Solo is an intensive time alone that varies from half a day to several days, and for many participants of Outward Bound, it is a unique and intense experience. As one participant described it:

This was the first time in my entire life that I had been quite alone. I married young, had three kids right away. To be able to sleep when I wanted to, to shout and dance around, have no one dependent on me—that was heaven. Perhaps this isn't exactly what Solo is for, but that's how it affected me. The Outward Bound literature talks a lot about personal growth. Well, I think I grew about ten feet during my Solo and I hope I stay that tall."[12]

Another participant in the Solo (sounding very much like Henry David Thoreau) said:

> I built a shelter, inspected my little domain, contemplated the tides, the sea birds, the changing skies. . . . Although I had pencil and paper along, I did no writing and no deep thinking. Afterwards, I realized that the value of Solo for me lay in taking a complete rest from the intense activity of my everyday life.[13]

A third participant commented simply: "I never knew how great it is to be alone."[14]

So positive solitude can be experienced momentarily, or it can be a major part of your life. Just as people who experience positive solitude have found various paths to that experience, so they will find different things when they get there. The experience of positive solitude is individual and unique. Some people will find solace and sanctuary. Others will find a renewed ability to concentrate. Others will discover spiritual peace. Still others will discover vigor and creativity. Though their common experience is positive solitude, the outcome of their experiments with it will be unique to them as individuals.

As fulfilling as solitude may be, it nevertheless brings its own problems. For example, people who have chosen to be alone for long periods tell us that while solitude is wonderful in and of itself, it also creates a mode of being that is uncomfortable when one wants to return to society. Clearly, just as one may need to learn how to be alone, after being alone one may need to relearn how to live in society. One writer on solitude, J. Ralph Audy, a human ecologist, spent much time "alone" with tribesmen in Africa and Asia and alone with Nature. Though he says he never felt lonely in either circumstance, he notes that when he wanted to return to society, his experience alone had changed him:

One dreams much of beer and sweet water in deserts. After perhaps an overdose of solitude during two years of Somaliland, I arrived in Nairobi and escaped from my hotel in search of beer. On opening the door to the bar in Torr's I saw a vast sea of faces, groups of close friends laughing together, a babel of voices, both masculine and frighteningly feminine. I was utterly unable to pluck up the courage to go to the bar. I backed out, and had beer in my hotel room. It took over a week to get used to such crowds of one's people and of strangers.[15]

Author Gretel Ehrlich, who left a large Eastern city to live more quietly on a ranch in Wyoming, related a similar story. In her book *The Solace of Open Spaces,* she recounted her increased understanding of the effects of being alone:

For someone who lives in a remote spot, arriving at a ranch or coming to town for supplies is cause for celebration. To emerge from isolation can be disorienting. Everything looks bright, new, vivid. After I had been herding sheep for only three days, the sound of the camp tender's pickup flustered me. Longing for human company, I felt a foolish grin take over my face; yet I had to resist an urgent temptation to run and hide.[16]

Most of us will live our lives within society. We want to, and must, adapt to that society. Yet, we also want to be independent and self-fulfilled. In modern America, it is time to turn away from conformity and togetherness and toward the experience of positive solitude. Disputing the beliefs that we Americans have acquired during our lifetimes, those who have spent significant times alone convey that solitude can bring increased self-knowledge, confidence, and times of pure joy. If the experience of solitude is not entirely easy and positive, let us remember that the experience of being with others is not all easy and positive either. Love, relationships, society, and being alone all bring us various trials and discomforts. Ultimately, we want to forge the spirit of community, but first we must find the spirit that is within each of us.

Notes

1. Margaret Mead, "Loneliness, Autonomy and Interdependence in Cultural Context," in Joseph Hartog, J. Ralph Audy, and Yehudi Cohen, eds., *The Anatomy of Loneliness* (New York: International Universities Press, 1980), 399.

2. Renate Wilson, *Inside Outward Bound* (Charlotte, N.C.: East Woods Press, 1981), 139.

3. Ibid., 400.

4. Carin M. Rubenstein and Phillip Shaver, "Loneliness in Two Northeastern Cities," in Hartog, Audy, and Cohen, eds., *The Anatomy of Loneliness,* 327.

5. Ralph Waldo Emerson, *The Transcendentalist,* in Carl Bode, ed., *The Portable Emerson* (New York: Viking Press, 1981), 100.

6. U.S. Department of Commerce, Bureau of the Census, *Current Population Reports, Population Characteristics. Households, Families, Marital Status and Living Arrangements: March 1987,* Series P-20, No. 417 (Washington, D.C.: U.S. Government Printing Office, August 1987.

7. U.S. Department of Commerce, Bureau of the Census, *Projections of the Number of Households and Families: 1986–2000,* Series P-25, No. 986 (Washington, D.C.: U.S. Government Printing Office, 1986).

8. Richard Jefferies, "The Story of My Heart," quoted in William James, "On a Certain Blindness in Human Beings," in Josephine Miles, ed., *Classic Essays in English* (Boston: Little, Brown & Co., 1961), 230–31.

9. Quoted in Helena Znaniecki Lopata, "Loneliness: Forms and Components," in Robert S. Weiss, ed., *Loneliness, the Experience of Emotional and Social Isolation* (Cambridge, Mass.: MIT Press, 1975), 110.

10. Emerson, *The Transcendentalist,* 100.

11. May Sarton, *Journal of a Solitude* (New York: W. W. Norton & Co., 1973) 207.

12. Quoted in Wilson, *Inside Outward Bound,* 142.

13. Quoted in ibid., 144.

14. Quoted in ibid., 142.

15. J. Ralph Audy, "Man, the Lonely Animal: Biological Roots of Loneliness," in Hartog, Audy, and Cohen, eds., *The Anatomy of Loneliness,* 114.

16. Gretel Ehrlich, *The Solace of Open Spaces* (New York: Viking Penguin, 1985), 5.

5
Managing the Loneliness Crises

When is man strong until he feels alone?
—ROBERT BROWNING, *Colombe's Birthday*

Loneliness crises are those times when a person feels "terribly lonely" or "desperately alone." You feel depressed, helpless, empty. Life seems to have no meaning. A loneliness crisis most often happens when you lose someone close to you, someone you have depended on for a large amount of feedback and often someone you depended on for many different kinds of feedback. The loss of a lover means the simultaneous loss of a source for sex, laughter, information, social support, material security, and intimate talk. With the exception of sex, the loss of a close friend or a family member brings similar deprivations. Such major losses mean that large blocks of your time are left suddenly unfilled. The unexpected death of a spouse or the sudden end of a relationship leaves you without other sources of feedback.

When changes in relationships are anticipated, a wise person will think ahead to a new life and plan new ways to fill the feedback gap.

You realize that you will miss your daughter when she goes to college, so you take on new challenges at work. You know that you will soon be divorced, so you become interested in new activities and new people. Yet planning for the loss is one thing; living through it is another. A loneliness crisis may still occur. Loneliness crises are characterized by intense emotions. All normal people will experience them at some time in their lives.

In addition to feeling normal sadness, people who experience a major loss are often terrified. Consider the case of a woman in group therapy who suddenly burst out sobbing and related her story:

> Everything was going all right until all of a sudden I became so lonely. This awful loneliness just came over me and dug into me. I couldn't get rid of it; and I don't know why. There was nothing I could do about it. It was terrible. I couldn't stand it. I wanted to die.[1]

A woman in her early forties described the anxiety in her own loneliness crisis this way:

> I wanted to get away from the situation and be with the kids in another country. So we left the country. I mean we really got away. And the feeling I had was of even more acute loneliness. Like I was walking through Barcelona. The kids didn't want to hang around, so they took off. So I was walking down a street and trying to visit some of the sites. And it was a very kind of empty feeling, having nobody to share any of these places with, not even the kids. It was very hard.[2]

Author Thomas Wolfe is well known for his dramatic depictions of loneliness. In his autobiographical novel *The Web and the Rock*, he described the loneliness of lovers who have decided to separate forever. First, read Wolfe's dramatic description from Webber's, the man's and his own, perspective:

> He had come away to forget her: He did nothing but remember her. He got sick with the pain and the thought of her, he got physically sick, and there was no medicine for his sickness. . . .
>   At night, after prowling about feverishly through the London

streets until three or four o'clock in the morning, he would go to bed and fall into a diseased coma in which events and people of his past life were mixed with the present, but during which he was yet conscious that he dreamed and that he could break the pestilential trance at any moment. Finally, in the early morning when people were going to their work along the street, he would fall soundly asleep and lie as if drugged until noon.[3]

The restlessness and despair of the loneliness crises could hardly be more powerfully depicted. The woman Webber left behind in New York was Esther Jack. She also suffered, alone:

To the swarming rock October had come back again with all its death and eagerness, its life, its lifelessness, its stored harvest and its barren earth, its prophecy of ruin, its hope of joy. It was October, and there had been autumnal sunset, and now brisk stars were winking in the Park.

Esther sat upon a lonely bench and thought of him. Four months ago today he left her. What was he doing now—now that October had come back again?

Was it the one red leaf, the last of its clan, that hung there straining in the wind? The dry leaves scampered down the path before her. In their swift-winged dance of death these dead souls fled along before her, driven with rusty scuffle before the demented wind. October had come back again.

Is it the wind that howls above the earth, is it the wind that drives all things before its lash, is it the wind that drives all men like dead ghosts fleeing?

All things were lost and broken in the wind. . . .[4]

We know that we must all face the inevitable fact of losing other human beings. Over a lifetime such losses will accumulate. You will lose lovers, parents, brothers and sisters, children, and friends. You can never have fewer losses than you have at this moment, and unless you decide to close yourself off from relationships altogether, in the future you will probably have more.

It is especially at the times of great loss that you must self-consciously confront your life. Positive solitude may seem enormously remote, even a cruel joke, in the throes of these bad times. Yet, if the loneliness can be suspended for even moments at a time, if health can even be glimpsed, you can make progress. Patiently, you must take the first steps toward self-sustenance. If ever a person needed their self—their intelligence, humanity, nurturance, creativity, and love—it is now.

How can you be sure to find love in your life? How can you always be in love? Be in love with yourself.

During a loneliness crisis, the memory of the lost other is fresh, perhaps infinitely dear. It is natural to want to hold that memory for a time, even though holding it will be poignant and perhaps actually painful. You understand that the memory will fade, and you both abhor and welcome its loss—abhor it because your memories are the precious remnant of your love, welcome it because living the memories is living in the past. You are alive and in the present, and some part of you wants to go on. Your aloneness is new and raw. You are probably frightened and disoriented.

Understanding the Full Extent of the Crisis

In these times of crisis the most important thing to do first is to understand fully what is happening. Recognize that this change in your life is profound. It will affect you enormously. Above all, human beings are feedback driven. It is our very ability to recognize and to think about environmental feedback that has assured the survival of our species. Disruption of our feedback systems is unnerving and disorienting for all of us, but dealing with the disruption is also our human strength.

So while part of you is mourning, part of you—the part that knows positive solitude—should be figuring out what to do. The voice of reason, the problem-solving abilities that most human beings contain within them, may be totally shut out at first. But gradually, as mourning takes its course, it will grow louder. This voice is the part of you that seems outside your emotional self, the part that watches you respond. It is the part of you that is standing back and giving wise counsel: "Yes, this is normal. Yes, this grieving is necessary and healthful. Yes, this pain will pass." Realizing that this grieving is happening helps a person to accept it.

Understand that you will greet people in life and then, eventually, you will pass them by. They leave you or they will die. You will leave them or you yourself will die. You need to understand that the loss *is* out of our control. But understand, too, that as long as you live, replacement of the lost feedback with new, positive feedback is within your control. This understanding is the beginning of hope.

Part of this process is allowing yourself the full expression of your feelings. To "own" your own feelings is to accept their existence, to express them, and to be responsible for expressing them appropriately. You must accept the existence of all your feelings, too. You must accept not just the socially acceptable feelings like sadness and hurt, but the darker, less acceptable feelings like anger and guilt. You must express these feelings in some way, whether through writing a journal, talking with a trusted friend, or seeing a professional counselor. Finally, you must be responsible for developing appropriate control of your feelings—working them through by expressing and understanding them, but also controlling them and moving on.

A part of experiencing loss is the natural tendency to withdraw emotionally and intellectually from the world. This regression is natural. You have been wounded, and you need to devote time and energy to healing. To pull back, deliberately to shut out new encounters and other new stimuli for a while is sensible. It is healthful to allow this regression. Allow yourself to feel childlike, dependent, nurtured. For a time you may have no energy for, and no interest in, filling the feedback gap. You may not want to think about personal meaning or about creating new options. You may simply want to be and to rest. Time out is emphatically okay. There is a time for expressing emotions, and there is a time for doing nothing, for indulging yourself.

Grieving Alone; Recovering Alone

But, you say, one of my toughest problems right now is that I have to go through this crisis alone. How can I endure this time of pain alone? It is normal to believe that a major part of the loss is having no one to grieve with. Regressing to a childlike state may be fine, you think, but when I do, who will take care of me?

When grieving alone, it is especially important to be absolutely clear about your own needs and abilities. Children, when ill or unhappy, cannot take care of themselves. They need the actual presence of a nurturing person. Adults, on the other hand, can act as nurturing parents for themselves. Unless they are physically disabled, they can adjust their environment to make retreat and healing possible. They can, for example, arrange to take time away for themselves. They can choose where to spend that time and they can create a nurturing environment for themselves during that time. Adults can be sweet and indulgent parents to themselves, in some ways better than any actual parents because these self-parents know their own needs absolutely and fully.

In times of crisis you have to ask yourself, "What feels good? Is there anything at all that would feel good to me now?" And then you have to listen to your own answers—childlike, absurd, unusual though they may be! Do you like baths? Make a ritual of taking luxurious oil baths. Give this time to yourself and treasure it. Get all the sleep you need, for without it little else will feel good. This is not a time for the rules and regulations of self-discipline. This is a time of acceptance and indulgence of that part of you that is still childlike and undisciplined and needy. For a reasonable length of time, as long as you are doing no harm to yourself either immediately or for the future, it is actually wise simply to do anything you feel like doing.

During this nurturing time, the character of your self-talk is crucial. What is your inner monologue saying to you? If you emphasize that you are "all alone" with "no one to take care of me"—if you focus on the absence of an other as opposed to the presence of your self—the healthy regression may turn into unhealthy feelings of depression and helplessness. Emphasize instead how well you are taking care of yourself. Notice the nice, creative things you are doing for yourself and how good you feel about them. Instead of listening to that inner voice that is always worrying about calories, for once enjoy the ice cream.

A problem you may have is that you, like many people, may not actually know how to nurture yourself. For one thing, you may not *believe* that you can rely on yourself for nurturing. If this statement is true for you, you can make good use of professional counseling. A professional therapist can guide you in examining your erroneous belief that your nurturing self can never be depended on. And counseling is an excellent framework in which to help the nurturing part of you to become stronger.

Often a person's times of rest and healthy regression include periods of sadness. In fact, in the early stages of mourning a relationship, you may be sad most of the time. Amid this sadness, make a conscious decision to notice the positive solitude experiences that occur. The sunlight on a pond or the deliciousness of a raspberry— some such delights will occasionally intrude upon your melancholy.

In spite of your belief, you are not *totally* sad. One counterintuitive way to encourage inklings of happiness is to focus—intently—on trying *not* to be happy. Take a few minutes to push all happiness out of your mind. Definitely do not let any happy memory, sensation, or plan intrude. Most people cannot do so. This experiment can get you in touch with the realization of your innate capacity for joy. Noticing your moments of happiness, you will spontaneously build on them and gradually begin to heal.

During a loneliness crisis, then, you need to understand the process that you are going through at the moment and the process you will go through to heal. You need to feel the loss, in whatever emotional form that feeling takes for you, and to allow yourself to regress and to rest. Gradually, you will find the energy to think about filling the feedback gap with joy and meaning instead of with sorrow and regret. Eventually, you will be willing to face the anxieties of building a different life. Not all at once, but soon, you will be willing to trade the depression of hopelessness for the anxiety of exploration. And, eventually, you will settle into a renewed life, a life filled with a new and probably different set of satisfying feedbacks.

Characteristic Dilemmas

Certain problems seem to emerge systematically during a loneliness crisis. The first one is succumbing to the urge to run away. I am not talking now about the urge to escape psychologically, to belittle the problem of the crisis itself but, rather, the urge literally to move, leave, roam, flee. In stressful situations, most animals exhibit the well-known flight-or-fight syndrome. They will either stay and do battle or attempt to escape. Humans are also adapted either to fight or to flee. Intense loneliness is more closely associated with the propensity to flee. Examples we have just seen are the divorced woman who took her children to Barcelona and Thomas Wolfe's character, Webber, who fled to Europe. We all know of people who have gone away to forget.

The anxiety of being thrust into a new life, not knowing where the next feedback fix may be coming from, can be enormous. Often your physical surroundings will evoke unhappy associations, and you will feel compelled to escape. Here is what one man says about being alone at home when his family is far away:

> "All the space in the house, except for my sanctum, the study, is associated with my wife and daughter, so that I feel a sense of incompleteness when they do not share this space. The feeling vanishes when I go to my study or to the University, to sites where solitude is an expectation, as it might be in a chapel."[5]

Associations to physical settings are real. If by flight you thereby discover a new feedback set, a permanent feedback set that will transfer to your "normal" life situation, then flight is fine. But if fleeing does not fill the feedback gap, if instead you are left forlorn on the streets of some foreign place, then flight has been counterproductive.

If it does any good at all, fleeing is only a temporary remedy. Traveling is almost always disconnecting and uncomfortable in some way, even for someone who is experienced at it. There is no reading light when you want one. You can't find a good bookstore. Your neighbors are a budding rock group. Emotionally, traveling is not likely to be any better than staying home and facing the feedback gap. With your home sanctum as a base of comforts, you are well prepared to develop new associations and a new feedback set.

While some people clearly take their loneliness with them, others are able to leave it behind. Usually, a walk in the country or a weekend escape is enough of an experiment to tell you what your own tendency is. But in all events, think carefully before you buy that ticket to Australia. The urge to flee is a primitive urge that during a loneliness crisis needs to be rationally considered before expensive commitments are made.

The flight syndrome can emerge even though you do not actually leave town. You may wander the streets or frequent bars. Well-meaning friends often will counsel you to go out a lot. But such activities and such advice must be carefully considered. Do you actually feel better when you are out? What does your wandering achieve? Do you feel good in a bar? Are your good times mostly dependent on filling your life up with people? Do you feel incapable of having a good time alone? You need to learn to have a good time all by yourself, and you need to make your home a place in which to have that good time.

The second major dilemma during a loneliness crisis is the tendency to make sudden decisions, decisions that lead to choosing the wrong things to fill the feedback gap. You may become overconfident. You may counsel yourself, "Trust your instincts. Go with the gut feelings." And you may jump headlong into trouble.

Habit is strong, and during these times when our emotions run high, reason does not always control habit as well as you would prefer. Thus people take off around the world. Or they take up the temporary solace of drugs. Or they jump into harmful relationships. The divorced person who gets involved with someone very much like the former spouse is making this mistake. Some people believe that they get involved with the carbon-copy mate because of some basic psychological need in themselves, but it may also be true that they make the mistake simply out of habit. They have grown accustomed to a certain type of feedback system. The system is comfortable, and in the exciting early stages of a relationship, the consequences of such a bad habit are forgotten. Unfortunately, as loneliness researcher Robert S. Weiss pointed out, "Attachments that develop in response to great need are likely to carry a large risk, which may at first be overlooked. . . . As long as they last, they are fulfilling."[6] But, unfortunately, such attachments do not last. A divorced woman who was interviewed by Weiss had gotten involved with a friend's husband and subsequently found that he could not leave his wife. She said:

You look for something to fill that emptiness. You start going out. You go with the girls meeting people. Wrong people, right people, it doesn't make any difference. . . . Then all of a sudden you wake up one day and find yourself in the middle of something. . . . It's something new in your life. It's something that's filling the emptiness. It may not be the best thing, but it's still something to look forward to, to get up every day for, to dress up for, to comb your hair for, to get a little happiness out of.[7]

As Weiss noted, such unwise attachments tend to end, and "one never becomes accustomed to their ending, just as one never becomes accustomed to physical pain or to moral humiliation."[8]

The third pitfall in the loneliness crisis is passivity. Making no changes at all in your life can be harmful. Widowed individuals and people who are not the initiators of their divorce are prone to this mistake. They hold on: They visit the same old haunts, stick with the same friends, take vacations in the same places, keep the same interests. For a time, a period of weeks or a few months, these pursuits may be necessary for you to maintain some sense of equilibrium and continuity. But eventually, you must realize that life is now different, that the decisions made during and for the relationship no longer need to be made nor should be made. Activities once enjoyed together may not be as fulfilling for the self alone. They may even be occasions for mourning or for wistful remembering. At a certain point you will want something more fulfilling for yourself.

Recognize that many decisions that were made within the relationship were compromises. Decisions were made to benefit the couple, not the separate individuals. The couple compromised on where they lived, where they vacationed, and what they ate for dinner. They played golf because he loved it and bridge because she loved it. The individual alone should expect to live differently—not better or worse, merely differently—than he or she lived when part of a couple. Some of the old ways will no longer be as satisfying as they were when a spouse was included. Concerts enjoyed together will now be experienced differently. Perhaps the concerts had been enjoyed primarily because they were a mutual activity. If it is true that they were primarily a social occasion and that the music itself was in some ways secondary, going to the same concerts when you are alone will seem empty. You simply may not enjoy the music itself enough to make continued attendance seem worthwhile. It is time to find other pursuits that you personally enjoy.

Old activities now have unpleasant associations. You can still get pleasure out of them, but many will not be as thoroughly enjoyable and comfortable as they once were. You must seek new pleasures. You may enjoy cross-country skiing, but you may also have skied with the loved one who is lost. Now is the time, at least temporarily, to take up downhill skiing. Now is the time to do anything that is uniquely your own. Now is the time to fulfill individual dreams and fantasies. If later you still want to go back to cross-country skiing, you will be stronger and your memories will be weaker. You will be ready to quell the old associations and to fill the feedback gap with your own fulfilling new ideas and explorations.

During the bad times, when loneliness is felt most acutely, when you are feeling hopeless, it is important to make a decision about every single form of feedback that you pursue. You must ask yourself, "Is this activity, this feedback that I am now choosing, going to help me to heal and to grow? Or is it going to lead me along the same path that I am now on, a path of suffering?" Habits that were once rewarding and self-actualizing may now be doleful and deadening. You must think this question through before you choose the old ways—wonderful and nurturing as they were.

Another problem that often arises during a loneliness crisis is the failure to recognize *all* the emotions involved. What is the full spectrum of feelings that you are experiencing? Some emotional complaints are more socially acceptable than are others, and even within ourselves this "acceptability" inclines us toward acknowledging some of our emotions but not others. In fact, there is a range of social acceptability for all our mental distresses, from most acceptable to least acceptable. For example, people may say that they are "depressed." This is a relatively acceptable ailment: People often say they are depressed. It is also acceptable, though somewhat less so, for people to say that they are lonely. It is be considerably less acceptable for them to say that they are afraid, which may imply weakness, or anxiety, which others may see as a sign of instability.

Though loneliness is not the most acceptable distress, it is not the least acceptable either. A major pitfall in a loneliness crisis is hiding behind the loneliness and denying to oneself or to others the other important feelings that have taken control and may need to be resolved. These feeling include anger, jealousy, anxiety, disorientation, fear, rage, and helplessness.

For example, consider widowhood—a major loneliness crisis. In a well-respected study by Helena Znaniecki Lopata, 40 percent of the widows Lopata talked to said that they are rarely or never lonely.[9] The other 60 percent said they do feel lonely, and these women showed a distinct tendency to repeat old, maladaptive emotional patterns that had been adopted *before* their spouses' death. A significant difference between the most lonely and the rarely lonely widows is the presence of anger. The very lonely women, in contrast to those who are seldom lonely, recall being angry with other people frequently before their husband's death. In the crisis of widowhood, these angry women lack people to whom they can turn for emotional and social support. Presumably, their anger drives such people away. Such sad individuals have a dual problem in the bad times: to deal with their anger while figuring out how to deal with the feedback gap.

A final dilemma is hopelessness. Whether or not you will feel hopeless depends, in part, on how you define the problem of loneliness. If you believe that loneliness will be assuaged only by finding someone and if you believe that finding someone is difficult or impossible, then your hopelessness has the force of logic and will be unshakable. If, however, you adopt the precepts of this book, then you believe that loneliness can be assuaged not in one, but in many ways. You know that you control these ways yourself. Thus, if you believe in positive solitude, your feelings of hopelessness are unlikely to continue for long.

If, after reading all that is said here, you still feel hopeless or if you find that the feelings of hopelessness consistently return, then you must find someone who will help you to take the first steps toward believing that things will get better. A friend or therapist who guides you toward self-nurturance is useful in these times. Sometimes the impetus need only be a small, thoughtful gesture that gives you a moment of solace. During one of my own loneliness crises, a friend who lives a thousand miles away sent me some bubble bath. That simple, loving gesture helped to get me started on my own self-nurturing journey. Sometimes the help comes in the form of modeling—you meet some people who are very nurturing to themselves, see their productive self-loving habits, and learn from them. Through such observations, you may come to believe that hope is not, after all, so hard to come by, and you begin the journey of positive solitude.

Notes

1. William A. Sadler, Jr., and Thomas B. Johnson, Jr., "From Loneliness to Anomia," in Joseph Hartog, J. Ralph Audy, and Yehudi Cohen, eds., *The Anatomy of Loneliness* (New York: International Universities Press, 1980), 34.

2. Robert S. Weiss, *Marital Separation* (New York: Basic Books, 1975), 57.

3. Thomas Wolfe, *The Web and the Rock* (New York: Harper & Row, 1973), 575.

4. Ibid., 627.

5. J. Ralph Audy, "Man, the Lonely Animal: Biological Roots of Loneliness," in Hartog, Audy, and Cohen, eds., *The Anatomy of Loneliness.*

6. Robert S. Weiss, ed., *Loneliness: The Experience of Emotional and Social Isolation* (Cambridge, Mass.: MIT Press, 1975), 140.

7. Ibid., 140.

8. Ibid., 141.

9. Helen Znaniecki Lopata, "Loneliness in Widowhood," in Hartog, Audy, and Cohen, eds., *The Anatomy of Loneliness,* 237–58.

6
Decision-Making
Alone

*The choices and decisions that we make in our times of
aloneness are ours and ours alone. We tap our inner resources
and make decisions that only we can make, in the process
coming more gradually to trust our own resources.*
—IRA J. TANNER, *Loneliness: The Fear of Love*

When we are suffering from problem emotions, it is natural to
devote our energy to dealing with them. Yet, managing practical
matters such as basic decisions should not be neglected. Your emotional well-being depends in part on your skill in making good decisions for yourself. In particular, people who are alone need to understand their strengths and weaknesses as decision makers. Inevitably,
the decision-making process for single people differs from the decision-making process practiced by couples or families. There are
major differences, for example, in the way goals are set, the number
of opinions that need to be processed, and the way a solution is
developed.

Consider a major decision like buying a new car. Picture, if you
will, a person in the process of making such a decision. One image

that is likely to come to mind is of Dad. Dad is sitting at a desk littered with bills and other ominous-looking missives (probably life-insurance plans). His brow is furrowed: Can he afford the car that he wants? Can they afford the car the family needs? What does his wife think? Should he get automatic door locks to protect the children? As Dad ponders, his focused desk lamp illuminates only his work, leaving the rest of the room in darkness. Through a doorway we see that in the next room the children are cooperating in the decision by keeping the television low or, better yet, by quietly studying. Mother is coming from the kitchen, where she has been making coffee, to confer with Dad. This idealized image conveys that this is a modern family, in which there is still one central decision maker but in which problems are, in some ways, shared.

Often the mode of decision making is similar for the decision maker who is alone. You may find yourself sitting in a darkened room, at a desk with a similar stack of bills and papers, with the familiar scowl. But though your mood may be alike in its focus and serious-ness, your situation is really different in a number of important re-spects.

On the down side, you may feel uncomfortable simply because you are alone while making your decision. Our culturally conditioned expectations of how decisions are made seldom includes the person alone, unless that person is some kind of hero. In fact, the traditional image that we Americans have is much like the scenario I've just described. In our culture, especially as presented on television, "good" decisions are made within supportive family structures. Ev-eryone in the family has a particular role in the decision-making process, and each acts that role well to ensure the best outcome. Even the children have a job, which is to leave Daddy and Mommy alone to make the decision. If you are alone, you may be sensitive to the fact that you must play all the roles. There is no spouse standing by with a cup of coffee or, for that matter, with helpful ideas. You may feel some loss on this account. If you are really feeling sorry for yourself, you may feel that the absence of children or of a partner in your life undermines the very meaningfulness of the decisions you face. You say to yourself, "Why worry so much about this decision anyhow? It only affects me. It's not such a big deal."

Yet, on the positive side, there is much to be said for not being a party to the traditional decision-making scenario. As a lone decision maker, you have no one to please but yourself. You do not have to take the time and emotional energy to consider the goals and satisfactions of others. In a process uncomplicated by spouse and children, you can simply go ahead and decide. When you need information to make your decision, you can get outside help. The telephone on your desk connects you with people who are at least as knowledgeable about the facts needed in the decision, and no doubt less opinionated, than a spouse would be. Because you don't have to spend time compromising with the family, you have time to make your own coffee, exactly as you like it. Furthermore, if the truth were to be told about the idealized family decision, the children aren't really sitting with the television turned low anyhow. They are arguing about which program to watch. The good wife is not making the coffee either. After a hard day in the office, she has collapsed into a nearby chair hoping that her husband will make it.

People who make decisions alone lack appropriate role models and may not have a strong image of themselves as effective, efficient decision makers. By recognizing some of your disadvantages and your advantages in the decision-making process, you can learn to cope with the former while taking advantage of the latter.

Decision making is often thought of as simply the act of choosing between two alternatives, but really it is an entire process. Making a decision includes many steps: identifying the problem or problems, gathering information, creating alternative actions, deciding what action to take, implementing that action, and, finally, living with the results.

Each step suggests the need for certain personal skills, knowledge, time commitments, and attitudes. When decision making is a social process, it is complicated greatly by differing goals and emotions and by the need for communication, clarification, debate, and compromise. Organizations, which can be thought of as social systems designed for collective decision making, often deal with this complexity by dividing up the steps of a decision-making process among many people. Families develop their own decision-making habits. People who are alone will follow the same decision-making steps that organizations, families, couples, and other groups use, yet their approach to each of the steps will necessarily be adapted to their particular needs.

Consider the initial step in decision making: the identification of the problem to be solved. Focusing on a problem is a different process for singles than it is for couples or for families. The person alone has fewer of others' problems to contend with, an obvious advantage. For the person who is *not* alone, the problems of the other people become topics for discussion, and the entire group has to discuss or consider each person's issues.

When you are alone, you can concentrate on your own issues. With freedom comes responsibility. You must assume the responsibility for identifying your problems. This is not as straightforward a process as it first appears. Often, out of habit, we rely upon others to help us see ourselves and gain a different perspective on issues. Alone, you must compensate for the lack of other perspectives by being more observant and thoughtful about yourself and your environment. Since making personal decisions is your responsibility, and only yours, you should focus even more strongly on your own problems. You need to focus your energies and to be judicious in allowing yourself to become distracted by the problems of others. When you are alone, this selfishness is healthy.

At the same time, such intense self-awareness will have its disadvantages. For one thing, it may be seen by outsiders as self-centered. When alone, you need to counteract this impression by making an extra effort to put others at ease or by helping them to understand your situation. A related problem is that because you become so used to identifying your problems by yourself, you become less open to the valid observations of others. It is unlikely that people alone will hold the *only* valid interpretations of their behavior; they will often be able to profit from the observations of others. You are often party to conversations that tell you something about yourself: "You seem tense." "Do I?" "Yes, you are frowning a lot this morning." "Really? I guess I've just been so busy that I didn't notice how I was feeling." Yet just as when you are with others you may have the tendency to rely on them too much, when you are alone you may tend to rely on yourself too much. Your friends may need to point out some of your problems for you. The best stance is to find a balance between healthy selfishness and openness to the input of other people.

The next step in the decision-making process is collecting information about the problem. Suppose the problem is finding a new apartment. To do so, you need to assemble a lot of information about apartments, locations, comparable rents, parking, security, leases, and so on. You will invest a significant amount of your personal resources in time, intellect, and imagination. In this situation, the individual alone is obviously at a disadvantage. A couple who is making the same decision has twice as much time and two creative minds instead of one, and a family or network includes even more resources. Under favorable circumstances that foster cooperation and open discussion, groups make better decisions than would an individual who is alone. When a group or couple is open and relaxed, it can tap a larger knowledge base. Since individuals will each think about the problem somewhat differently, the group or couple will also have more different approaches to a problem and will be able to select the best one. The individual alone has a relatively limited amount of knowledge and will have a limited set of alternative approaches to a problem.

Suppose you want to find that new apartment across town. You read the newspaper ads for the community you have chosen and ask a friend who lives there to look around for you. Soon you have some leads, and you make appointments to see the apartments after work for several evenings in a row. After visiting half a dozen apartments, you settle on one and take home the lease to study it. Satisfied, you return across town the next day and give your deposit to the landlord. You have followed a reasonable process. Yet, compare it with what a couple could do in the same situation. Harry and Sally each have friends in their target community, so they get more leads than you do. Sally has to work late one night—just like you do so often—but instead of canceling an appointment with a landlord, Harry goes. In reviewing the lease, Harry and Sally pool their collective experience in such matters, which, while it may not be exactly twice yours, is certainly more. Satisfied, the next day Sally drops the lease off because their new apartment happens to be on her way to work.

Of course, you are a more efficient decision maker than are either couples or families. You avoid meetings and arguments. And it is true that you can use the time you thus save to seek additional information and to create more approaches to the problem. Still, the adage that two heads are better than one does hold some truth. Because much of their knowledge will overlap, two people may not always have twice as much knowledge as one, but they typically have more knowledge than the individual alone does. A family or group has even more.

Realizing this fact, as every person alone must, can increase your fear of being alone. We live in a competitive society, in which singles must compete with couples for such daily necessities as housing and for such luxuries as hotel rooms. In a species that has survived by its intelligence, any perceived deficiency in decision making that comes from being excluded from a group is bound to increase anxiety. However, in the twentieth century, our primitive fears of exclusion are allayed by the fact that the individual does not really need to know very much to survive. We do not need to know how to build a house or grow crops or treat illnesses to live safely, eat well, and stay healthy.

Some decisions do, however, require in-depth knowledge. It is one thing to plunk down the money to rent an apartment. It is quite another thing to buy a house. You not only shop for the house, but you try to get a good buy, arrange for the mortgage, and manage the upkeep. Personal financial planning is another area in which you will need broad expertise. Even twenty years ago, investment decisions were relatively uncomplicated. With today's proliferation of financial instruments and the volatility of world economies, such decisions require a great deal of knowledge. For these kinds of complex decisions, you must learn to compensate for living alone.

Consider lowering some of your expectations. For example, when you are making a complicated decision alone, you should expect to invest a great deal of time in gathering information. You may not be able to make your final decision quickly. Because of time constraints, you may want to simplify some of your decisions, investing, for example, in mutual funds instead of more volatile individual stocks.

At the same time, you can compensate by choosing to spend some of your time systematically learning about those complicated issues that you face. Major decisions—buying a house, planning investments, providing adequate insurance, developing a career—seldom arrive unexpectedly. When important and complex decisions do occur, you can be prepared. Couples, lulled into complacency, often fail to continue learning about life's more complicated business. It is not uncommon for responsibility to become diffused within the couple. Each relies on the other's knowledge, which may be outdated or simply wrong. One says, "My spouse knows a lot about the stock market, so I don't need to know more." When you are alone, you cannot afford not to know, and you will not blindly rely on others to know. You wisely learn the basics and continue to update your knowledge.

In summary, when you are alone it is important to fight the primitive feeling of anxiety that comes from being "excluded" from the tribe. It is important to distinguish those problems that require detailed knowledge from those that do not. Reserve your energy for studying those problems that in our society are complicated and risky, especially financial matters, major purchases, and health-related decisions.

Moreover, when you are alone you should make systematic efforts to identify experts who can help you to expand your knowledge. In identifying lawyers, accountants, doctors, and others, singles tend to have fewer immediate contacts than do others. They simply have fewer opportunities to make them, and they cannot rely on their spouse to know people to enlarge their networks. One coping strategy is to realize this weakness and compensate by taking systematic advantage of the contacts you do have. Make a special effort to join professional and recreational and other networking groups. Happily, a person alone can elicit outside help from experts without offending a partner who believes himself or herself to be the in-house expert. Thus unfettered, you can always chose the best possible counsel.

When you are alone, you will solve problems according to your own personality and experience; you will tend to use certain problem-solving approaches over others. For example, if you are what has been called a right-brain dominant individual, you will solve problems more intuitively and holistically. If you are a left-brain dominant individual, you will tend to solve problems more logically, sequentially, and analytically. Individuals' decision-making styles also differ in terms of their ability and training to think logically, manage time, and maintain self-discipline. Savvy corporations take advantage of the fact that their employees have different styles by creating problem-solving teams that combine people with different approaches. The same strategy will work well for individuals. Often the individual who is alone should seek others whose decision-making styles differ from their own. Creative, intuitive persons might seek out analytic types, for example. Thus, you can assure that you will see a problem from various angles, and you will be better equipped to ensure its happy solution. The person who tends to make hasty decisions would do well to find a consultant/friend who is more methodical. The person who tends to focus on the general framework of a problem would do well to find a consultant who is detail oriented. When you are alone, you must know what your own problem-solving style is, and you should learn to complement it. Identify friends with complementary styles who are willing to help you to make some decisions. You may also be able to compensate by learning additional new styles.

Once information is gathered and different approaches to the problem are adopted, the next step in the decision-making process is to select a solution. People choose different solutions in large part on the basis of their ability to implement them. Though couples and groups may be highly focused and committed to a solution, compared to the person alone they are usually at a disadvantage. It is less likely that any one solution will please all group members, and when the solution is implemented, some members may resist. This resistance will be time consuming, annoying, and potentially sabotaging to the solution. Because you alone have done all the decision making, you will have a clear focus on your problem and a strong commitment to your selected solution. You are more likely to take Mark Twain's view that you should put all your eggs in one basket—and then watch that basket! This effect on implementation of the desired solution is widely known in business start-ups. Entrepreneurs are focused, single-minded, and motivated. It is not surprising, then, that it is the person alone, not couples or groups, who most often establishes a successful new company.

Yet in implementing a solution, you must also keep in mind your limitations. As the one person to implement the decision, you have relatively less time. You have fewer hands to perform necessary tasks. Consider household work. Although some housework is simplified when one person does it, some is made more tedious by being alone. In every household, whether populated by one or many people, there is one electric bill, one telephone bill, and one rent bill to be paid. The checkbook still needs to be balanced, too. Alone, you cannot share these burdens. Individuals who are alone are less likely to have a backup system in the form of another person to do these chores, to say nothing of earning the required money, if they cannot or do not wish to do them. These complications suggest that people who are alone need to be especially well organized so busy times do not find them falling behind in such essentials as paying bills. The accompanying luxury, of course, is that if you really want to let a job slide, you are free to do so.

In general, making effective decisions alone requires that you be literally and figuratively *centered.* In part, being centered means having an appropriate physical space: a well-organized decision-making center. Albert Einstein did not keep all his knowledge in even his astonishing brain—he had a marvelous library, and he knew where things were in it. You require a desk with plenty of file space, an efficient phone system, excellent reference books, and a systematic listing of contacts. You will probably want a phone answering machine. A personal computer is useful for complicated financial records and analyses and for gaining valuable knowledge through various on-line networks. Such a decision-making system should be thoughtfully selected to serve your particular decision-making needs, be they as simple as paying bills or as complex as tracking real estate.

Having this central place for decision making will contribute to your psychological sense of being centered—that combination of self-awareness, confidence, and openness that often characterizes the well-adjusted individual. Centered persons recognize the problems inherent in making decisions alone and take steps to remedy them.

They recognize that their time and energy are finite and they do not push themselves to attempt too much. They seek challenges that match their abilities. They recognize their need for expert assistance in some aspects of their decision making, they begin to collect contacts with experts well before they desperately need them, and they are well organized.

Most of all, if you are alone, you recognize that making effective decisions does not require the presence of an intimate companion. While it does require your own thoughtfulness, knowledge, and creativity and it does require resourcefulness in finding trustworthy expert advice, it is something that you can accomplish effectively alone.

Ultimately, a decision is implemented, and your solution succeeds or fails. You have to live with the results of your decisions and actions. As a person alone you have only yourself to blame for failure. And only yourself to credit with success. You cannot realistically blame your consultants. A consultant, such as a personal financial analyst, is removed from the personal consequences of the decisions that are made. The consultant's legitimate role is to give advice, not to make decisions. You cannot rightfully blame your helpful friends either. Close friends will give advice, but they will most assuredly not wish to take credit for a decision. (If they do, they do not often stay friends.) Of course, this clear delineation of decision-making responsibility is not true in couples and families. A partner is, by definition, a person with whom one makes a decision. Together a couple shares the consequences of a decision, and they may exult or console one another as necessary. They may also fight and blame each other when a decision turns out badly. The person alone has all the decision-making power, and, if things go well, all the resulting glory. Yet, whether the result is glory or ignominy, you must be prepared to handle the consequences—emotional, interpersonal, or financial.

Take particular care to forecast the personal consequences of the solution you choose and to figure out what your emotional reaction to failure will mean. Will you blame yourself? Will you fall into the loneliness trap of desperately wishing you had a partner in the decision? Or will you realistically assess your decision-making process, analyze your strengths and weaknesses both as a decision maker and as a *solitary* decision maker, and go on to the next problem?

Choice implies uncertainty, and the decision-making process is always accompanied by some uncertainty. When people are alone, this uncertainty can be heightened. Perhaps they realize some of the advantages of collective decision making without figuring out how to compensate for them in their own lives. They may not yet have realized some of the advantages of being alone in a decision. They feel doubtful and uncomfortable.

The uncertainty of decision making alone will be especially high for the person who is newly alone. If you are recently separated from a major decision-making partner like a spouse, the occasion of even a minor decision may cause extra anxiety. Since your new decision-making process represents a significant change from former modes, your anxiety about coping with this new situation is not unreasonable. You have to develop a whole new decision-making process, yet you may be only dimly aware of how to do it. Not only are you coping emotionally with the ending of a close relationship, not only are you in need of adopting a new and unfamiliar decision-making process, but at the same time important practical problems—such as a divorce or the settling of an estate—are likely to accompany the end of the recent relationship. Often in these circumstances the safest first step is to do nothing for a time. Unless you have a trusted friend to handle your affairs, you should delay major decisions for at least weeks, possibly months. Feeling lonely and uncertain, lacking confidence, an individual alone is prey at these times to the suggestions of many people who do not have his or her best interests at heart. Defer decisions until you figure out what the most effective decision-making process will be for you.

When newly alone, your tasks are, first, to fill your feedback gap by yourself and with yourself; second, to become accustomed to your new life circumstances; and, third, to regain or increase your own confidence. When you have made a good start on these tasks, you should learn how to make an effective decision along the lines suggested here, and you should learn to assess your own abilities to do so objectively.

All people who are alone, whether newly or not, will be acutely aware that no matter what they learn or know, they are likely to be stereotyped as relatively weak decision makers. What do most of us really think about people who are making decisions primarily alone? In truth, we may question whether their decisions are good ones. For the logical reasons I have already pointed out, most of us would guess that their decisions are less likely to be effective than are those made by couples or groups. The person alone senses these prejudices. The woman alone is particularly susceptible because she comes from a category of individuals about whom there are already many prejudices: The quality of women's judgment has only recently been accepted. Still, as a decision maker the woman alone is sometimes seen as less than half a couple, and because she senses this disapproval, her confidence in her own abilities as a decision maker may be low. The single man may also experience prejudice. For example, the assumption often is that he needs to be helped to find a suitable partner. Society has always stigmatized the individual alone: as a loner, an eccentric. (At one time in Puritan America it was even illegal to live alone!) The implication is that the lone person must be a little bit crazy. Without a firm belief system of your own to sustain you in your aloneness and a firm knowledge of your ability to make decisions, you can indeed be a weak decision maker. Your judgment may waver, or you may fail to effectively implement your own goals.

The problem of the negative stereotype cannot be solved by individuals. Only as singles take a full and strong role in our society will prejudices against them be defeated. But people alone can gain enough confidence in their own decision-making abilities to give up caring what others think. You can realize your weaknesses, your uncertainties, and your self-doubts as a decision maker, and you can learn to compensate for them. You can build on your strengths. In so doing, you can become a model that others will come to respect and emulate.

Remember that there are significant advantages to making decisions alone, not the least of which is escaping from some of the negative aspects of decision making that exist for couples and family groups. Not only is it difficult for two people to negotiate clear goals, but their separate perceptions of those goals may be not quite the same and may diverge even further over time. A person alone will have clearer goals than will people together. The negotiation of goals and the process of deciding consume time; typically, the larger the group, the more time is required. The person who is alone can make routine decisions quickly. Couples and groups are also subject to pressures for conformity, and sometimes even though their decision is bad, it will be agreed to and implemented anyway. The person who is alone can do exactly as he or she pleases.

When you know how to make decisions alone, you take pride in doing so. You express yourself. You alone have the final word.

When you are alone, you may, because of your unique personality, follow highly idiosyncratic decision-making processes. Such creativity in decision-making can exist only when you are free of external constraints. You may be as eccentric as you wish. You can analyze the problem in detail or you can go with your intuition, and no person can criticize you for not approaching the problem "properly."

When you are alone in your decision, no one can cloud your unique vision.

7

Sensuality Alone

BOGART: How'd you like it?
HEPBURN: Like it?
BOGART: White-water rapids!
HEPBURN: I never dreamed. . . .
BOGART: I don't blame you for being scared. Not one little bit. Nobody with good sense ain't scared of white water.
HEPBURN: I never dreamed that any mere physical experience could be so stimulating.

—*The African Queen*

In solitude it is just as important to tend to your physical needs as it is to tend to your intellectual and emotional needs. It is especially important to remember that your physical well-being is inextricably intertwined with your emotional well-being. The depression and anxiety so often associated with loneliness are always felt physically in different heart and respiratory patterns or in changed levels of activity that leave you feeling either sluggish or overtired.

Sometimes your feelings originate not in your situation but in a change of activity level itself. For example, for some reason related or not to your solitude, you may choose to be less active than usual;

as a result, you will begin to feel sluggish. Because you feel sluggish, you may start to think that you are becoming depressed—all because you failed to attend to your physical needs in the first place.

Physical well-being is a prime source of joy in solitude. As you look inward in solitude, you will discover an expanded sensuality, and, happily, you will have the time and energy to explore it. Discovering and developing your sensuality can become not only an enormous pleasure, but an important source of centering and well-being.

Unfortunately, commonly approved notions of sensuality, like so many aspects of our culture, tend to focus on relationships. In America today, sensuality implies sexuality. Among all possible sensualities, sexuality is the type that is most often touted in the media. In the age of the velvet mouth, the glistening body, and the phallic lipstick, sex is a sensuality that sells. Our society promotes it as a major tool of advertising, movies, television, and magazines; as the central issue in human relationships; and even as a human rights focus. We place relatively little value on the broader experiences of sensuality—the use of our eyes, ears, and other sensory organs for the pursuit of pleasures not associated with sex.

Of course, being in sex is wonderful. Great, intense sex with a great, intensely sexy person is, yes! great and intense and sexy. But all our emphasis on sexuality can result in a serious obstacle for anyone who is pursuing positive solitude. It often becomes a loneliness trap. When you think of sensuality primarily in terms of sexuality, you buy into the belief that you need someone else around to fulfill your sensual needs. By focusing on sexuality, you are ignoring all the other wonderful sensualities that your mind/body offers to you. You severely limit yourself.

Each of your senses has something wonderful to offer. Sight gives you the delight of colors, shapes, nature, the human body, clothing, architecture, and art. Hearing offers birds and oceans and music. Smell brings you lilacs, perfume, and spring air. Taste introduces chocolate, potato chips, and spices. Through touch you experience warmth, fur, and velvet. Through your kinesthetic sense you take pleasure in walking and swimming and dancing.

Yet for many of us, sensuality is a mere acquaintance, rather than a close friend. After all, our time is limited. We work hard. Americans in the latter part of the twentieth century are working more hours than they did twenty years ago. It is obvious why sensuality came more naturally in our youth—we had more time for it! We become tired, and out of habit and convenience we fill our lives with pastimes that are more active than sensual. Yet sensuality is always central to a full life. You should find time for it no matter what your age. You must actively pursue it by discovering environments that engage all your different senses.

Focusing on Sensuality

To become reacquainted with your sensual self, you must first make experiencing your sensuality a goal. A person never loses the capacity for sensuality and this capacity doesn't even fade much until you are quite old. Yet over the years one tends to forget about it more and more. "I am too old for that," we say to ourselves. We start limiting ourselves by such thoughts even when we are children: "I'm too old to play with blocks!" By forty, we are experts at limiting our options: "I'm too old to take up a musical instrument." "People my age cannot learn to ski." We put on our boring business clothes and go back to work. We express surprise when a fifty year old takes up scuba diving, when a sixty year old starts a new business, or when a seventy year old enjoys sex.

A lot of the pressures not to indulge our sensuality come from society. When we think of California as sunny and New England as cold, we are not noticing only the weather. The acceptability of sensuality also differs in these distinct social climes. The challenge is to let your sensual self be heard no matter what the social rules.

After you encourage your sensual self to speak, pay attention to what you hear. It is often said that your most important sexual organ is between your ears. Your most important sensual organ is there, too.

Sensuality involves your intellect. Ignorance narrows your experience instead of expanding it; it deadens your sensuality. Through experience, you can develop an aesthetic sense at any age. In recent decades the tradition of aestheticism has been overpowered by the cult of youth and sexuality. It is waiting to be rediscovered. There is good reason to mourn the decline of liberal arts in education, for such early training predisposes adults to feeling comfortable with many different sensual explorations. One good art history course at age twenty allows you to walk into a museum at age forty and have a place to start. Throughout life, the liberal arts enliven the mind for a broad appreciation of life—opening your thoughts to music and literature and painting and an appreciation of the natural world.

To enhance your sensuality, you must suspend your automatic judgments of what it is OK to feel. So often we allow only specific, predetermined types of sensual stimulation to give us pleasure. Many men emphasize sexuality, sports, music, and food. It is acceptable for a man to have a fur rug on his bed, but less acceptable for him to enjoy a fur coat. A woman's sensuality is likely to focus on her environment, clothing, touching, food, art, or music. She less frequently emphasizes sex or sports. Part of the pleasure of being sensual alone is the freedom to break out of these stereotypes and to find out what truly turns you on. Men alone can do more with touch, smell, and aesthetics. Women alone can do more with kinesthetics, including both sports and sex. Be creative! (After all, nobody is watching.)

As with anything you will do alone, it's important to take matters into your own hands. A day filled with sensuality is not likely just to happen. So, plan a sensual day alone. You might sleep late, waking up to a fine cup of coffee and a croissant served on your most beautiful dishes. Read in bed a while, make love to yourself, sip a glass of champagne. You might indulge yourself then in a scented bath or a long shower, dress beautifully, and go out to see something engaging and visually wonderful—an art museum, a forest, a city market alive on a Saturday morning. You might occupy yourself at such a scene by walking through it, photographing it, or talking to strangers you meet. Lunch would be whatever your mood desires. In the afternoon you might try a sensuous activity or sport, sculling perhaps, swimming at the beach, or a nature walk. Spend an hour or two reading a good book or listening to music.

Of course, if you are constantly thinking, "Gee, I sure do wish so-and-so were here now," you will not enjoy a positive sensuality. You must have enough confidence in your self, enough control of your positive thought processes, to handle such intrusive thoughts. Yes, it might be nice if someone were with you. Yet, you are alone, with your own feelings and sensuality, and that is terrific, too. Think it and feel it.

Enhancing Your Sensuality Through Solitude

Listening to your sensual self is actually easier in many ways for people who are alone. When you are with other people, your sensual pleasures are defined by your very togetherness. What you will do at any moment is a compromise of the wishes of all the people present. Sometimes you compromise just with one other person; sometimes there is a whole family or group involved. With all the distracting social stimulation in your environment, staying in touch with your own needs and pleasures is difficult. Even if you can do so, expressing them fully when you must compromise with others is impossible.

When you are with persons of the opposite gender, male-female rituals in touching and in dress and even in the way you look about the room will distract you from your self. Maintaining a deep and peaceful focus becomes impossible. A person touches your arm, and your attention is drawn to that touch. Your companion points out something lovely, a flower or a phrase of music, and you drop your own perceptions and center your attention on what has been pointed out. You may or may not agree that it is lovely.

Solitude can enhance your sensuality. When you are alone, you will not be distracted. You can take stock of your mood and do exactly what your sensual self feels like doing. Often you will find that your mind will be at peace and at rest. Being apart from business, talk, and action, you will heighten your awareness of your senses, your surroundings, and your natural rhythms. You can express your individual aesthetic sense. Have you ever noticed that the loveliest apartments are often designed by single people? In the art and furniture they collect, they can express themselves with an aesthetic sense that requires no compromise.

Sensuality has a lot to do with mood. Your mood at any particular time predisposes you to particular sets of sensual experience. If you are part of a couple, it seems natural to "set the mood": actively to

create an environment that encourages sensuality. In positive solitude, too, even if it feels a bit unnatural at first, think about setting
the mood for your personal sensuality.

The sensual moods that you probably know best are associated
with relationships, especially sexual ones. These moods represent
socially acceptable sensuality. The mood of couple sensuality is so
acceptable that it is a cliché: you dress carefully, select a good bottle
of wine, and lower the lights—all to promote mutual sensuality and
sexuality. Hard-rock sensuality—the sexual sensuality of clubs and
music—is a different kind of couple sensuality—livelier, tougher,
widely pursued. A rare sensuality in which it is acceptable for people
of the same gender to touch and admire each other is sports. The
comaraderie of the field, and especially of the locker room, creates
a mood of highly charged sensuality involving all the senses.

People who are alone have other sensual moods to pursue. Many
become outdoor enthusiasts and nature lovers. For instance, hunters
describe their delight at being alone in the woods. They are attuned
to sounds, smells, shapes, and shadows. Experiencing an environment that is simultaneously beautiful and hazardous, they are intensely present in their sensual selves. Trout fishers note the same
intensity: concentration on the stream and the fish, broken occasionally by gazing up at the natural setting.

I have been a member of the Appalachian Mountain Club for
many years now. This is what I wrote in my diary about the sensuality
of a day spent at a club retreat:

> At this moment, this day, there is no place in the world that I would
> rather be—my back propped against a rough rock, the ground warm,
> my feet up on a fallen birch, the lake lying gentle in front of me. Fifty
> yards out is a rock cairn making an entrance to our harbor. A hundred
> yards out, at the edge of a small, treed island, the wind on the water
> is steady.
>
>   Wow! Nature news breaks at my very feet! A tiny snake—no
> more than six inches long—has a one-inch toad by the head. One of
> them—the toad I presume!—is squealing. The little wide-eyed snake
> is determined—there they go thrashing through the dry leaves, his/her
> body curling (happily? greedily?) *Greedily.* But now the toad leaps and

throws off his persecutor! He rests. Is his eye bloodied? Meanwhile the snake slithers deep under the leaves. I reach out to measure the toad with a length of my finger and he jumps out of range in one effort. All is quiet. Ah—I find him and he leaps off again, to fall down a boulder-cliff to safety. And the snake? Will he climb into my shoe? Up my pants leg? Where the devil is she/he? I take up a stick and poke it into the leaves and acorns. I tease Snake away along a wide rock. He won't be back.

[A few minutes later]. Goddamn! Something black and furry—I hope it was a weasel, not a rat!—just darted down my slope not more than two yards from my shoulder! Searching around the rocks by the shore, I cannot find a trace—a weasel then! My God, what a place! Observe, feel, keep/guard/protect/enhance my own thoughts, my own spirit. This is a place for such keeping.

Another, quite opposite type of sensuality focuses not on intellectual energy but on intellectual surrender. This kind of Zen sensuality usually develops in a place where silence, reflection, and solitude are honored and protected. It involves clearing your mind of its constant thinking so that other, sensual stimuli may enter. It has been called by many names—letting go, centering, and meditating. Zen practitioners say that it is "seeing the truth *through your everyday eyes.* It is only the heartless questioning of life-as-it-is that ties man in knots. A man does not need an answer to find peace. He needs only to surrender to his existence, to cease the endless, empty questioning. The secret of enlightenment is when you are hungry, eat; and when you are tired, sleep."[1] You can bring Zen sensuality into your life in many ways. Practicing meditation and lying in float tanks are among the trendier pursuits. Gentle walking and simply resting are other ways. The goal is to rid yourself of expectations. Just surrender, in a quiet place, to what happens.

Many people who are alone discover a heightened aesthetic sensuality. Freed from the preoccupation of organizing a household complicated by other lives, they can focus on making their living space an extension of themselves. They discover their own taste. They make a point of collecting art and other things that satisfy their aesthetic sense.

I have one friend whose apartment is a delight to visit. At every turn my friend has placed something joyful or droll or serious—pictures and bowls and sculptures, all with character, that she has collected in her travels. Everywhere are textured things you are dying to touch—and can indeed touch because you are not in a museum. I have another friend whose apartment is basically white, the better to show off the sculpture lights she collects and the few colored pieces she owns. Yet another is a sensualist whose lovely home is graced with fragrances—soaps, foods, and flowers.

People like these are turned on. They have created wonderful places to experience on a daily basis. They have made sensuality a theme of their positive solitude.

It should come as no surprise that in these lovely environments sensual people make love to themselves. Masturbation is such an ugly word for love. Who invented that word anyhow? Better to think of solitary sex as self-love, which is less clinical and infinitely more sensual.

What is it that sex with another person gives you? Let us leave aside the affectional side for a while (see chapter 14: "And Who Are All These Others?") and concentrate on the physical. There is no debating that sex with another person does provide certain mechanical perks. It also entails the fascination of risk and surprise: What will your partner do next? How will he or she react to what you do? Although these interactions cannot be replaced, when you are alone you can do a great deal to have a similar good time.

You know, for example, what it is that physically pleases you. If you cannot do these things yourself, there are dozens of healthy products available in discrete catalogs to help you out (maybe even some you wouldn't dare to try with a partner). If you miss the excitement of another person, add excitement with your new toys, or with fantasies imagined, read, or watched. Choose fresh environments for your self-love. Take yourself away for a fantasy weekend at an inn or outdoors. Refresh your sensuality by finding new moods. It is important to get away from the repetition of your daily life to turn your mind on again.

I believe that refreshing ourselves is even more important as we get older and sameness looms on the horizon. One reason why people love nature is that it is constantly changing—light from sunrise to sunset, and then darkness and stars; animals ranging about; and plants germinating, growing, fruiting, and dying. It is all so engaging to watch! As I write these words, I am looking out at an old apple tree, snow covered, where eight male blue jays have come to a feeder. Just beyond, the road curves into a village at the base of a small mountain. I have taken myself to this small bed and breakfast in Vermont to get away—to work, to be sure, but also to refresh my senses—and as I feel more rested, more joyful, I know this trip is worthwhile.

Travel of any sort, whether it be hours or minutes away, opens new opportunities for sensuality. When it is vacation travel, unencumbered by work or other activities that structure your time, it can also be used to open a deliberate feedback gap, to create anticipation. In an intellectual mood, you might ask yourself, What shall I do today? In a sensual mood, you might ask yourself, What shall I feel today? Single people are often warned, "Never go to such and such a place alone. It is too beautiful!" or "It is too romantic!" While I would not suggest that your first travel forays alone should be to a romantic inn, maybe your fourth or fifth trip could be. Alone, you, too, will enjoy the drink by the fire, the candlelight dinner, and the flannel sheets.

Inhibitors of Sensuality and How to Manage Them

Of course, experiencing a positive sensuality at all times is impossible. We have other things to do. We become tired. Positive sensuality can be lost through long-term boredom and mental stagnation. It can be cut off by illness.

There is an effect of our environment, too. Some environments are truly antisensual, as was one cold dark afternoon that annoyed Henry David Thoreau:

> The landscape is barren of objects, the trees being leafless, and so little light in the sky for variety. Such a day as will almost oblige a man to eat his own heart. A day in which you must hold on to life by your teeth. . . . Ah, but is not this a glorious time for your deep inward fires? And will not your green hickory and white oak burn clear in this frosty air?

Now is not your manhood taxed by the great Assessor? . . . A day when you cannot pluck a flower, cannot dig a parsnip, nor pull a turnip, for the frozen ground! What do the thoughts find to live on?[2]

Contrast this description to a day in Thoreau's life in August of the same year:

My heart leaps into my mouth at the sound of the wind in the woods. I, whose life was but yesterday so desultory and shallow, suddenly recover my spirits, my spirituality, through my hearing. . . . For joy I could embrace the earth; I shall delight to be buried in it . . . now I have occasion to be grateful for the flood of life that is flowing over me. I am not so poor: I can smell the ripening apples; the very rills are deep; the autumnal flowers . . . feed my spirit, endear the earth to me, make me value myself and rejoice. . . . I thank you, God. I do not deserve anything, I am unworthy of the least regard; and yet I am made to rejoice . . . the world is gilded for my delight and holidays are prepared for me, and my path is strewn with flowers. . . . Ah! I would not tread on a cricket in whose song is such a revelation, so soothing and cheering to my ear! Oh, keep my senses pure![3]

Although we cannot change the seasons, we can be aware of their effects on our emotions and we can appreciate the different sensualities they bring—the warmth and freedom of summer, the rest and coziness of winter.

Another barrier to experiencing our sensuality fully is the image we have of our own bodies. How would you describe your body? How do you see it? Experience it? Does it annoy you? Does it please you? Unfortunately, society is often the mirror in which we see ourselves. In our American culture, women and men who should be much less self-conscious dwell on their bodies. Women are concerned with weight and breast size. Men worry about their muscles, their hair, the size of their penis.

What is your body image? Some of us feel that our body is something we drag around with us. When we are in a hurry, it cannot move fast enough; it pleads to be fed and watered; it inconveniently bleeds. Perhaps you think of your body mainly as a tool—as hands that do work, arms that are strong, and feet that get you where you want to go. Perhaps you do not think much at all about your body; it is "over there" while the "real" you is "over here."

Your image of your body affects your experience of it and your use of it. If it is primarily a drag on you, out of shape, tired a lot, and unkempt, you will feel annoyed by it. In such cases, you are more likely to try to ignore your body, and in ignoring its needs, to abuse it. If you view your body as a tool, you will tend it more carefully. Because you realize how much you need them, you will take care of your hands, your eyes, and your pitching arm.

Consider imagining your body as a wonderful toy. If you think about it this way, not only will you avoid abusing it, not only will you take the time to tend it, but you will also enjoy it. You will creatively explore its various sensualities. You will learn that different parts of your body have different sensations of touch and temperature. You will figure out how to appreciate more fully the wonders of seeing, of hearing, of smelling, of moving. A broad sensuality is flexible; as we go through the stages of life, we may need to compensate for the loss of one sensuality with a gain in another. Being experienced and enriched in all our senses will make this adaptation easier. The body can be such a wonderful toy that even if we lose one or more of our senses, the others can entertain us endlessly with new intensities and varieties of sensation.

Another inhibitor to sensuality is our basic beliefs about touch. Sometimes people who are alone say that they yearn to be held or hugged. They suggest that when they spend much time alone, even a particularly warm handshake or a friendly touch becomes significant to them. Research has even suggested that human touch is related to the healing of disease. The touch of another human being, be it nurturing or sensual or sexual, sometimes seems magical.

No definitive research has been done that will give us guidelines as to how much human touch we each need. Probably, as in most things, the range of human need differs. We must each take responsibility for discovering our own needs. This discovery is best done in times of peace and emotional well-being, rather than in times of crisis: though it is in times of crisis that we may yearn to be held, it is in times of relative calm that we can realistically assess ourselves and prepare ourselves for more difficult times.

Our self-assessment should include all our senses, not touch alone. Though it may be touch we yearn for, often it is simply sensual stimulation, *of any sort in sufficient intensity and duration,* that we really need. Sensuality is an urn that can be filled with a blend of many pleasing oils, it can be filled to the top even though one particular oil is not available.

If your other senses are well satisfied and yet you still yearn to be touched by another person, there are two courses to be taken, and perhaps, to be on the safe side, both should be pursued simultaneously. On the one hand, you may guess that "Yes, I, for one, really do have a need to be touched. Since I am alone, this is a problem." What are your alternatives?

First, a caution. Do not seek to meet your need to be touched through a person of the opposite sex until you are satisfied that you *can* satisfy most of these needs yourself. This statement may seem like a contradiction. However, since touch is so important to you, if you are very needy, you can be controlled by it in a relationship. Such control often leads to disappointment and dependence for you at best, and to sexual exploitation and grief at worst.

Certainly there are ways for you to get your desires for touch met apart from intimate relationships:

Get a regular body massage.

Hug your friends, especially friends of the same sex. They may decide to hug back.

Spend more time with little children. They love hugging and touching and are more needy of it themselves and more willing to offer it to others.

Make love to yourself. You are the person who knows how to touch you best.

Go into therapy and ask for what you need: Get all the hugs you want and get held when you need to be held. (Find out more about where these needs originate for you.)

Become a toucher yourself—touch people on the arm when you talk to them. Touch family members more often. Be open when they reciprocate (and understanding if they don't.)

All these avenues to touch are under your control. Through them, you receive touch independently, without obligation by either party. They allow you to preserve your individuality and to strengthen it while still meeting your desire for contact.

At the same time, you may want to consider reducing your need for touch. As we have already suggested, one way to do so is to make sure that the vessel of your senses is filled. Another way is to challenge the belief that being physically contacted by others is a *need*. While being touched *may* be a need, this need is far from proven. Millions of people live happily without regular physical contact with others—people who choose to live alone, such as the elderly, the single, and the religious, and people who live in cultures in which touch is simply infrequent. Many Americans have lived for long periods without significant amounts of touching—in homes where touching is negligible, in college dormitories, in long periods spent concentrating on work. Many are happy, satisfied individuals, for whom the "need" for human touch is not an important influence.

We must also challenge the primacy of the "need" to be touched because it is intimately intertwined with the erroneous belief that we must have a companion to be content. Touch and love inevitably go together. The belief that we cannot exist without loving companionship strengthens our belief that we cannot exist without touch from another.

When we are alone and are feeling lonely, the one thing we cannot have, by definition, is companionship. When we are alone, we cannot, by definition, be actually touched by another. It is human nature to focus on the problems of existence, rather than on its positives: Isn't it interesting that when we are alone we tend to focus on the one thing that we cannot have, that is, companionship? It is natural, too, to focus especially on a wonderful part of companionship: touch. Our focus is like that of a young child who, in a room full of dolls, wants the one doll, the only doll, that her little sibling is playing with. We want most what we cannot have.

Will the hug keep you happy and healthy—and unlonely? Maybe it will. I adore Leo Buscaglia, the wonderful teacher who has spread hugs from coast to coast, but I also believe that the mania for hugging should be tempered. In earlier times in our society much was made of the shy smile. Love itself could be inferred by the touch of gloved hands. In modern times it is the small child in us who keeps the wish for hugs so vividly alive, and this child whithin can be nurtured in other, more independent ways.

Making a Habit of Sensuality

One way to know whether you are committed to a broad sensuality is to recognize whether you are willing to spend time on it. You enjoy the outdoors, but how often do you actually go there? Another way to recognize your commitment is to see whether you are willing to spend money on it. You loved the massage you received as a gift, but how often do you actually arrange one for yourself? You may love art, but have you brought it into your home?

Sensual highs are all the more precious because they cannot be remembered easily. You can recall activities (like ceremonies), places, and personalities much more readily than you can your fleeting feelings. One way to establish your commitment to sensuality is to write about it. Consider keeping a journal. Tapping your creativity in this way will help you to remember and will encourage you to be more aware of your sensual self on a daily basis. In your recording, be sensitive to the social taboos we all face in expressing our sensual selves. Thoreau wrote things like "This is a delicious evening"[4] and did not risk being banned from the local library. It is one thing for us to experience all this great stuff; it is quite another to write it down and worry about having it be discovered by Aunt Tillie or Uncle Cal. Still, with proper security precautions, the risk is worth it. Isn't finding a little excitement part of what love is about?

Notes

1. Sheldon B. Kopp, *If You Meet the Buddha on the Road, Kill Him!* (New York: Bantam Books, 1976), 187.

2. Quoted in Joel Porte, *Emerson and Thoreau: Transcendentalists in Conflict* (Middletown, Conn.: Wesleyan University Press, 1965), 145.

3. Quoted in ibid., 146.

4. Henry David Thoreau, *Walden* (Boston: Houghton Mifflin Co., 1960), 47.

8
Finding Solace

Those that he loved so long and sees no more,
Loved and still loves,—not dead, but gone before,
—He gathers round him.
—SAMUEL ROGERS (1763–1855), "Human Life"

A woman happily weeds her garden. A mechanic carefully lays out his tools to begin the day's work. A man places stamps in his collection. A child falls asleep clutching her tattered blanket. Can you imagine what these people have in common? The woman and the mechanic are working, while the stamp collector is playing. The child is merely sleeping. At first glance, they all seem to be doing different things. Yet in one important way, these people are actually having the same experience. If you could know what each of them is feeling, you would realize that they are all experiencing a sense of peace and connectedness. They are all experiencing that special sort of content-ment that is called solace.

Solace is the emotional experience of a soothing presence. In a turbulent world solace calms us. In the face of adversity it gives us composure. It reminds us to be contented when we are alone. Un-doubtedly, one of the reasons that people say they are lonely is the absence of solace in their lives. When you lack solace, you lack serenity. To live a life without solace is to live a life of denial and, often, of despair.

The solacing presence you experience may be an actual or a remembered one. A young girl who lies in her mother's arms experiences the actual presence of maternal soothing. Her mother is helping her to accept her life as it is now—not the perfect life of the womb and of infancy, but the real world of dangers and challenges. The girl is being comforted. Through solace she acquires an equanimity that helps her to face real life.

A solacing presence can also come from a memory. An old man who sits reading a book that was once valued by his father experiences such a soothing memory. In his old age, even in the face of death, the memory of being close to his father brings him a sense of timelessness and peace.

How likely is it that this soothing, which is so closely attached in our minds to a nurturing presence, can exist when other people are not close by? Does solace exist in the lives of people who are alone? The answer is that the potential for solace is within us, and each of us can find and tap this potential. Indeed, we must find it, for knowing solace is essential to achieving positive solitude.

According to psychiatrist Paul Horton and others, solace is evoked partly by our *selves* and partly by our experience of symbolic *objects* in our environment.[1] On the one hand, solace comes from our actual experiences and memories. Almost all people who had normal care as infants experience solacing memories as adults. These memories are usually of being with a parent or other close relative or of specific moments of great contentment. Adults have within them the ability to soothe themselves with these memories.

On the other hand, solace also comes from seeing or holding or otherwise experiencing those objects that have come to symbolize contentment in our lives. These objects do not necessarily conjure up specific memories, but they elicit in us the feeling of being soothed. Just having them near us is a pleasure. With a bit of effort, we all can recognize objects that to us symbolize comfort and peace: jewelry owned by your mother, a lamp your father used in college, a trophy earned under the guidance of a beloved coach. Whether solace comes from memory or from an object, people who are alone are fully capable of achieving it. Understanding the potency of solace in our lives is the first step.

The technical term psychologists use for the process of solace is *transitional relatedness.* Despite its pedantic sound, it is a good term because it describes the way solace actually works in our lives. Solace is a straightforward process that all normal human beings experience beginning in infancy. In their *relationship* with their mothers, infants gain a sense of security and well-being. Psychoanalysts suggest that the original psychological internalizations of the mother's soothing presence are unconscious. Psychologists practicing within a cognitive behavioral framework believe that infants quickly learn to associate contentment with the presence of their mothers and that they soon learn to associate other objects, such as a favored toy held while in their mother's presence, with this contentment. Later, as children separate physically and emotionally from their mothers, the memory of the first soothing relationship is symbolized by things in their environment. As they mature, children then make age-appropriate *transitions* from one soothing object to another. All these soothing objects are called transitional objects. We make such transitions as long as we live—throughout childhood, adolescence, and adulthood—keeping solace alive in our inner world. Thus, we can see that our *relatedness* to a soothing presence goes through *transitions* that allow us to experience solace even though we are alone.

Examples in Childhood and Beyond

In the cartoon *Peanuts,* the character Linus always carries his treasured blanket. Linus is viewed as just a bit odd, but actually he is in the majority, for most normal children will identify soothing transitional objects. A child may choose a Teddy bear, a stuffed animal, a nursery rhyme or song, a religious figure, an imaginary companion, or even a scent or a texture. When the child outgrows a soothing object, most often the object is carefully stored rather than thrown away. Then more age-appropriate objects are chosen. With experience, a person learns, unconsciously, that almost any object can be a soother. In this way, for example, as psychiatrists point out, a musical piece like Beethoven's Fourth Symphony can be experienced as much more than a technical masterpiece. Listening to it can become a highly personal and meaningful event, an experience that is unique and solacing to the individual listener.[2]

Again, experiencing solace through both memories and symbolic objects is normal. It is the person who purports not to need anybody or anything, whether from his or her past, present, or future, who is abnormal. Such unfortunates become "wrapped in [their] separateness as though an insulator."[3] They experience not positive solitude, but a desolate solitude. One wonders just how the childhood of such a person differs from that of normal children. Is such a child consistently deprived of his favorite blankets and toys to "toughen him up"? Was his belief in Santa Claus and other soothing illusions squelched too early by perhaps well-meaning parents? Whatever the cause, such a child learns to turn away from solace, setting himself up for intense alienation in later life. In *Citizen Kane* newspaper mogul Charles Foster Kane (Orson Welles) was toughened up all right, as his ruthless lies and personal life demonstrated to all who were close to him. But the key to his life was symbolized by a transitional object, an object of solace that he never gave away: his boyhood sled named Rosebud. Because he was deprived as a child, Kane never made healthy psychological transitions to objects that could provide solace for him in adulthood. Fervently murmured by the great newspaper mogul on his deathbed, "Rosebud" was the symbol of the emotional life Kane had forever buried.

In early childhood a typical example of solace is attachment to some precious object, such as a blanket or a scrap of material. However, it is not always easy to predict just what object, or what it is about an object, that a child finds solacing. It may be the sight of the object itself, or it may be its color, its texture, or its smell. Children have definite, persistent attachments to an object and will express their emotions most vehemently when the object is removed or lost. Any parent who has been so unenlightened as to wash the favored object, thus removing some essential quality like scent, knows this attachment first hand. Unfortunately, often no substitute object can replace the one chosen by the child. The choice of solacing objects is highly personal, based on an individual's unique set of experiences and sensitivities. If any other person changes the object, he violates the cardinal rule that the object should be creatively chosen by the owner. A fierce individual independence on this score not only shows itself early in childhood, but probably persists throughout life.

Psychiatrist Paul Horton has written one of the most insightful and practical books on solace. In it, he cites many adult examples of transitional objects—art, religion, sailboating, a spouse, one's own creative writing, and the symbol of the magic carpet. From his practice of psychotherapy, he also clearly explains how the transitional object can be important in our lives.[4] For example, he tells of an eleven-year-old boy who was admitted to a pediatric service for urinary tract infections, but who seemed not to respond to family visits or toys. The boy was withdrawn and sometimes tearful. When he cried, he told the psychiatrist that he was thinking of his stamp collection. He had worked on this collection extensively with his grandmother, who had died when he was nine, and whom he saw as especially nurturing. "My mother was always having a baby . . . my grandmother gave us *warm* cereal." The psychiatrist requested that the collection be brought to the boy in the hospital. Because the collection had not seemed important to the child during the past year, the parents doubted it would be of use. However, when the collection was brought, the child shed his depression and began to show interest in other toys.

The same kinds of transitions occur in adult life. In one of Horton's cases, a professor recalled a series of transitional objects during his life: a Teddy bear; several blankets, each of which became the lining for the next; music, including songs he recalled from the age of five; a mystical experience, which occurred at a point where his mother was unwilling to console him; fantasies of an ideal woman, to be wooed through his musical talents; additional mystical experiences related to family tragedies; and, finally, more music.

Transitions from one solacing object to another become increasingly sophisticated, until it is not a simple matter to detect what object may be transitional for a particular adult. Anything can be used: clocks, books, a globe, persons, paperweights, baseball games, music, poetry, and colors. When several years ago, I visited a dear friend who lives in the country and keeps sheep, she ranted about having to chase the sheep all over the countryside when they escaped—which was just about daily. Late that summer, after sending them off to be butchered, she swore never again to keep such dumb animals. But last time I visited her, there were more sheep! I suspect that for my friend her sheep are transitional objects, a reminder of the farm she grew up on, with its herds of cattle. Today, on her seven-acre rural lot, merely having kids, cats, dogs, and two huge gardens is not enough. They don't evoke the full sense of the farm she grew up on. And so she has sheep!

Which brings me to an important point. The choice of solacing objects is not always wise. We must remember that the choice is emotional, not rational. A particularly widespread and unwise object of solace is television watching. Today generations of people have been conditioned throughout childhood and adolescence to "relax" in front of the television. As very young children, they lay in front of it clutching their favorite blankets or toys. Later they ate in front of it, and they probably watched it alongside their parents. Favorite programs and music from childhood television become solacing to them as adults. This sort of transitional relatedness is to be expected and, depending on the type of programs watched, may not be a problem. But, more profoundly, watching television *itself* may become the solacer. Psychologically, television *is* Mom. Because solace is an emotional rather than a rational experience, as adults one of the things we should do to nurture ourselves is to examine the wisdom of our choice of solacers.

Finding Solace When Alone

Solace is common to all who have had normal parenting as infants, and for adults it is a natural ability that we have within ourselves. There is no reason to believe that normal people who happen to be alone have any greater or any weaker ability than do others to have solacing memories or to value solacing objects. Nor is there any reason to believe that normal people who happen to be alone have any more or any less innate need for solace than others do.

Nevertheless, the desire to experience solace does create several challenges that are unique to people who are alone. The most obvious issue is that, like everyone else, people who live alone may hold the mistaken belief that soothing comes primarily from other people, rather than from their own internal resources and experiences. Since they are alone, moreover, they may be especially prone to falling into the loneliness trap that says: "I can solve my problem only through other people, and since I am alone this is impossible, and so I am helpless." They may yearn for solace from others so strongly that they are hardly in touch with the reality that solace is at their own personal command.

Another problem is that individuals who are alone may be less likely, on a daily basis, to see others who are themselves experiencing the phenomenon of solace. For example, they do not live with a child who clearly gains great pleasure from dragging around a battered old doll. They do not vicariously experience the solace a spouse gets from collecting stamps. Thus, they are not reminded that it might feel good to wear their favorite old shirt when they are in a blue mood. They are not reminded of the simple pleasure that seeing solacing objects can bring to them.

Do we need really to be reminded? Absolutely. As adults it is so easy to get caught up in *"important"* things—our work, our friends, our exercise. We fall into the routine of spending our time—of organizing it, filling it, making it productive—and thus we ignore emotional needs.

A related problem is that in our consumer society we are often tempted to buy new furniture, new housewares, new clothes—in short, to show off a bit. Old comforts and objects may often get crowded out of our modern life, and with them goes our solace. Because it is easy to forget the human importance of solace, for people who are alone it may be especially useful to identify some symbols of solace, perhaps some very old ones, and to place them in obvious places where they will serve as reminders.

Still another challenge comes from the fact that when you are alone, you may want to make a virtue out of what seems to be a necessity. You may deny your emotional needs, becoming especially resistant to the idea of the need for solace. Such resistance probably originates in the American belief in individualism. From childhood onward, you are taught to "stand on your own two feet" and "stand up for yourself" (yet not to be alone or to *enjoy* being alone!). Men are indoctrinated with the ideas of individualism more than women are, though both are encouraged to be far more individualistic than are men and women of other modern cultures. Thus, when Americans are introduced to the ideas of solace, which involve a certain kind of emotional dependence, it is natural for us to resist them. "I shouldn't need anyone or anything! I am free and independent" is our reaction. This attitude, so admirable in many respects, simply does not fully account for the emotional richness of human existence.

In positive solitude the point is to fill our emotional needs ourselves, *not* to deny them. Feedback that we give ourselves in the form of emotions should be used, not ignored. The beliefs of positive solitude should not be confused with such widespread slogans of individualism as "Be tough," "Be strong," or "Stay loose." These slogans really admonish us to be unemotional and insensitive, while in positive solitude you want to be just the opposite—sensitive to other people's emotions and, most important, in touch with your own. Some advocates of positive solitude may, in the Zen tradition, wish to control the emotions in their lives, but all will recognize their importance. Positive solitude is adamantly not a philosophy for escaping our emotions. Thus, ignoring the need for solace is not likely to make the need go away. The thing to do instead is to find the solace that does indeed exist in your life.

Sometimes people choose other people as solacing objects, and when this is true, the person who is alone will obviously have some problems. It may be true—though to my knowledge there has been no research to substantiate it—that human beings become solacing objects more readily than do objects. There is no reason to believe, however, that when a person is a solacing object, he or she is any more *powerful* as a solacing object than is, say, a treasured twenty-acre wood lot in the country. Human beings may have other characteristics that enhance their attractiveness, but as solacing objects per se, they are on a par with others.

Having another person as a solacing object has its pitfalls because, unlike inanimate objects, people can easily go away. If you married your husband because he reminded you of your loving father and then your husband dies or leaves you, you will suddenly become bereft of important solace in your life. When a solacing person-object has been lost through divorce or other means, short-term regression to objects closer to earlier solace is healthy, since it allows the individual to "recharge" his or her self-solacing abilities. For most people, solace takes many forms, and many forms of solace often remain, or can be developed, when one form is lost. The person who is alone needs to be especially cognizant of this fact and needs to develop reliable solacers.

A benefit for people who are alone is that solitude itself may be solacing. Of course, people who are alone have more access to the solace of solitude than do others. In this case I do not mean that when you are alone you have more time and more ability to focus on remembered people and events, though this is also true. Rather, I mean that the act of being alone *itself* has meaning, and perhaps for you it symbolizes solace. If as a child your times alone were often peaceful and contented, when you are an adult your times alone should be reminiscent of those earlier times. When you were a child, did you spend some of your times alone quietly—reading, being with nature, or experiencing something beautiful? If so, you are fortunate because solitude now can be solacing for you. Was a favored solacing object company to you at these times? If so, it can now remind you of your solacing solitudes. If, however, your times alone were filled with apprehensions and stress or with stimulants like television or Nintendo, it may be more difficult for you now to find solace simply in being alone.

The Value of Ritual

For many people ritual is an important source of solace. Rituals provide recurring connections to the past and to the future. Especially significant rituals, such as major holidays, ceremonies upon entrance into adult life, and funerals often give participants a sense of timelessness, of continuity in the face of human mortality. Less public rituals, such as family and household traditions, can be a way to remember the best of the past and to build future memories. Of course, not all rituals are solacing. Ritual can also be a way of formalizing an event to avoid intimate contacts. It can be a way of forgetting—of filling up time to avoid painful memories.

For people who are alone, rituals can pose various concerns. Major holidays can be difficult because they are designed primarily to celebrate togetherness. Christmas and Thanksgiving, certainly, but also New Year's Eve, Mother's Day, and Father's Day, all emphasize being with others. During these togetherness holidays, people who are alone sometimes feel excluded or, at least, not included. As a society we continue to emphasize these holidays partly because of their commercial emphasis on gift giving. Alternative holidays celebrating the joys of individualism and positive solitude would not be likely to elicit our merchants' support! People alone need to recognize the overwhelming emphasis on these togetherness holidays and to treat them realistically. To avoid feelings of exclusion, one can find a group that is truly inclusive. Singles may want to spend these holidays with other singles or among people with similar interests (skiing or traveling, for instance). A more courageous choice, and one more in line with a pure form of positive solitude, is to spend the holiday alone. Being alone and trying simply to ignore the existence of the holiday is likely to fail; the social influence all around you will probably be too overwhelming. Rather, put your own holiday into the holiday, by directing some thought to creating a special time for reflection, for beauty, for peace, for excitement, for learning—for whatever is meaningful to you.

Another thing that people who are alone can do is to make a point of emphasizing other kinds of holidays—the timeless holidays instead of the togetherness holidays. For example, the changing of the seasons is an excuse for a ritual that can be designed around yourself. I have known several individuals who make seasonal pilgrimages annually to beloved places. One goes each spring to a particular room in a hotel on Cape Cod. Another goes hunting in the mountains during the same week every autumn. Your birthday is also a fine excuse for a self-made, self-centered ritual—a solacing, centering time to look forward to every year and an experience to look back upon with fond memories.

Rituals also play a role in your everyday life. The way you rise in the morning, the way you work, the way you spend the twilight hours—all these acts may include solacing rituals. For people who are alone, the household rituals remembered from earlier years may be associated with family settings. Reenacting them may seem pointless and even painful. But such memories may become good ones. Although those times are past, there is much positive about them that deserves to be remembered. Find the solacing spots in your home life and build rituals around them. These rituals may be as simple as treating yourself to fried potatoes every Sunday morning or tending a garden every spring. Some of the rituals may be old family ones renewed; some may be of your own unique design. Whichever they may be, recognizing their contribution to the solace in your life is paramount.

When Solace Is Threatened

These, then, are some of the special challenges in finding solace that people face when alone. Some additional problems arise in crisis. Both people who are alone and people who are not alone should be aware that certain life experiences threaten the loss of their transitional abilities. Sometimes a person who is depressed "forgets" how to use transitional relatedness. This forgetting may be caused by a severe disillusionment, such as might be experienced in combat, or with the death of one's mother. A continuing lack of success in finding transitional objects may lead to deep discouragement. People have compared this lack of relatedness to "a light having gone out" or "the growing awareness of an inner void."[5] It is not unlike what some people call loneliness. The individual who experiences such a loss has to find new memories and new symbols of solace. Doing so will take time. Sometimes, through therapy, one must extensively relearn transitional relatedness.

There are some things we can do to prevent or lessen the major emotional trauma associated with the disturbance of our ability to find solace. It is logical, of course, to enhance your stability deliberately by recognizing and creating a variety of controllable sources of solace. This strategy suggests that you should pay particular attention to your needs for solace when your primary solacer is a person who can be lost to you. However, precious objects can also be lost. Through a fire, a daughter lost all the things she had kept in memory of her deceased mother. She carefully replaced them, selecting things that reminded her of her mother or that she knew her mother would have wanted her to have.

Solace is an enduring and powerful force in our lives, whether we are alone or are with others. One of the best protections of your ability to be self-soothing is to maintain a close contact with your childlike self. The child in us is freest when she or he knows that the solacing parent in us is also powerful. Being able to play and to relax, instead of being perpetually overworking and vigilant, is an indication of a solacing force at work in your life, one of the essential ways in which we understand, and love, ourselves.

Notes

1. I am indebted to Paul C. Horton for developing many of these basic concepts in his book *Solace, the Missing Dimension in Psychiatry* (Chicago: University of Chicago Press, 1981). Responsibility for the interpretation of these ideas is, of course, my own.

2. P. C. Horton, J. Louy, and H. P. Coppolillo, "Personality Disorder and Transitional Relatedness," *Archives of General Psychiatry* 30 (May 1974): 618–22.

3. Horton, *Solace,* 147.

4. Ibid., 108–9, 112, 119–21.

5. Ibid., 121.

9

The Challenge
of Laughter
and Celebration

A merry heart doeth good like a medicine. —Proverbs 17:22

Merriment—the very thought of it brings to mind children, holidays, families, pubs, and parties. More than any other facet of life, merriment is equated with togetherness. When we think of joy and laughter, we seldom envision the person alone. Maybe we are even incapable of that vision. Can you imagine the person alone enjoying a good laugh at the dinner table? Maybe if the television is on. . . . Or the person alone skipping gleefully along a country path? We would most likely think, "Where's the other person? No one else? What is he, loony or something?" Merriment is difficult to imagine for people alone, yet it is one of those pleasures that none of us wants to miss.

In recent years medical science has begun to accept the possibility that humor actually has healing properties. In a book investigating this idea, physician Raymond A. Moody informs us:

> Over the years I have encountered a surprising number of instances in which, to all appearances, patients have laughed themselves back to health, or at least have used their sense of humor as a very positive and adaptive response to their illnesses. These remarkable recoveries . . . have suggested to me the possibility that there may indeed be something therapeutic about humor, just as folk belief has long assured us.[1]

The most famous example of such healing is Norman Cousins's self-treatment of a life-threatening collagen disease by immersing himself in humor. Cousins reasoned that since negative thoughts have been shown to predispose a person to illness, positive thoughts might have a healing effect. Cousins equipped his hospital room, and later a hotel room, with an extensive collection of funny videos, especially "Candid Camera" reruns. He did recover. Today his idea is being widely explored and debated.

Smiling and laughing probably do cause us to feel better physically. When we smile, we contract some major muscles that influence the flow of blood to the brain. The result, as one scientist has put it, is like taking an oxygen bath. Our cells and tissues receive an increased supply of oxygen that causes a feeling of exuberance.[2]

Smiling and laughing also may make us feel better psychologically. Having a sense of humor allows patients to cope better with their pain.[3] It helps all of us to deal better with our problems. The ability to laugh at ourselves, at key figures in society, and at society at large all allow us to accept the vagaries of life. If we are this ridiculous and yet have muddled along this far, we console ourselves, perhaps things will turn out all right after all. An early book on humor and healing put it this way:

> The best formula for the health of the individual is contained in the mathematical expression health varies as the amount of laughter. . . .
>
> Laughter makes one expansive in outlook and is very likely to give

the feeling that the future need not be the subject of quite so much solicitude as is usually allowed for it.

The effect of laughter upon the mind not only brings relaxation with it, so far as mental tension is concerned, but makes it also less prone to dread and less solicitous about the future. This favorable effect on the mind influences various functions of the body and makes them healthier than would otherwise be the case.[4]

A few years after he wrote his famous book on dreams, Sigmund Freud wrote a lesser-known book on humor, laughter, and the comic. In it, he asserted:

> Humor has in it a *liberating* element. But it also has something fine and elevating . . . What is fine about it is the triumph of . . . the ego's victorious assertion of its own invulnerability. It refuses to be hurt by the arrows of reality or to be compelled to suffer. It insists that it is impervious to wounds dealt by the outside world, in fact that these are merely occasions for affording it pleasure.[5]

Merriment, joy, laughter, humor. There is more than one good case for including them in our lives: Our health can be enhanced, our sense of well-being can be enhanced, even our self-hood can be enhanced.

Laughter in America is closely related to spontaneity, to body language, and to a sense of personal freedom. In our country it is common to relate our joy with a loud, expressive guffaw, or merry chatter, or broad movements. Yet though it is characteristically American to laugh out loud, even here we should expect variations among individuals in the types of stimuli that make them laugh, in the expression of that laughter, and in the very sensations that humor produces in individuals. If you are not laughing out loud, perhaps you are laughing inside.

Laughing Alone

The easiest path to merriment is with other people. Laughter is created between people playing off each other in their conversations and interactions. Even laughter about nothing in particular can be contagious, passed from person to person merely because one person begins to laugh. In a laughter workshop I attended, all the participants lay in a big circle, each with his or her head on the next person's stomach. One person started the game by saying "Ho, Ho," and each was to add a "Ho." Between the hos and the giggles from feeling the next person's head bouncing on your stomach, we were all giggling in no time.

For people alone, finding opportunities to experience joy and laughter is more challenging. Singles face the rejection I already alluded to, the stigma placed on them when, unaccompanied by another person, they openly express laughter and joy. People give them odd looks when they are caught "laughing to themselves." Given this social reaction, you may wonder about your own sanity when you are alone. Talking to yourself is definitely considered eccentric. Laughing to yourself may be perceived as the next worse thing.

To the extent that people who are alone spend more time at work, their lives may be more filled than average with the serious details of the business world. They may be in special need of the balm of humor. Author Louise Bernikow notes that career women seem especially to want men with a sense of humor. Perusing a file of applications to a dating service, she observed that most women did not want to be dependent on men and did not want men to take care of them or to provide them with any particular identity. What they did want was fun, something very different from what they experienced every day on the job.[6] It is a safe guess that men who are alone need the same thing.

To enjoy laughter, the person who is alone must contend with these problems. The first and most important step is to commit yourself to having laughter and joy when you are alone. It should be possible to do so whether you are totally alone, as in your own home, or whether you are alone in some social context. To experience joy and laughter is natural for every human being. It is your right, too, to experience them on your own terms. If you laugh out loud and someone looks at you in askance, consider it their problem. More often than not, it will be your joy, rather than your craziness, that will reach others. And if you are alone when you laugh, you should not feel odd about your behavior. Whether together or alone, learn to accept laughter as a normal part of your life.

Henry David Thoreau described a solitary wood chopper who visited him at Walden, a man who exemplified and symbolized spontaneous joy: He was "so quiet and solitary and so happy withal; a well of good humor and contentment . . . overflowed at his eyes. His mirth was without alloy. Sometimes I saw him at his work in the woods, felling trees, and he would greet me with a laugh of inexpressible satisfaction. . . . When I approached him he would suspend his work, and with half-suppressed mirth lie along the trunk of a pine which he had felled, and, peeling off the inner bark, roll it up into a ball and chew it while he laughed and talked. Such an exuberance of animal spirits had he that he sometimes tumbled down and rolled on the ground with laughter at anything which made him think and tickled him."[7] Charming as he is, this character is unusual. Typically when you are alone, more of your laughter will be inward. When you are with others, the external expression of your merriment is reinforced by them. In a humorous situation, you catch someone's eye and it is difficult not to laugh. When you are alone you are more likely to feel amused without showing it or by showing it only slightly.

In developing a personalized sense of humor, the person alone does have some advantages. Humor in America is often homogenized. Sitcoms, monologues, and cartoons are all designed for the widest possible audience. They are all right for what they are, but the individual alone has the time and focus to be sensitive, in addition, to personal quirks. Search not for what the jokesters in Hollywood think is funny, but for what you think is funny. The person alone has more time to read and to develop this individualistic taste for humor. Through reading, especially, we enrich our native abilities to gain perspective on a situation and to make light of it.

Another advantage for the person who is alone is a predisposition to peak experiences, that kind of internal laughter that is the joy of total focus. Solitude is a major contributor to the creation of the peak experience, one of the prime characteristics of what Abraham Maslow termed the self-actualized individual.

Nevertheless, the person who is alone needs to pay special attention to creating situations that will encourage merriment. For one thing, laughter is not likely to blossom when you are tired, depressed, or otherwise physically low. You will be more predisposed to laughter if you are energized and aroused. Keeping in good physical shape—eating well, exercising regularly, getting enough sleep— will provide the healthy medium in which laughter can grow.

Creating a "humor environment" is another possibility. For an experiment designed to test whether merriment promotes social harmony, a group of British researchers created just such an environment.[8] Among other things, they left silly toys around, decorated with printed cartoons and jokes, provided clothing and masks, and piped in amusing sound effects. A visit to this environment did, indeed, improve people's spirits. Put some fun and amusement into your environment via amusing videos, a daily joke calendar, bathtub toys for adults, creative clothing, or funky art.

As adults we tend to decorate our living space for beauty and attractiveness. Yet, whimsy also deserves our attention. Not long ago, while house-sitting for six weeks in the apartment of strangers, I developed quite an affection for the taste of my hostess and host. Their stuff was wonderful. The kitchen was full of charming cups and vessels. The plates were either beautifully crafted or had little people and animals crawling on them. In the living room, among the serious books and antiques and modern furniture, were a three-dimensional cutout of a white pig and a troll-like thing with a wide-open mouth and ridiculous stubby arms outstretched. The bedroom door sported a clay face with a yawning mouth on a sock for collecting spare change. Everywhere I went in the apartment there were amusements—tiny wooden figures on a pedestal to pick up and admire, a precious doll, delicate laquer-ware cups, silly little wooden animals whose heads wobbled, Kliban pot holders (the Chefcat flipping mice and cheese in a pan), mobiles, and plants. The pièce de résistance was in the bathtub—a plastic whale you wound up by pulling on a fish that came out from its mouth; as you let the fish go in the water, the whale gobbled the little fish back up.

I especially appreciated this apartment because I myself am not good at collecting the funky. I keep trying, but either I don't buy it because it's too silly or I buy something else because it is practical. I shared this frustrating weakness with a friend of mine one day while we were in a creative artisans' shop, and on my birthday, my thoughtful friend presented me with this great ugly thing I had admired there. It is a casserole with a droopy, mean dragon on the top for a handle; when you put the top on over hot food, steam comes out of the dragon's mouth. I often put flowers in Dragon's mouth and serve mushrooms from its belly. I adore it, but I could *never* have bought it.

Another strategy is knowing amusing and joyful people who can give you models to emulate when you are alone. It is not so much that you will consciously copy them, but that laughter is contagious, and you will remember it. Fun people can be found in many churches, dance groups, personal-development classes, and clubs. You know them because true joy emanates from them; you experience their centeredness, and even radiance, when in their company. It is wonderful to have a joyful person as a therapist. Some therapists are serious and heavy-handed, even though one of the more powerful tools of their trade is the modeling of positive emotions.

Humor that is meaningful to you is humor that is most likely to stay with you. Meaningful humor usually touches your life directly. As a college professor, I tend to be touched by jokes that point out professorial foibles. I can learn about my own rigidities from these jokes, and I can experience the sense of human control that comes from surviving in spite of my own absurdity. When I experience such humor, I not only *laugh,* I *know.* Such laughter is much more central to my life than, say, the laughter I experience during the average TV sitcom. The latter also fills the feedback gap and is worth pursuing as part of a program to increase your fun, but I don't believe that it should be a steady diet. One of the reasons the "Candid Camera" TV series was so popular was that it portrayed the foibles of real people. We viewers could see the true ironies and absurdities in our human condition. These kinds of humor that allow us to gain perspective on ourselves and our lives are the most healing kinds. Not only do they give us the physiological boost that all healthy laughter gives, but they give us the psychological boost as well.

Celebrating Alone

Surely one of the most challenging things to do alone is to celebrate. Holidays, special events, and personal successes all traditionally call for high energy and laughter. Doing them alone requires careful attention and practice.

I once deliberately spent Thanksgiving Day alone: my first positive solitude Thanksgiving. What a wonderful time! I bought a turkey and all the trimmings exactly as I like them, and I enjoyed preparing the meal for myself. I smelled the delicious turkey cooking all that morning. I put a great bottle of white wine in the freezer so there would be just the beginning of ice when I opened it. I set a beautiful table. When I sat down to eat around one o'clock, I had already spent a considerable amount of time reflecting on the meaning of Thanksgiving, and this special Thanksgiving for me. I counted many blessings and remembered many happy times. I saluted new adventures to come. I drank half a bottle of wine and ate a terrific meal, capped by pumpkin pie from the best bakery of pumpkin pies that I have ever found. I recalled with tears friends and loved ones now gone. I thought about Thanksgivings in the future. Then I took a delicious, deep nap.

I didn't have Aunt Harriet and Uncle Mike. I didn't have merry greetings at the door and a house full of guests. I didn't have conversation with anyone but myself. But for what Thanksgiving is about, I had it all. The point is that I planned it that way. I knew that if I spent Thanksgiving alone without a celebration, I could feel deprived, so I figured out what it is about Thanksgiving that matters to me, and I made sure it happened.

Vacationing Alone

Going on vacation alone is another challenge. When you are alone, vacations, like holidays, must be carefully planned in the psychological sense. You cannot simply adopt the norms that are followed by couples and families (is it uncharitable to add "Thank goodness!")? To enjoy yourself on a vacation alone, you have to adopt a different mindset than do others around you. It is best to have acquired a number of positive solitude skills like sensuality and decision-making. You need to be able to eat alone happily. Know some individual sports—golf, windsurfing, biking, fishing. Be willing to celebrate a beautiful sunset even though no one else is doing so. Be able to put some variety in your days. When you return, be prepared to deal with people who think of vacation primarily in terms of socializing with other people. Take lots of photos and keep a journal, and relive your vacation through them rather than through someone else.

Bringing laughter and celebration into our lives is a definite plus. When you are alone, you need to devote to them an extra bit of forethought, and not a little creativity, but you can certainly have them in your life.

Notes

1. Raymond A. Moody, Jr., *Laugh after Laugh: The Healing Power of Humor* (Jacksonville, Fla.: Headwaters Press, 1978), xi–xii.

2. Robert B. Zajonc, "Emotion and Facial Efference: An Ignored Theory Reclaimed," *Science,* April 5, 1985: 15–21.

3. Mark Zborowski, *People in Pain* (San Francisco: Jossey-Bass, 1979).

4. James J. Walsh, *Laughter and Health* (New York: D. Appleton & Co., 1928), vii, viii, xi, 127.

5. Sigmund Freud, quoted in Moody, *Laugh after Laugh,* 114–15.

6. Louise Bernikow, *Alone in America* (Boston: Faber & Faber, 1986), 91.

7. Henry David Thoreau, *Walden* (Boston: Houghton Mifflin Co., 1960), 101.

8. S. G. Brisland *et al.,* "Laughter in the Basement," in Anthony J. Chapman, ed., *It's a Funny Thing, Humor* (New York: Pergamon Press, 1977). Noted in Moody, *Laugh after Laugh,* 104–5.

10

Feeling Lonely in a Crowd: Alienation at Work

Old friends seemed to fade away. It wasn't in my makeup to work at building friendships in or out of business hours.

—An entrepreneur,
quoted in DAVID E. GUMPERT and DAVID P. BOYD,
"The Loneliness of the Small-Business Owner"

It may never have occurred to you that you can experience loneliness at work. You probably think of loneliness primarily in terms of your personal relationships (or lack of them), and you associate it with the bad feelings you sometimes have when you are physically alone. Often loneliness at work is harder to recognize than is loneliness in your personal life simply because you work in the company of others. You see people interacting with each other throughout the workday—you interact with them, too—and no one *seems* lonely. The feedback gap seems to be filled.

Yet it is important to reflect a bit on this idea of feeling lonely in a crowd because a common place to feel lonely in a crowd is at work. Even though others nearby seem to have the potential to fill your feedback gap, you can feel depressed and sad in their company.

For some reason you do not thrive on the feedback that comes from them. Perhaps their input is meaningless to you—these are not people you particularly care about. Or you may not be ready for their feedback because it is not really the kind of feedback you want right now. Being lonely in a crowd is especially difficult for people who do not understand the principle of the feedback gap: If you erroneously believe that togetherness should heal your loneliness and if you still feel lonely even when company is clearly available, you will blame yourself for your sadness. Clearly, such self-blame will not increase your positive solitude.

Alienation at Work

It is sometimes hard to get in touch with the fact that you are feeling lonely in a crowd, and it is especially difficult at your job. Many of us put on our business role along with our business suit, hiding our true selves and our true feelings, even from ourselves. Sometimes the role you play is so habitual that you do not recognize your own loneliness. Yet, there are many reasons why, in the business environments in which we work, people often fail to receive the feedback that they need.

The word *business* itself is derived from the Anglo-Saxon word *bysig,* which means "to be occupied and/or diligent." Business actually does mean busyness—filling the feedback gap with activity. Some business is fulfilling, and some is not. As we have already seen, filling the feedback gap indiscriminately—as with popular music or with meaningless television programs—leads to increasing your loneliness rather than to reducing it. Busyness, activity merely for its own sake, is counterproductive to self-fulfillment. Many people know this intuitively. Americans' intense interest in entrepreneurship and small business is one indication of people's strong need to find meaningful work for themselves.

The detrimental effects of busyness are usually subtle. Keeping busy can keep you preoccupied and superficially happy. You may recognize only vaguely that the work you do is meaningless to you personally; or that because you are so busy, you are accumulating months and years of unfulfilling activity; or that your relationships at work are superficial.

Because you are busy, you may simply not have considered that there are better ways to fill the feedback gap. Most people hope to live meaningful lives. They want to grow and to develop themselves, to enjoy the world around them, to contribute to the well-being of their family and friends, to alleviate the distress that they see around them in their communities and in the world. But it seems to most of us, too, that there is always a lot of business to be accomplished. Sometimes we let this business dominate our daily lives. Busy people may get sidetracked from their life goals.

We cannot forget, either, that business is also about making money. In our capitalist society a primary goal of a business is to create as much money as possible so that the people who earn it can *then* use it to pursue meaningful lives. Unfortunately, to earn their living, many people do work that is otherwise meaningless to them, and if anything in life is a challenge, it is spending eight hours every day putting off who you really are. It is hard to put off really living until you receive your paycheck, to put off meeting your own needs until the office closes. When you do work that is personally meaningless, you can easily become lonely for yourself. In a job that has little meaning to you, for as many hours a day as you work you will be split off from yourself. You will become one more alienated worker.

In fact, one of the biggest problems in business today is the creation of meaningful work. Everyone knows that too many jobs are dull or stressful, but often the jobs cannot be changed without hindering productivity.

American businesses have not done a good job of encouraging people to find the meaning that does exist in their work. Yet, if you believe in your company's mission and your own job contributes to that mission, no matter what your job is, it is important. Every job that contributes to the welfare of the company is valuable. Whether it is as an accountant or janitor, production worker or president, each employee is necessary for the smooth functioning of the whole. But we Americans seldom point this fact out. In our business culture we emphasize competition, rather than cooperation, and we measure personal value by the amount of money that is made. In the end, the contribution of the guy who makes a lot of money turns out to be "meaningful," while the contribution of the guy who makes only a little money does not. Besides, our attitude is that the little guy can easily be replaced. No wonder it is difficult for many people to enjoy their jobs—jobs whose meaning to the company is often obscure and in which their own goals, the meanings *they* wish to pursue, are certainly not important.

Contrast this situation to that of the Japanese, who often emphasize to all employees the importance of their jobs. Japanese companies have recently achieved a measure of fame for sending employees to so-called hell camps that train them in harsh discipline and company loyalty through long hours of physical exertion and even deprivation. Less known is how each employee at these camps is taught to believe in the importance of his or her personal contribution to the whole. In one instance, the employees at a camp were sent into the town around the training center to beg for menial work for the day. If they found work that was too challenging—like bartending—the trainers made them move on to something less interesting, like sweeping. At the end of the day, the students reconvened to discuss their work. All felt grateful for the opportunity to help someone out. They had enjoyed their work because they had made useful contributions, however small, to the companies that had "hired" them. Of course, the trainers urged the employees—most of whom were beginning a banking career at the entry-level job of teller—to remember these feelings whenever they get bored in their work: *All* work, even if it is simple and not well paid, contributes to the general welfare of the company and its people, and, if you adopt this attitude, even menial tasks can be done with joy.[1]

Why is there alienation at work? One reason is that today work has become highly specialized, a fact that has enhanced productivity but reduced psychological satisfaction. A legal secretary may prepare the forms for a case but never meets the client. A doctor sees a patient only for a few minutes and, often, focuses on only one particular part of the patient's body. Both workers know that their job is less meaningful than it might be because they are not seeing it through.

Another reason for alienation is that in modern times workers are primarily employees, and it is sometimes difficult to fill the feed-back gap in meaningful ways when you are working for someone else. No longer are we a nation of independent farmers and small business-people. Working in a modern corporation, people have less control over the type of work they do, the scheduling of their time, and the design of their personal surroundings. They have little say as to what the overall goals of the company will be.

Of course, you can choose what type of company to work for. Often today companies are too large and bureaucratic to offer mean-ingful work to most of their employees, so you can choose a smaller firm. You can choose a company whose product you believe to be important or useful. Working as a receptionist for a company that makes a product you like (good food, sports gear, or books) may be better, emotionally speaking, than working as a manager for a com-pany that makes a product that you believe to be harmful (cigarettes). Also, you can choose to join a management team that you respect.

Unfortunately, companies usually change without consulting their employees. The company may grow so large that your own job seems small and unimportant. Or the company may simply change its mission, assuming that employees' jobs—your job—must change to meet the company's new goals. You may accidentally end up in a job that is no longer meaningful to you.

Companies design their reward systems to increase the behav-iors that they want. At the same time, all companies suppress, in the sense that they fail to reward, behaviors that are not directly in line with their own goals. They are not being malevolent or even manipulative. Companies are merely being rational in pursuing their goals. However, rewarding all or even most of *your* individual goals, talents, and ideas is not in the company's plan, and it never will be. Most likely, you will be rewarded in relation to how well you meet such corporate goals as producing profits or increasing sales or taking on additional responsibilities. Sometimes your monetary rewards will even be high. But typically, a company will not think of you, or treat you, as a whole human being. It will ignore large chunks of who you are—maybe even your creativity, your values, and your initiative. Every person has to ask herself or himself whether the feedback she or he gets at work fills the feedback gap well enough. Does it really further your career? Your life goals? Does it make you feel good about yourself? Does it make you feel good to be alive?

The individual for whom there is a close match of company rewards and personal goals is, indeed, fortunate. Sadly, many employees don't find such a match. Because companies reward only a small portion of their potential, these workers feel alienated.

One especially important cause of personal alienation on the job is the inability to express your own moral convictions. Today this area of business concern is receiving a lot of media attention, without, unfortunately, causing much real change. Most companies do not solicit individual employees' opinions on such moral issues as divestment of investments in South Africa or the impact of the company on the environment. You will not be encouraged to express your opinions, and if you do express them you may face punishment. It is not often that you, the whole person, can really contribute to your company's ideas. It is typically the top management's or the stockholders' ideas of morality that dominate.

In our society you are, technically at least, free to leave any particular job. However, this freedom is often illusory. Leaving a job is not as easy as it sounds. If you have roots in the community or if you are older or narrowly skilled or otherwise difficult to place, you will have a hard time finding new work. Economic recessions can affect even the most skilled. Thus, many of us are forced to stay and to try to cope with our alienation. We must live with a feedback gap every working day.

Some people try to reduce their alienation at work by making friends in the workplace. Unfortunately, loneliness at work is often complicated, rather than helped, by the kinds of friendships you will discover there. Sometimes it is difficult to make truly close friends at work because the intense competition in your company will keep people apart. When promotions, salary, and interesting jobs are in scarce supply, being in competition with your friends is bound to weaken some relationships. You develop "business friendships," but you seldom find the kind of intimacy in which you share a great deal of yourself.

Also, it makes sense to be wary of intimate on-the-job friendships. Close friends at work may seriously, even if inadvertently, hurt your career. For example, they might sympathetically mention to someone that you are concerned about a serious health problem in your family—thus, through the inevitable grapevine, alerting the management to your family's tendency toward heart disease. At a certain age, this information could squelch your chances for promotion.

If you have puzzled over your inability to make real friends on the job, consider that these pressures make intimacy especially difficult in the workplace. Sadly, being with people all day and not getting close to them will increase your alienation.

Burnout

A variant of job alienation is burnout. Burnout is the kind of loneliness you feel when your job requires you to act one way even though you really feel differently. You burn out when you are forced by circumstances to match your behaviors to the demands of the situation, rather than being allowed to express your true feelings and beliefs. Burnout is actually worse than filling the feedback gap with merely meaningless activities because you are filling it with behaviors you actively disagree with and do not want to do.

There are many situations in which burnout may occur. Sometimes people are forced to hide their emotions as, for example, when they feel they must be nice for a while to a customer whom they detest. In other instances a person has to put on an act every minute, all day. For example, a waitress must seem polite, positive, and energetic even if she happens to be feeling surly, negative, and tired. A funeral attendant may be feeling happy, funny, and expressive, but he has to appear grave and subdued.

If the difference between how people actually feel and how they are forced to act on the job is large or if they must control themselves over a long time, they burn out to a point of depression or anger. Burnout is especially likely to occur if they disagree that the job really requires them to put on an act. For instance, whether a flight attendant should be required to be polite to an obnoxious passenger is a matter of considerable debate between attendants and management.

Of course, all jobs require emotional control. This is normal and expected. Disneyworld is famous for creating a dual world of "on stage" and "off stage" for its employees. On stage includes any time the employees are in contact with the public. Off stage exists in employee-only areas—the system of tunnels that underlies Disneyworld. When an employee is on stage, he or she is expected not just to do a job, but to play a role. An employee handbook suggests:

> First, we practice a friendly smile at all times with our guests and among ourselves. Second, we use friendly, courteous phrases. "May I help you." . . . "Thank you." . . . "Have a nice day." . . . "Enjoy the rest of your stay," and many others are all part of our daily working vocabulary. [Walt Disney Productions, 1982][2]

At McDonald's, desirable traits for people who greet customers include sincerity, enthusiasm, confidence, and a sense of humor.[3] For the team that designed the Macintosh computer, Apple Computer chose only those people who expressed great enthusiasm about working on the machine.[4]

The question is how to distinguish between acceptable and stress-producing roles. At the Mary Kay Ash cosmetics company, salespeople are expected to sing cheerily, "I've got the Mary Kay Enthusiasm" and to take a vow of enthusiasm. The total emotional commitment required can alienate an employee. Quashing their true thoughts and feelings, employees work hard to accept their own acting. Some learn to rationalize their faked enthusiasm as "just part of the job." Other employees, however, are not as successful at adapting. They may not believe that their continual smiles should be part of the job. These employees fake their smiles *in bad faith,*[5] and they are troubled by not being in touch with themselves. They burn out and act out:

> A young businessman said to a flight attendant, "Why aren't you smiling?" She put her tray back on the food cart, looked him in the eye, and said, "I'll tell you what. You smile first, then I'll smile." The businessman smiled at her. "Good," she replied. "Now freeze and hold that smile for fifteen hours."[6]

This woman is breaking the unspoken rules about how she should act emotionally on the job, and she is annoying her customers in the process. Her alienation from herself is a threat to her employer, and it is a danger to her, for it may lead to both emotional and physical health problems.

Authorities believe that even smiles faked *in good faith* can lead to health problems. Psychologist Christina Maslach has pointed this out in her work with burned-out professionals.[7] The worst problems occur in the helping professions. Burnout happens often among nurses, mental health workers, and physicians. It also occurs among educators of all ranks, and it is significant among people who work in service positions, including salespeople, judges, and referees. The social worker who must extend empathy to every client clearly believes that the client needs the empathy. Yet she does not always feel empathy for every client, nor does she personally feel empathic in every session. The flight attendant who *does* believe that he should smile at customers all the time—and sometimes slips—is in a similar dilemma.

Burnout occurs to some extent in all jobs. You may feel that you have to smile at the boss even though you are angry with him. You are polite to a lazy co-worker even though you are furious at her because you have had to do her work. Whatever the extent of your alienation from your emotions, it will affect your well-being. When you feel helpless to change the norms for emotional expression in your job, you may become depressed. You may become angry at the system or at yourself. Your self-esteem suffers.

Most drastically, when you cannot express yourself in your work, you may develop the habit of not expressing your true emotions at all, whether inside or outside the job. You may even get to the point of not *feeling* your emotions as much as you used to. After all, you are being trained in this schizophrenic existence 8 hours a day, 40 hours a week, 2,000 hours a year. This training can result in the deepest alienation—an alienation from alienation, from all feeling itself, which is the ultimate consequence of what starts out as the simple rationalization, "It's just part of the job."

Obviously, whether it leads to burnout or alienation or worse, loneliness at work is a significant problem. Because people spend significant parts of their lives at work, it is a problem that can have an important impact on their ability to achieve.

Whai Can Be Done?

Some companies today recognize the problems of alienation and burnout and try hard to put meaning back into jobs. Instead of putting people to work on an anonymous assembly line, they may put people to work in groups, with each group responsible for a particular component or product. Working in groups not only allows people to interact with others on the job, it gives them the sense that they are doing a whole piece of work for which they are responsible. They have an increased sense that they "own" the work—that their personal values about quality and productivity directly affect it. Meaningfulness is increased by other forms of participation as well. An engineer, for example, may be encouraged to participate, along with a salesperson, in meeting customers. Employees may be encouraged to know not just one job, but many. Employee-involvement groups pose and often solve company problems from the bottom up.

Some companies encourage employees to take more responsibility for decision making. Participative-management techniques like quality circles and employee-involvement teams have been widespread since the middle 1970s. More recently, the concept of entrepreneurship within a business has become popular under the name *intrapreneurism.* This management technique encourages employees to express their creativity and independence even within their large companies. Like employee involvement, intrapreneurism attempts to give back to the employee the sense of meaning that is lost when work is specialized or when people must work in large, bureaucratic organizations.

A company may also try to give its employees the sense that they have a stake in the productivity and welfare of the company as a whole. One way to do so is financial, through providing stock options or profit-sharing plans. Another way is to pay increased attention to the development and publication of the company's overall goals and values with which employees can relate. Often these goals and values give the employees a sense of unity and pride.

These kinds of programs can allay alienation to some extent. Nevertheless, although being responsible for building an entire carburetor is better than merely putting one bolt on it, building a carburetor is not as challenging and craftsmanlike as building an entire car, and it seems a long way from, for instance, solving the transportation problems of the elderly in one's local community. Furthermore, there will always be jobs in which employees must interact extensively with the public, and in these jobs there will always be pressure to be emotionally robotic. There are limits to what a company can do to help you find or develop meaningful and emotionally reasonable work. There will always be limits on the amount of good work to be found, and there will always be competition for this work.

So, in many instances it is going to be up to the employees to solve their problem of alienation. As a consequence, you, as an employee, need to understand the problems of loneliness and alienation discussed here. You must take responsibility for filling your own feedback gap with meaningful activity, not just with busyness. Changing the meaningless work in your company is a worthwhile goal that you, in partnership with others there, can pursue. Yet, if the work remains alienating, since you yourself want to avoid this kind of loneliness, your ultimate choice may be to seek meaningful work elsewhere.

Executive Alienation

People sometimes dream of the time when they will have moved up to a leadership position in their company. Maybe they will become a vice president, or chief executive officer (CEO), and *then*, they think, they will be in charge of the company and their own work life. *Then* they will not feel alienated. *Then* they will do meaningful work. If you actually manage to make it to the top, this is all true—but only in part. You will indeed have more to say about what you do every day. You will have more influence on the goals and activities of your company. But ascending to that company leadership spot is many difficult years away and arriving there may not be as satisfying as you think.

Those CEOs who are frank often report that moving to the top of a company brings its own new forms of alienation. It is indeed lonely at the top.

Top executives point out that they must constantly be responsive to the needs of various constituencies in their companies—employees, customers, and other executives, to name but a few. Excessive demands are put on their time by activities like civic affairs. Yet they are alone in their decisions.

One of the important tasks of a president or CEO is to be a model of strength; publicly admitting loneliness would hardly enhance this image, so studies of executives who admit that they feel lonely or alienated are rare. Among the few CEOs who have gone on record, "isolation" and "alienation" are key experiences.[8] They commonly report feelings of emptiness and sterility, as do other lonely people. Executives, too, feel personally alienated when their daily activities match their business role more than they match their personal goals, beliefs, and values.

An executive may be unsure of how to make a particular decision, yet he may be forced by constraints, like time pressures, to decide. Afterwards, though his feelings about the decision are still mixed, the executive must exude total confidence to convince others to back his choice. This necessity to maintain a public facade in spite of strong counterindicative personal reactions can be extremely self-alienating, yet it is a persistent part of the executive's job.

Executives may actually feel hurt or angry when criticized, but they attempt to appear unruffled. They desperately want to appear confident even when they have serious doubts. They even fake attention and politeness. Since time is a precious commodity, executives learn to give visitors the impression of having plenty of time to listen to them when, in reality, they are counting the minutes. As one realistic administrator put it:

> Social functions . . . all [require] the administrator's presence . . . at times when other matters [are] much more pressing or when overwork [makes] one yearn for a quiet evening at home or a lunch of cheese and crackers in the privacy of one's office. The task of engaging in small talk, having just emerged from an emotionally charged meeting . . . is

no simple skill. It requires either a high degree of concentration which allows for the submergence of matters that normally would be uppermost in the mind, or a skillful display of polite attention in which nods, facial expressions, and assorted vocalizations succeed in giving the impression the listener's thoughts are where they are not. With experience, I grew adept at both methods . . . Either tactic, however, was almost invariably accompanied by the recurrent sense of distancing, of being oddly apart from others.[9]

Executives also experience the social alienation of being separated from others. Of course, they are not physically separated, but they are separated as human beings because of their role.[10] It is easy to see how they are separated from lower-level workers in the company; they do not take them into their confidence in such matters as salaries or company strategy or work schedules. In fact, they are removed and alienated from almost everyone over whom they have power. They frequently make basic decisions about salaries, promotions, layoffs, and staff redistributions. Whenever they must make decisions about people's lives, they cannot take them into their confidence.

In addition, executives experience isolation every day in dozens of their interpersonal transactions.[11] To begin with, they are inevitably seen as special, and they are highly visible at all kinds of events. People constantly seek their opinions and are curious about all aspects of their work and lives. Part of their problem is that since they are treated this way, they begin to *feel* special, too; they begin to see themselves apart from other people, and alone.

The executive is also alienated because he possesses a great deal of confidential information. If his company is small, he may know more about his people than does anyone else. Paradoxically, he will feel both close to his people and removed from them, for with his intimate knowledge comes the responsibility for acting wisely. Knowledge about salaries and budgets is especially sensitive. The constant sense of knowing the whole picture when in conversation with people who see only a part of it can increase the sense of aloneness.

The executive's satisfaction in personal relationships suffers both on and off the job. Long hours and high mobility add to his problems. When he is not happy in his job—in spite of his own expectations and society's belief that he should be—the executive feels guilty. He experiences a feeling of powerlessness. Because he, like everyone else, believed the corporate myth that satisfaction would be found at the top and because he invested many years only to learn a sadder reality, he feels naive and hopeless. Seeing that others around him also believe the myth and are trying desperately to make it to the top only increases his alienation.

Entrepreneurial Alienation

Even becoming an entrepreneur, the ultimate dream for job independence, can be lonely. *The Wall Street Journal* describes the entrepreneur's life this way:

> Here's a blueprint for loneliness: Don't join a large organization that provides a colleague-oriented atmosphere; instead, go off on your own. Let your business dominate your life to the detriment of relationships with family and friends. Confide in no one.[12]

In a recent study on stress and loneliness among entrepreneurs, 52 percent said they experienced a recurring sense of loneliness, and 68 percent reported that they had no confidante with whom they could share their deepest concerns.[13] Their experience was related to physical stresses like back and chest pains, headaches, impaired digestion, and insomnia. Their loneliness and stress did not diminish over time: The heads of older companies said they have just as much loneliness and stress as did the heads of younger companies.

Running a business alone, the entrepreneur normally has no one who shares his or her overview of the business. Decision-making pressure is high, yet there is no one with whom to brainstorm strategies or the solution of problems. Pressure to project a strong image is high. If owners allow their private fears to be aired, employees worry about the well-being of their companies and the rate of turnover among employees climbs.

Entrepreneurs are psychologically different from other people, too. They are constantly oriented toward innovation, while employees value stability. They become immersed in their companies and neglect the interests of family and friends. Entrepreneurs are competitive and impatient. Even in their personal lives, they tend to go it alone. Their favorite sports tend to be solitary ones like sailing, flying, and swimming. A typical comment from them is, "Hang gliding is something you can do when you're really alone. You depend on yourself." Of course, there is some solace to be found in activities like these. As one CEO put it, "When I am on my boat, nothing else matters. The only problems are natural (wind, weather and tide) which I cannot change. Thus I am forced to accept what is and flow with it. Simply put, the world outside my sailboat does not exist."[14]

Solutions

Clearly, loneliness in business is widespread, from employees to top administrators to entrepreneurs. Although it may not always be called loneliness—alienation is the more typical term used in the business world—it comes to the same thing. People fill the feedback gap, in this case, the work portion of their lives, with activities that are not meaningful to them and that do not allow them to make honest and full contact with other human beings. They are busy, they fulfill their roles, and they work hard. But they do not feel connected, and they are not satisfied. Their feelings are the same as those of other people who say they are lonely—emptiness, vulnerability, depression, and impatient boredom.

Both individuals and companies need to recognize these problems of loneliness and alienation at work. Individuals need to address for themselves the question, "What is meaningful work—to me?" Imagine that you are at the end of your life, looking back on your work. What will you think about it then? Was it more than merely a way to make a living? Were you able to express yourself in your work?

Attempting to compensate for these problems outside work may be helpful. Putting an extra effort into your involvement with your community and family may replace some of the intimate personal connections lost at work. Discussing work problems with a spouse may be of some use, though often the spouse is simply not knowledgeable enough to be really helpful, and it may be burdensome for you to describe and relive a work problem. Precious time for simply relaxing is thereby lost. Sometimes it is better to use your free time to escape.

Companies can be run by executive committees instead of individual CEOs. This way of organizing has the virtue of bringing several different perspectives to bear on decisions. Informed insiders exist, at the same level, who are in a position to give meaningful feedback. The alienation felt by the solo CEO is thereby reduced, and the total responsibility for decisions is shared. However, I should point out that the use of executive committees is the exception, rather than the rule. Most companies prefer the strengths traditionally associated with the individual decision maker—speed, decisiveness, and the aura of the leader. It is usually left up to the individual executives to find positive solitude at the top.

Entrepreneurs who feel alone and alienated have several alternatives. They can establish a board of directors, drawn from people outside the company, to advise them regarding difficult and complex decisions. Although the buck stops with the entrepreneur, such a board can give valuable information and emotional support. Another thing entrepreneurs can do is to join peer groups, such as groups of entrepreneurs in noncompeting businesses (Rotary Clubs and Young Presidents Clubs, for example).

Although there are some remedies for loneliness at work, the feedback gap in business is not going to go away. From the psychological point of view, many jobs will continue to be overspecialized. Especially in large organizations, employees and top managers alike will continue to be separated from each other. Humanizing organizations will continue to be one of the great challenges of our time. Until this effort succeeds, it is up to the individual person to identify, understand, and remedy his or her own job alienation. Since we all spend so much time at work, dealing with our loneliness there will make a crucial contribution to our positive solitude.

Notes

1. Thomas P. Rohlen, *For Harmony and Strength* (Berkeley: University of California Press, 1974).

2. Quoted in Anat Rafaeli and Robert I. Sutton, "Expression of Emotion as Part of the Work Role," *Academy of Management Review,* 12 (1987): 27.

3. M. Boas and S. Chain, *Big Mac: The Unauthorized Story of McDonald's* (New York: E. P. Dutton, 1976), 84.

4. S. Tyler and J. Nathan (producers), *In Search of Excellence* (film) (New York: Public Broadcast System, 1985).

5. Rafaeli and Sutton, "Expression of Emotion," 32.

6. A. R. Hochschild, *The Managed Heart* (Berkeley: University of California Press, 1983), 127. Quoted in Rafaeli and Sutton, "Expression of Emotion," 31.

7. Christina Maslach, "The Client Role in Staff Burnout," *Journal of Social Issues* 34, no. 4 (1978), 111–24.

8. See Philip W. Jackson, "Lonely at the Top: Observations on the Genesis of Administrative Isolation," *School Review* 85 (May 1977): 425–32. See also Abraham K. Korman, Ursula Wittig-Berman, and Dorothy Lang, "Career Success and Personal Failure: Alienation in Professionals and Managers," *Academy of Management Journal* 24, no. 2 (1981): 342–60.

9. Ibid., 430–31.

10. Korman, Wittig-Berman, and Lang, "Career Success and Personal Failure," 344.

11. Jackson, "Lonely at the Top," 428ff.

12. "Owner's Isolation Can Result in Loneliness and High Stress," *Wall Street Journal,* May 7, 1984, 35.

13. See David E. Gumpert and David P. Boyd, "The Loneliness of the Small-Business Owner," *Harvard Business Review,* November–December 1984: 4–8.

14. Ibid., 10.

11
Psychotherapy and Loneliness

I feel like a child now. Everything I see seems strange to me. . . . Never in my life did the world look so beautiful to me.
—Client involved in one of Japan's "quiet" therapies, quoted in DAVID K. REYNOLDS, *Morita Psychotherapy*

At some point a person who feels lonely may look to therapy for answers. Just as you would seek a therapist who supports your own system of values, you should seek a therapist who understands the goals of positive solitude. There are many therapeutic approaches that will support you in your growth toward positive solitude. Three that are particularly promising are behavioral therapy, restricted environmental stimulation therapy (REST), and logotherapy.

Behavioral Therapy

Among the newer therapies that adopt a fully optimistic view of being alone, the best known is behavioral therapy. Behavioral therapy is widely known and practiced in a number of variants, including social learning theory, behavior modification, and cognitive behavior modification. Typically, the behavioral therapist's view of loneliness is both concrete and practical.

When a person comes to therapy with a complaint such as "I am lonely" or "I am depressed," the behavioral therapist naturally regards these comments as abstractions that should be explored and elaborated upon. The therapist tries to find out just what the person really means when he or she says "I am lonely." In the terms used in this book, I might put the therapist's question as, "Exactly what parts of this person's feedback system are not being well filled?" This question must be explored anew with each client because all individuals have a unique set of experiences that has led them to label themselves as lonely. The therapist will encourage the client to elaborate. What thoughts, feelings, and behaviors are associated with the expression of loneliness?

Researchers who have studied this therapeutic process suggest that it works this way: When a client tells the therapist that he or she is lonely, the therapist must figure out exactly what this statement means by asking the person to describe more fully the experience of loneliness. The best way to help the client to become less lonely is to find out the individual meaning of loneliness for that person. The person might describe, for example, feeling lonely and unloved. The therapist probes even further, and the person expands on all his or her perceptions of loneliness. Together, the client and therapist figure out that the original statement "I feel lonely" can be reduced for this client to difficulties in making friends, participating in groups, and relaxing on a date.[1] These specific difficulties can then be remedied. Clients learn how to make friends, how to be comfortable in a group, how to feel safe when at home alone, and so on. With guidance from the therapist, clients learn how to fill the feedback gap, step by step.

Therapist Jeffrey E. Young, at the University of Pennsylvania, works with chronically lonely adults using cognitive behavioral therapy.[2] In working with his clients, he focuses primarily on the lonely person's desire to build better social relationships. I should point out that although in this book I see positive solitude as an end in itself, Young sees it as one step in the process of reconnecting with others.[3]

The same method of therapy can be applied toward either goal, however.

Young typically works with people through six stages of personal growth, moving from less complicated to more complicated tasks. The goals of the stages are as follows:

1. To overcome anxiety and sadness about spending time alone.
2. To engage in activities with a few casual friends.
3. To engage in mutual self-disclosure with a trustworthy friend.
4. To meet a potentially intimate, appropriate partner.
5. To begin to develop intimacy with an appropriate partner, usually through disclosure and sexual contact.
6. To make an emotional commitment to an appropriate partner for a relatively long period of time.[4]

In each stage the client and therapist work on learning behaviors and cognitions that support each goal. They also work on learning how to perform each stage with a minimum of stress.

Setting a behavioral hierarchy like this and working through it step by step can also be a means to positive solitude. If one was doing therapy with the goal of achieving positive solitude, the stages might look something like this:

1. To feel physically safe when alone, both at home and outside the home.
2. To overcome anxiety and sadness about spending time alone.
3. To learn to feel comforted and not anxious when one is both tired (or sick) and alone.
4. To understand the principle of the feedback gap and to find interesting, personally enriching things to do every day when alone.
5. To build solace, tradition, and other long-term enrichments into your life.
6. To demonstrate to yourself that your life, lived alone, has meaning.

Generally, behavioral therapists encourage their clients to determine the hierarchy of goals. *You* must choose the final outcome. Do you want togetherness? Or positive solitude? Or perhaps both?

Once you clarify your goals, the next step in cognitive behavioral therapy is to work on the thoughts that prevent you from achieving your goals. To cope with our complicated environment, we humans are constantly making mental models of it. Sometimes our models are not well chosen. They lead to confusion and dismay. All of us have some automatic thoughts that are based on maladaptive assumptions. Our behavior and emotions reflect these counterproductive thoughts. To free ourselves of such negative thinking we need to get to the underlying problem: We must challenge the weak models and assumptions that we made in the first place.

From his therapeutic practice, Dr. Young has put together an excellent list of thoughts, assumptions, behaviors, and emotions that are typical of people who complain of being lonely. In therapy, he and his clients work to replace the automatically counterproductive thoughts and behaviors with positive and realistic thoughts and behaviors that are appropriate for each stage. You can use the same approach to work toward positive solitude, as can be seen in Table 1. With practice, you can learn to think positively about your solitude and to feel the positive emotions that go along with your new way of thinking.

To achieve positive solitude, you work with a behavioral therapist to change the repertoire of behaviors, beliefs, and attitudes that prevent you from feeling satisfied when alone. For example, you might need to change the way you think about solitude itself, moving gradually from negative assumptions about solitude toward adopting more positive ideas about it. Or you might need to work on changing specific things you do when you are alone that are finally counterproductive—excessive television watching, for instance, or other less-than-meaningful activities. Do not be discouraged if your list of counterproductive habits is long. When you have had little experience with being alone, a long list is normal. On the other hand, your problem may be small yet highly disruptive, as when a person who is otherwise content with his or her own company feels physically unsafe living alone. In either case, behavioral therapy, one of the most

Table 1. How Positive Solitude Solves Typical Loneliness
Problems

Problem 1: Feeling Discontent Alone

Typical Loneliness Assumptions	Typical Lonely Thoughts	Related Emotions
1. I have nothing to do alone. 2. I don't want to go out by myself. 3. I can't stand being alone. 4. I feel cut off when I'm alone. 5. I'll always be alone. 6. It's scary being alone.	1. Life has no meaning without someone to share it. 2. There must be something wrong with me if I'm alone. 3. I'm better off doing nothing than doing things alone. 4. I cannot cope with problems without help.	Bored, hopeless, empty, sad, anxious, isolated
POSITIVE SOLITUDE ASSUMPTIONS	**RELATED POSITIVE THOUGHTS**	**EMOTIONS**
1. Being alone is natural. 2. I can make my own life meaningful. 3. I can enjoy doing things alone.	1. I like being by myself. 2. When I'm alone, I realize that I still care about others. 3. There are lots of things I want to do. 4. I like having the time to do the things I want to do.	Love, affection, enthusiasm

Table 1. *(Continued)*

Problem 2: Not Trusting

Typical Loneliness Assumptions	Typical Lonely Thoughts	Related Emotions
1. I'm better off by myself. 2. I don't like most people. 3. I don't trust anyone.	1. Most people only care about themselves. 2. People will take advantage of you if they can.	Bitter, isolated
POSITIVE SOLITUDE ASSUMPTIONS	**RELATED POSITIVE THOUGHTS**	**EMOTIONS**
1. It's normal for people to watch out for themselves first. 2. When people feel secure themselves, they are best able to help others to feel secure.	1. I can rely on myself. 2. I understand healthy selfishness. 3. By taking care of myself, I can be available to help others.	Security, confidence

Problem 3: Not Able to Find an Intimate Partner

Typical Loneliness Assumptions	Typical Lonely Thoughts	Related Emotions
1. There's no place to meet men/women. 2. The men/women I get involved with always end up hurting me. 3. There are very few men/women I find desirable. 4. No one can measure up to my last lover.	1. I must find the perfect man/woman and not settle for less. 2. I should continue to pursue people I am strongly attracted to regardless of whether we are well suited in other respects.	Frustrated, hopeless, emotionally empty, bitter

Table 1. *(Continued)*

5. The partners I find attractive will not be acceptable to my friends or to society.

3. If I try hard enough, I can always get the man/woman I want to love me.
4. Meeting new people should be fun or I should not bother.

POSITIVE SOLITUDE ASSUMPTIONS	RELATED POSITIVE THOUGHTS	EMOTIONS
1. Having a partner is not essential to my well-being. 2. I should concentrate on being happy alone.	1. I like myself. 2. I am interesting. 3. I lead a full life.	Self-esteem, hope

Problem 4: Being Passive

Typical Loneliness Assumptions	Typical Lonely Thoughts	Related Emotions
1. The problems in this relationship are all my fault. 2. I can't seem to get what I want from this relationship. 3. I can't say how I feel or he/she might leave me. 4. I'm always being criticized.	1. If someone criticizes me, he/she must be right. 2. People should give me what I want without my having to ask for it. 3. When someone criticizes me, it means he/she is preparing to leave me.	Frustrated, helpless, anxious, insecure, angry, ambivalent

Table 1. *(Continued)*

POSITIVE SOLITUDE ASSUMPTIONS	RELATED POSITIVE THOUGHTS	EMOTIONS
1. I set my own goals and standards. 2. I evaluate criticism in terms of my own beliefs.	1. I am my values. 2. I make time to examine my beliefs, values, and attitudes. 3. I take a positive attitude toward solving problems.	Self-respect

Problem 5: Setting Unrealistic Expectations

Typical Loneliness Assumptions	Typical Lonely Thoughts	Related Emotions
1. My partner will not do certain things the right way even though I have asked him/her to change. 2. My partner is not the person I thought he/she was when we first got involved.	1. There are right and wrong ways of doing almost everything, and I know what they are. 2. I should not have to tolerate any faults in my partner. 3. People should live up to my expectations of them or they are letting me down. 4. It's better to live alone than to have other people disappoint me.	Angry, frustrated, impatient, hostile

POSITIVE SOLITUDE ASSUMPTIONS	RELATED POSITIVE THOUGHTS	EMOTIONS
1. There are many ways to accomplish my goals.	1. I can adapt to the changes life brings my way.	Confidence, patience, equanimity
2. I am willing to try different approaches to life.	2. I can rely on my judgment of others.	
3. People will live up to my expectations much of the time.	3. When it comes to my own interests, I am the most reliable person I know.	
4. I live up to my own expectations most of the time.		

effective approaches known today, can help you to deal with the problem systematically and thoroughly.

Rest and Related Approaches

REST is a newer and less widely known therapeutic technique advocated by psychologist Peter Suedfeld. Suedfeld argues that throughout history various types of solitude, from puberty rites to voluntary seclusion, have been used as a psychological healing process. REST is the modern-day version of this ancient tradition, in which solitude is practiced not only for its own sake, but as a means to solving other behavioral problems as well.

In this therapy clients are first taught the positive aspects of solitude. Then they are introduced into an environment that drastically reduces both their social and their sensory contacts. According to Suedfeld, the most effective version of REST tested so far places the client in a dark, soundproof room, usually for a day or less.[5] The client lies on a bed and communicates with the therapist through a monitor. In some versions of this therapy, therapeutic messages are communicated to the client through the monitor. In other versions, the client is simply left alone. Suedfeld published the full account of his research in his 1980 book *Restricted Environmental Stimulation*.

REST is not sensory deprivation, which is the total removal of sensory input to the individual. Perhaps because of the reputation of sensory deprivation for being disorienting, even torturous, the idea of it may unnerve you just a bit. Understand that REST is sensory *reduction,* not sensory deprivation. But as Westerners, we should understand, too, that our cultural attitudes toward both are probably similar: We often fear the self-stimulation that can occur under conditions of reduced environmental input. We have been taught to believe that any form of "talking to ourselves" indicates that we are crazy. The novel sensations, vivid fantasies, and visions that may be experienced in sensory deprivation are taboo in our culture. Yet, psychologists know from experiments with sensory deprivation that it is *normal* for an individual to replace external stimulation with internal stimulation when the external stimulation drops below a certain level. Under controlled circumstances, the novel experiences, however culturally unacceptable, are not to be feared.

It is normal in REST therapy, also, to fill the feedback gap with yourself. The personal challenge is to accept yourself and what you tell yourself in the novel REST environment. Usually, when an individual goes into an environment of reduced sensory input holding neutral or positive expectations, the experience is positive. It is only when you fear the experience that you experience it fearfully. The same may be said, of course, of any experience of being alone.

REST is based on Suedfeld's conviction that we need to ignore what society teaches us about being alone and to learn to think of it as a positive experience. Suedfeld notes that everywhere in society, from parents and teachers to social scientists and writers, being alone is seen as an aberration and as a symptom of individual maladjustment or illness. It is even considered to be the breakdown of society itself. According to Suedfeld:

Psychologists have for the most part accepted this tradition unquestioningly, in the same way as we have gone along with most of the major societal norms of our environment. . . . Most personality theorists assume that attachment to other people is basic, and that when such attachments are disputed, loneliness results. Positive feelings about being alone have been described as reaction formation, or the outward signs of distrustfulness and defensiveness, or the atrophying of the normal attachment system in old age. . . . Perhaps the most favorable thing that has been said about being alone is that people who are able to overcome its terrible effects may experience a strengthening and greater integration of their personality; the implication is that adversity is good for you and that solitude is necessarily a form of adversity. . . . There is no disputing the fact that solitude and loneliness can sometimes be unpleasant, stressful, and injurious. In my opinion, this is to a great extent a result of cultural norms. Modern urbanites and dwellers in technologically advanced societies have been taught that isolation is a bad thing, and they react accordingly.[6]

Suedfeld argues that mainstream research in psychology has ignored the view that solitude may have positive effects. Psychologists tend to hold on to their negative view in spite of the fact that many people find solitude to be pleasant, exciting, enlightening, and highly desirable.[7] The fact that the public reveres and stands in awe of people who have experienced long periods of solitude—people who have taken long voyages alone, for instance—is just one more indication that we do not really understand solitude. Indeed, it may indicate that we irrationally fear it.

We must remember that even the limited experimentation that has been done with solitude indicates that it can have important effects in helping people to change their behavior. REST, which involves one twenty-four-hour period of solitude, has been successfully used to help people gain weight, lose weight, reduce their intake of alcohol, reduce stuttering, eliminate phobias, and change many other behaviors. In one study, the combination of REST with a behavioral therapy program helped clients to stop smoking. About 50 percent of the clients who used both REST and the behavioral therapy program had stopped smoking completely one year after treatment; the success rate was only 25 percent if the clients used either the REST treatment or the behavioral therapy program alone.[8]

In the Japanese culture therapies that rely on solitude are widely practiced. In his book *The Quiet Therapies: Japanese Pathways to Personal Growth,* David Reynolds reports on five such therapies, all of which isolate clients and force them to live with their own thoughts. *Shadan* therapy may be translated as isolation therapy. Another term for this particular technique is *ansei,* or rest therapy. The rationale for this approach is that the mind becomes exhausted trying to solve its own problems and that it simply needs to rest. Education and advice are not necessary for a cure. The mind, when rested, will pursue a natural healing process. The therapy starts with a period of total isolation, during which the patient lies in bed, eats, and has no contact with people. Gradually, simple tasks, such as spending twenty minutes copying, are introduced. It is believed that when a person's thought processes are slowed, they are deepened as well. As one Zen master observed, "Most people who come here are students who, for the most part, are merely restless. They want 'hara' [a form of composure]."[9]

The most famous of the quiet therapies in Japan is Morita therapy. With this therapy, clients begin a month of treatment with a bed-rest isolation that lasts a week. They simply lie quietly in their rooms; they may not read, talk, smoke, listen to the radio, or do anything except tend to their physical needs. During the course of this week, the emotional cycle moves from boredom and doubt to a gradually deeper inner focus, to peak experiences, then to increasing boredom, and finally to the desire for activity. The fourth and fifth days of isolation are key. By this time, peak experiences are likely to occur and the desire for activity becomes stronger. What happens psychologically? Reynolds points out that Japanese therapies are marked by significant, long periods of silence aimed at the acceptance, incorporation, and transcendence of symptoms. The Japanese thinks, "My symptoms *are* me"[10] and comes to own them, whereas the Westerner aims to eliminate symptoms.

Japan is one of the most crowded countries on Earth. Perhaps as a culture, the Japanese have already learned what we now need to know: that modern life contains too much stimulation. Many of us are experiencing sensory and social overload. It is time to consider seriously that the various solitude therapies—and perhaps simply being alone—may help.

Logotherapy

At the same time as we are overstimulated, our lives seem to contain too little meaning. Especially when we are alone, the awfulness of this reality comes home to us. A third type of therapy, of which Victor Frankl's logotherapy is a key example, addresses this problem. Logotherapy signifies literally "meaning" therapy; it is an approach that helps people to find meaning in their existence.

Frankl is a psychiatrist who spent years in the Nazi concentration camps. Logotherapy derives from his experiences in the camps, which have been described in his internationally acclaimed book *Man's Search for Meaning.* [11] Frankl believes that people who survived the camps did so because they could perceive some meaning in their present or future lives. They had a book or other piece of work they wanted to finish; they loved someone; or, simply, they understood that it was meaningful, even living within the camps, to be able to choose their own *attitude* toward their terrible circumstances.

Frankl's recent research suggests that many Americans experience a lack of meaning in their lives. We Americans report being bored. We experience what he calls the "Sunday neurosis": Having been busy all week, when left alone for one day we do not know ourselves and we literally do not know what to do with ourselves. We recognize this problem, but we do not know how to solve it. A study of 7,948 college students done by Johns Hopkins University found that when the students were asked what they considered "very important" to them now, 16 percent checked "making a lot of money," while 78 percent said their first goal was "finding a purpose and meaning to my life." [12] Boredom, the Sunday blues, the lack of meaning in life—all these are often reported by people who say they are lonely. It is likely, then, that Frankl's ideas can help people who are alone and unhappy.

Frankl suggests that there are three ways to find meaning. The first is meaningful work. The second is love. The third is deciding what attitude to take toward the circumstances of your life. The first two ways are fairly self-evident (though for a full understanding, the reader should consult Frankl's work). The third was highlighted for Frankl by his experience in the concentration camps:

> We who lived in concentration camps can remember the men who walked through the huts comforting others, giving away their last piece of bread. They may have been few in number, but they offer sufficient proof that everything can be taken from a man but one thing: the last of the human freedoms—to choose one's attitude in any given set of circumstances, to choose one's own way.
>
> And there were always choices to make. Every day, every hour, offered the opportunity to make a decision, a decision which determined whether you would or would not submit to those powers which threatened to rob you of your very self, your inner freedom; which determined whether or not you would become the plaything of circumstance, renouncing freedom and dignity to become molded into the form of the typical inmate.[13]

Frankl came to believe that only the person who kept some sort of faith in the future could survive. Inmates of the camps could tell when another inmate had lost his faith. When life had lost meaning for him, the inmate would stop trying to live and would indeed die shortly thereafter. As Nietzche said, "He who has a why to live for can bear with almost any *how*."[14]

In contrast to Freudian psychoanalysis, which emphasizes introspection and recall of the past, logotherapy emphasizes present reality and planning for the future. Instead of believing, as Freud and his followers have, that the primary motivational force in life is to find pleasure, Frankl believes that the primary motivational force is to find meaning:

> Man's search for meaning is the primary motivation in his life and not a "secondary rationalization" of his instinctual drives. This meaning is unique and specific in that it must and can be fulfilled by him alone; only then does it achieve a significance which will satisfy his own *will* to meaning. There are some authors who contend that meanings and values are "nothing but defense mechanisms, reaction formations and sublimations." But as for myself, I would not be willing to live merely for the sake of my "defense mechanisms," nor would I be ready to die

merely for the sake of my "reaction formations." Man, however, is able to live and even to die for the sake of his ideals and values![15]

On the basis of its own logic, logotherapy is designed to be one of the least directive of all therapies. The meaning discovered should be the client's own meaning.

If you are having problems being alone, if you are failing to find positive solitude, you may be experiencing a lack of meaning in your life. Your realization of the lack of meaning will arise particularly when you are alone: You will label it loneliness, alienation, or, perhaps, boredom. You will not know what to do about it. Certainly, these symptoms of loneliness are similar to those that Frankl describes, especially the boredom expressed and the inability to face yourself when the activities of the week are over. It is certain hell to face each day with nothing really to live for. How horrifying to look back on your life and realize that it had no meaning! This is one reason why certain people seem so desperately fearful of being alone.

The ideas of logotherapy are pertinent to every person's life, but they are especially important to people who are alone. If you are alone, no one else will be there to remind you that your life is meaningful. If you are not raising a family or supporting a spouse, either financially or emotionally, you may question the meaning of your life. Even if you personally find your own life meaningful, you may not receive much support for your perception.

Because one of the ways to meaning is love, finding meaning in life may not be quite as obvious for singles as it is for those who live in couples or families. However, finding meaning through love when alone is certainly possible. It is merely more challenging and subtle than when one is intimately connected. For instance, love may be experienced through giving service to others, whether directly through volunteering or indirectly through charitable contributions. Service to society may or may not be seen and recognized by others, but it is recognized by the self. Who can tell, for instance, what subtle satisfactions are experienced by someone who makes anonymous donations to charity? People alone can find meaning in life through love; they only have to be creative about their goals.

Of course, as Frankl points out, meaning is not only found

through love. It is also discovered in work that we want to accomplish and through the realization of our basic freedom to decide our own attitudes. Whichever the way to meaning, the important point to remember is that individuals, alone, must discover the meaning in their lives. The initiative is theirs. Chapter 13 is devoted to the issue of finding meaning in your life alone.

Managing the Client-Therapist Relationship

Whatever the therapeutic approach, when a person alone enters therapy, some special issues arise. In terms of the interaction of solitude and relationships, first, what is the client's attitude toward the therapy and, second, what is the therapist's attitude toward the therapy?

Some years ago, a book, with the engaging title *Psychotherapy, the Purchase of Friendship,* was published. This title has often come back to me as, at various times over the years, I have considered therapy for myself or have considered recommending it to a friend. Perhaps the expense of therapy would not be necessary, I have thought, if a good friend were consulted instead. Maybe, too, therapy is a crutch that allows a person not to make the kind of intimate friend that is necessary for discussing really personal problems. These issues are particularly important for the person who is alone and seeking counsel about loneliness. If relationships are an issue, where does your relationship to your therapist fit into your life?

The therapist-client relationship can fill the feedback gap in powerful ways. It can take the place of normal friendships in a person's life. It can be an even more perfect relationship than a friendship because a client can tell the therapist everything. The therapist may seem to be the "best friend" that the client has yearned for. The therapist always listens, always counsels, and seldom gets angry; he or she is the perfect friend. Because of the power of this relationship, it needs to be handled with caution.

On the one hand, there are definitely times when such a relationship is desirable and even necessary. During particularly bad times, for example, when a person has lost his or her spouse or parent or other close loved one, the relationship with the therapist can be a bridge between the relationship that was and the new life that will be.

Perhaps the client has no experience being alone and needs to spend time learning this skill, but in the meantime is panicked because he fears the loss of human support. The relationship with the therapist is useful under this circumstance, to help the client make the transition gradually, with the minimum amount of fear. The therapist-client relationship is especially useful in emergencies, too, because the therapist, or at least *a* therapist, can always be found immediately. An intimate friend would have to be cultivated over months or even years.

The therapist-client relationship is also, fortunately, different from a friendship in the sense that the therapist is trained to be objective. Although as Suedfeld and others have rightly pointed out, therapists are quite humanly susceptible to cultural indoctrination, they are the best hope for objectivity that a person has. While the advice that a friend will give to a person who is newly alone almost inevitably gets around to "you should go out more," the therapist is more likely to know better. Her opinions will be more subtle. She may be able to help her client to appreciate the virtues of positive solitude. A good therapist *is* an excellent friend.

The danger of the therapist-client relationship lies in the tendency of the client to depend on it. The relationship can fill the feedback gap so well that the client may not feel the need to build the kinds of self-sufficiency that can take its place. The best therapists will point this problem out to their clients and help them to work toward self-sufficiency and the end of therapy. Others, unfortunately, will be content to have their friendship purchased for the hourly fee. This is a major pitfall for persons who enter therapy with the main problem of being alone and unhappy.

Realizing this pitfall, the client should, early in the establishment of the therapist-client relationship, consult with the therapist as to how the therapist will handle the end of therapy. The goal of therapy is clearly independence and an end to the therapeutic relationship. The client is best protected if the therapist offers concrete guidelines, such as behaviors and attitudes to be achieved, that will signal to both the client and the therapist that the desired progress has been made and that the relationship should end.

The therapist's attitude toward therapy with people who are alone is a factor to be considered. There is ample evidence that therapists, as do many others, often have a bias toward togetherness. To conscientious therapists, it may be enough merely to suggest this bias. Realizing that they may have a bias toward "helping" people reconnect with other people in traditional ways may be enough to help them reconsider their goals in the therapy. It may be enough to encourage them to study the ideas of positive solitude. Other therapists may need more convincing.

Many of the pessimistic views about the nature of loneliness and its susceptibility to treatment are based in psychoanalytic theory. Therapists who accept only narrow views of psychoanalytic theory are less likely to support the idea of positive solitude than are other therapists. They believe that behavioral change does not deal with underlying psychological issues. Some of them would assert that even if you do manage to achieve positive solitude, if you have not dealt with your subconscious impulses and needs, you will still not be mentally healthy. Frieda Fromm-Reichmann's is a widely respected psychoanalytic view of loneliness.[16] According to Fromm-Reichmann, loneliness, defined as the longing for interpersonal intimacy, stems from the infant's inevitable separation from his or her mother. Her theory asserts that the "longing for interpersonal intimacy" is an inevitable feeling of all human beings throughout life and that we are all threatened by its loss. In the psychoanalytic view, loneliness, like so many neurotic conflicts, is inevitable. It is the adult's unconscious longing for the mother that we all "lose" when, as infants, we learn about reality.

According to the psychoanalytic view, some people become especially susceptible to loneliness later in life because, as infants, they failed to make a successful transition from their infant sense of omnipotence to a healthy self of otherness. Consequently, the theory suggests, "the deeply seated triad of narcissism, megalomania, and hostility will be established, which is at the root affliction of loneliness."[17] Fromm-Reichmann argued that this "real loneliness," as she called it, is similar to other deranged mental states like panic and that it will eventually result in psychotic disturbances. She wrote: "Anyone who has encountered persons who were under the influence of real loneliness understands why people are more frightened of being lonely than of being hungry, or being deprived of sleep, or having their sexual needs unfulfilled."[18] Thus, while some psychoanalytic therapists assert that loneliness is inevitable for normal people, others suggest that it is terrifying for those who have had an unfortunate experience as infants.

Many criticisms might be aimed at these views, especially since they are based solely on experiences of early infancy. Psychoanalytic theory has itself come under strong criticism in recent decades, as psychologists and psychiatrists working with the individual's entire personal history, rather than focusing on childhood, have made great progress with clients in therapy.

If you accept the psychoanalytic view, then two problems occur in therapy. You would have to ask yourself whether the loneliness you acquired in infancy is really amenable to treatment. Certainly, such ills are difficult to treat, and psychoanalysts would argue that they are susceptible only to psychoanalysis. Since psychoanalysis is difficult and costly, this reasoning would leave most of us to suffer an inevitable loneliness. I believe that many persons' beliefs in the inevitability of loneliness, their beliefs that loneliness is simply part of the human condition, may be traced to the strong influence in our culture of the psychoanalytic view.

Another problem that occurs in this sort of therapy is the exclusively negative connotation put on being alone. The infant's screams and agony at being separated from his or her mother is the first, and dominant, association with being alone. The positive aspects of being alone—opportunities for personal growth, the expression of creativity, and the development of curiosity that are available to the infant—are not emphasized enough if mentioned at all. To place exclusively negative connotations on being alone is to fixate on the helplessness and rage of our infancy—not a pleasant picture of our adulthood and, in my mind, not a realistic one.

Fortunately, most people today do not find themselves faced with therapists who adopt a rigid view of the influence of the unconscious. Many therapists who were trained in classical psychoanalysis consider themselves to be eclectics who acknowledge the existence of unconscious thinking while recognizing the power of conscious thoughts and behaviors. Still, we need continually to be aware of the influence of this way of thinking on common understandings about loneliness and solitude.

Here is one psychologist's advice to therapists and clients who are concerned not only with their own relationship but with the nature of relationships in our lives. It is particularly incisive and a fine summary of the spirit of this chapter:

> We cannot continue to promote the clichés about love's selflessness, the intrinsic satisfactions of caring for another, and the notion of love associated with bowing to another's will. . . . We [should] listen more carefully to what our clients are saying about their relationships and help them prepare for a world with many more options than we and our parents were offered. . . . Love may be here to stay, but it is going to be a different kind of love and we had better keep ourselves tuned in to where it is going. To admit that one is not in love or capable of loving in the traditional sense is admitting a host of demeaning characteristics about one's worth. Love has been equated with maturity, self-actualization, positive reinforcement, and making the world go 'round. Perhaps when our theories can dissociate love from the ultimate of mental health and maturity, individuals can admit temporary or permanent absence of a love relationship without shame or panic, and we will be able to knock love off its virtuous pedestal.
>
> Psychologists have been long using concepts like love, maturity, femininity, and masculinity in the sense of culturally-approved behaviors. They then decree as pathological any behaviors that deviate from these cultural norms, thereby perpetuating traditional values, often beyond their usefulness.[19]

The opposite of loneliness is not togetherness. The opposite of solitude is not happiness. In modern therapy, done well, clients and therapists will confront these realities together, and they will work together to create new goals.

Notes

1. Leonard M. Horowitz, Rita de S. French, and Craig A. Anderson, "The Prototype of a Lonely Person," In Letitia Anne Peplau and Daniel Perlman, eds.,

Loneliness: A Sourcebook of Current Theory, Research and Therapy (New York: John Wiley & Sons, 1982), 193. Slightly changed from the original to reflect loneliness rather than depression as the concept described.

2. Jeffrey E. Young, "Loneliness, Depression and Cognitive Therapy: Theory and Application," in Peplau and Perlman, eds., *Loneliness,* 379–405.

3. Ibid. See also chapter 14, this volume.

4. Young, "Loneliness, Depression and Cognitive Therapy," 391.

5. Peter Suedfeld, "Aloneness as a Healing Experience," in Peplau and Perlman, eds., *Loneliness,* 54–67.

6. Ibid., 54–55, 64.

7. Ibid., 56.

8. Ibid., 63.

9. David K. Reynolds, *The Quiet Therapies: Japanese Pathways to Personal Growth* (Honolulu: University Press of Hawaii, 1980), 91.

10. Ibid., 110.

11. Victor Frankl, *Man's Search for Meaning,* rev. ed. (New York: Simon & Schuster, 1984).

12. Ibid., 122.

13. Ibid., 86.

14. Quoted in ibid., 97.

15. Ibid., 121.

16. Frieda Fromm-Reichmann, "Loneliness," *Psychiatry* 22 (1959): 1–15.

17. Ibid., 344.

18. Frieda Fromm-Reichmann, "Loneliness," in Joseph Hartog, J. Ralph Audy, and Yehudi A. Cohen, eds., *The Anatomy of Loneliness* (New York: International Universities Press, 1980), 348.

19. Annette M. Brodsky, "Perspectives of a Feminist Therapist," in Mary Ellen Curtin, ed., *Symposium on Love* (New York: Behavioral Publications, 1973), 104–5.

12
Women and Men: Different Solitudes

Male loneliness: "My ambition is wholly personal now. All I want to do is fall in love."
Female loneliness: "I've become a workaholic because I'm so lonely."
—LOUISE BERNIKOW, *Alone in America*

So far everything you have read in this book has been addressed equally to women and men. The central work of positive solitude is the same for both—understanding the feedback gap, becoming aware of the possibilities for positive solitude, changing habits, addressing specific problems, and exploring positive solitude as a personally fulfilling resource. My discussion here would be incomplete, however, if I failed to explore some of the separate issues that men and women will experience in their pursuit of positive solitude. When it comes to the attitudes held by society, the specific types of practical problems faced, and the style in which positive solitude is pursued, gender matters.

It would be a heartening step toward equality of the sexes if living alone was equally acceptable for men and for women in society's eyes. Unfortunately, this is not yet the case. The truth is that we, as a society, have different expectations for how men and women should live. Partly as a result of these different expectations, men and women who are alone face different psychological and practical problems and need to adopt different styles for being alone.

Hurtful Stereotypes

Society still does not respect single men and single women equally. Generally, single men are at least tolerated and often appreciated. Since the Sexual Revolution of the sixties, especially, they are often admired for escaping marriage and for leading an uncommitted lifestyle. They are welcome additions to dinner parties and other couples functions. In contrast, until recently, single status for women indicated a major failure in life. A man alone has always been a bachelor, but a woman alone has always been an old maid. In recent decades, this attitude toward single women has faded a bit. Still, as recently as 1988, an article in a major women's magazine referred, quite in earnest, to this "dreaded old-maid status."[1]

For women who are alone, many other unflattering stereotypes still exist. Ask newly single women and they will agree that the following attitudes toward them, in comparison with attitudes toward newly single men, are often true:

> He is dating, she is looking for a man.
> He loves his work, she sacrificed everything for her career.
> He is single again, she is divorced.
> He should find someone and start a new life, she should find someone to take care of her (or to take care of).
> He wants to spend time alone right now, she hates men.
> He has a great lifestyle, too bad her life fell apart.
> He has a lot of outside interests, she joins every group she can.
> He will settle down after a while, she will get used to living alone.

The perpetuation of these stereotypes hurts both men and women. Certainly, it impairs women's self-esteem. Any newly single woman who is facing these stereotypes for the first time will find them especially painful. She will have to deal with them even if she is young enough to be considered marriageable, and the longer she remains single, the stronger the stereotypes become. Whatever her personal adjustment to her single status, her "failure" to reconnect with a man increases the negative images of her. Some people will see in her a bitter man hater or a desperate neurotic, a social joiner or a depressed loser. It is not surprising, then, that a woman's reaction to her single status is a combination of anger, anxiety, and bewilderment.

Men are also hurt by the stereotypes. In actuality a man's terrific singles lifestyle may not feel so great. The man may not want to date around. He may not want an unsophisticated young wife. He may not want to be with a woman at all. Because society expects men to be fully in charge of their choices, men feel uncomfortable expressing their anxieties about their single role. They tend to suppress their feelings, and, ultimately, they even forget how to feel. As singles living up to society's stereotypes, they may never realize that their ability to be in touch with their true thoughts and emotions has been impaired.

Different Life Experiences

In addition to the different attitudes that they face in society, men and women who are alone simply have different life experiences. Such common interpersonal situations as work, friendships, and marriage differ for them and lead them to experience being alone in different ways.

For example, consider the isolation that men and women feel when they lose their jobs. Both women and men derive social stimulation from their work. Employed women and men both report about the same amount of isolation in their lives overall. Naturally, when they become unemployed, both report significantly more isolation than when they were employed. However, the unemployed men suffer more emotionally from the isolation than do the unemployed women.[2] While a woman may need to work, a man is still expected to work.

Men and women also differ in the relationships they have with family and friends and in their tendency to feel isolation because of these relationships. Single men tend to be more isolated from their own families than do single women. Single women, on the other hand, tend to be more isolated from ties with people *outside* their families.

Both single men and women experience more isolation when they are poor. Of course, more women than men are poor and so more women are isolated. Where one lives is also a factor in isolation. Men and women are alike in that when they did not grow up in the city, the longer they live in a city the more isolated they will feel.[3]

Marriage brings problems of isolation to both genders. Overall, while married people are less lonely than are unmarried people, it seems that marriage fills the feedback gap more fully for men than for women. It also appears that marriage may actually create a feedback gap for women. Research shows that men who are married are not likely to feel isolated from family ties: The marriage itself fills a man's need for family. Married women are more likely than are married men to feel isolated both from family ties and from friendship networks.

Age is also a factor in isolation. Among older people, single men are the loneliest, married men are the least lonely, and women fall between the two. Being both single, divorced, or widowed and old is experienced more negatively by men than by women. Men do not expect these outcomes in their lives and have not prepared for them. Older married women have greater decision-making problems as their husbands age because the decision-making burdens of the household fall to them. Their discomfort with this unaccustomed role is exacerbated by the fact that their husbands seldom take on their share of the household chores.[4]

The end of marriage has a greater impact on women than on men. It is a simple fact that women are more likely than are men to lose their marital partner. For example, among adults over age sixty-five, women are three times more likely to be widowed.[5] More women than men will experience the feedback gap left by an ended marriage. Because of the lack of available partners, they are also much less likely to remarry than are widowed men.

Because of these societal expectations and life experiences, it is natural that men and women develop different attitudes toward loneliness and toward being alone. These attitudes are best understood in the context of men's and women's attitudes toward relationships.

Men seem to expect less from relationships and to value existing relationships less than do women. Perhaps men can afford to take their relationships for granted because they can be reasonably sure that should a feedback gap occur, they can readily fill it with a new one. Most men, it seems, do not anticipate being alone, and they do not plan for it.

Some men—those least in touch with their emotions—may devalue relationships entirely. Author Louise Bernikow (Alone in America) asserts that for these men, merely existing in a woman's presence on a daily basis seems to constitute an adequate relationship. Bernikow cites the case of one man who, after separating from his wife, replaced her by turning on the television. After discovering many similar men in her research, Bernikow concluded, "Men took it for granted that there would be 'someone' there. It was as though, for many of them, they felt that if they did what was expected of them—namely, got good jobs and made decent livings—the rest would somehow fall into place. Often enough, it did. I had the impression, particularly with men who had been left by women, that those women had been background noise, like the television set turned on. They had been 'someone' there at the end of the day."[6] Men like this are not functioning as fully developed human beings. Not only do they fail to enjoy the relationships they have, their lives revert to the mundanity of television when the relationship fades.

More subtle examples of the devaluing of relationships also exist. One of the men Bernikow describes spent a long period allegedly enjoying his solitude. The man confidently asserted to her that he relished his time alone—even though he often could not eat alone or go to the movies alone or play music alone. Nevertheless, he was proud of his passion for solitude. (As I will discuss later, it is socially unacceptable for men to say otherwise.) One day the man simply decided that he wanted to be in love. Though he was an educated person, he chose to marry a woman much younger than himself who could not match him intellectually. He asserted that their "rhythm" together was wonderful. Although by objective standards the relationship was far less emotionally and intellectually intimate than it might have been, he said that it met his needs. His young wife did not work outside the home; she was always there for him. Obviously, he had filled the feedback gap, but we may question whether he filled it meaningfully. I would predict that, as time passes, he will feel lonely within his marriage, though we know that it is unlikely that he will admit it.

In spite of progress toward gender equality, men still feel responsible for initiating relationships, and they feel a strong sense of failure when they do not succeed. Men feel pressured by the widespread expectation that a man will easily reconnect with a new partner. If there are twice as many woman as men in a given age group, a man appears inadequate if he does not have a partner or, at the least, an active sex life.

A special problem for men is that when they *are* enduring that set of negative emotions called loneliness, they are more likely to be shunned if they let their feelings show. Canadian researchers asked two groups of their students to read a case study of a lonely individual who felt depressed, inferior, and rejected. All the details of the case were identical for both groups, except that for one group the individual was named Jim and for another group the individual was named Sue. The students were then asked such questions as how acceptable Sue or Jim would be as an acquaintance, close friend, or date. They were also asked how disturbed Sue or Jim was. The results showed that when a man lets his loneliness show, people reject him more than they would reject a woman in the same situation. Women rejected the lonely man more often than men did. These findings were similar to those of other studies that have shown that the depressed and lonely man is more rejected and more devalued and is considered more emotionally impaired than is the depressed and lonely woman.[7]

Even many men who do value relationships and intimacy and who feel the emptiness of the feedback gap deeply cannot express their emotions. To understand this difference between men and women better, let us again refer to some of the psychological research. Researchers measure loneliness in one of two ways. First, they can measure it directly. They ask people to describe whether they are lonely and to rate how intense their loneliness is. Second, they can measure it indirectly, by asking people a number of specific questions about how often they interact with others, how intimate they are with others, and how they feel when they spend time alone. Comparisons of answers given under these direct and indirect approaches reveal that many men secretly harbor important problems with loneliness in their lives. Under direct questioning, men are less likely than are women to admit to being lonely. But under indirect questioning, men actually report being more lonely than do women. The man who asserted his positive solitude but could not eat alone is a good example of this tendency. Under direct questioning, lonely men reveal that they actually do experience negative emotions like depression and anxiety, and they experience them more often than do lonely women. The lonely men also put themselves down more often. They tend to attribute their loneliness to personal failure, rather than to external, uncontrollable causes.[8]

Patterns of aloneness and emotional expression are different for women. Like men, women's experience of aloneness must be seen in the context of their view of relationships. Women have broader expectations for relationships than do men. It is rare that a woman considers her husband to be background noise. Surveys almost always tell us that women desire fully intimate relationships that include affection and good two-way communication. Women actively work to build such relationships, if not with their husbands, than with friends.

Women's choices for relationships are limited compared to the choices available to men. Even if she wanted a husband who could be treated like background noise, a woman is unlikely to find such a compliant man. (If nothing else, a compliant woman is usually younger than her mate, and women marry men younger than themselves less often than men marry younger women.) If she is financially successful, it is also less likely that a woman will meet a man who is willing to be financially supported by her. It is less likely that she will meet a man who can love her in spite of, or for, her intellectual or business interests. Add these issues to demographic realities for women in older age brackets and it is clear that women's choices are, indeed, limited. Aside from the intrinsic value of relationships, this relative lack of opportunity itself may lead women to value relationships more highly than do men.

The scarcity of relationships leads many women—especially those who are not familiar with positive solitude—to fear the end of the relationships they do have. Some women say that they desperately fear being alone. The brave ones admit that they cringe at the thought that while their husbands and lovers are comparing them with other women, they are comparing the husbands and lovers with solitude. This fear leads them to rationalize staying in bad or mediocre relationships, as this woman does:

> If you're lonely, you might go out with somebody you don't like or else you might stick with a marriage to somebody who treats you badly. He'll change, you say. Or, he needs me. . . . What you are really talking about is being terrified of going on alone. Even though you're already lonely. The fear of being alone is so overwhelming, you won't even consider it. You may shout at each other to leave, you may say, we're through, I never want to see you again, but you don't sit down in a calm, very serious way and say, This is it. We can't go on like this. That is too scary.[9]

Such blind fear leads women to make undignified choices. Because of it, they stay in mediocre, or worse, relationships. Because of it they may become mistresses, a role that—although enhanced by recent titles like "man sharer" and "new other woman"—is demeaning.

On the positive side, women are less surprised than are men at being alone. They expect to be alone, if not now, then someday. They are well aware of the statistics on widowhood and divorce. For many, preparation to be independent, psychologically and otherwise, becomes an eminently logical goal. It is no coincidence that the author of the book you hold in your hands is a woman.

Different Styles for Coping

Given these differences between men and women, it is not surprising that men and women have developed different styles for dealing with being alone. I have already pointed out the first difference in styles: that women are more likely than are men to admit their loneliness. Most researchers agree, too, that women are more likely to admit to themselves and to others the sadness or anger or fear that they feel when they are alone. Men keep their feelings to themselves and, therefore, often fail to deal with them.

A second difference in styles is that during their lives, women develop more interpersonal skills than do men. From childhood onward, men are oriented to seeing their world in terms of achievement, while women see their world in terms of relationships. Each has its advantages and disadvantages, but because women are more in touch with the emotions on which relationships are based and because they expect one day to be alone—that is, without an intimate partner— women usually develop better friendship-forming skills. Studies have shown that when they are newly alone, women more easily establish a variety of new supporting relationships. Married men typically meet their emotional needs by relying on their spouses to create their social lives. Often a wife even chooses a couple's friends. Thus, as new bachelors, men are relatively weak in the skills necessary for developing close friendships.

In young adulthood, these differences in relationship-building skills have not yet become apparent. When men and women are in their twenties and thirties, the difference in their friendship-forming skills is masked. Work is a convenient source of friends for the men during this stage of life, and the women's greater skill is not visible because they are so busy with their jobs and their families. In later years, however, a person's friendships result more from personal initiative. Typically older women continue to make new friends, while older men are less likely to do so. One study found that among people over age sixty-five, women had 38 percent more friends than did men.[10]

Over their lifetimes both women and men pick up some positive solitude skills. However, they tend to have different strengths and weaknesses in positive solitude. Given men's greater socialization toward responsibility in business and financial affairs, we may realistically expect them to be stronger at making decisions alone. They will have the kinds of knowledge that will facilitate their decision-making alone. They will also have ready access to experts, many of whom are male. Often men are raised specifically to be independent decision makers. This independence is, of course, a weakness when collective decisions are called for, but in comparison to being raised as a help-mate, when you are alone it is a strength.

Women have more of the expressive abilities that help them to find solace. Women pay close attention to their home environment. They have the homemaking interest and skills that help them to create a solacing personal space. Probably, too, a woman's home becomes solacing for her because it is closely involved with what she learned about homemaking from her mother. Men may not be able to find such solace in their home environments. They are unlikely to inherit their mothers' methods of homemaking. They are less likely to own solacing objects that were their mothers', such as the old rolling pin or favorite jewelry. They are more likely to own objects that remind them of their fathers, but there is some doubt that associations to one's father are quite as comforting as those to one's mother. It may be that men's intense interest in sports, especially the ritual of learning statistics and reading the sports pages, is a way of maintaining solace and tradition. These may be the masculine ways of maintaining ties to such comforting childhood activities as collect-ing things.

Another difference in style is that women are much more likely than are men to enter therapy. In general, they give themselves more opportunities for personal growth. They are more likely, for example, consciously to develop their ability to put more fun, or more sensual-ity, or more learning, into their lives. Of course, entering therapy is not particularly useful if the therapy focuses on developing better or more relationships while ignoring positive solitude. Both women and men need to be continually aware of how well their therapists incor-porate positive solitude into the therapeutic experience.

The challenge of developing a meaningful life that includes both self and others also differs for women and men. For many, the issue of family is basic. Many women believe that having a family is the most meaningful thing they can do. If they are alone, this belief becomes a major issue: There is no socially accepted standard for building this particular type of meaning into their lives. What is family life when the socially endorsed image of husband, mother, and children is not possible or perhaps not even desirable? Today women alone are finding alternatives. Some choose single parenthood through birth or adoption. Some become an active aunt.

Men start from a position of having learned that making a living is meaningful in and of itself, and they can readily take their identity from it. Many ignore the issue of family. However, when family is important to them and they are alone, they, too, must find imaginative alternatives to create this kind of meaning in their lives. Because of social stereotypes about parenting and nurturing, this task may be particularly challenging for them. Thus, single men adopt children far less often than do single women.

For many people, work outside the home is highly meaningful, and many find emotional closeness with business friends. Yet, as we have seen, the workplace is not always a good place to get close to others. Again, gender has an effect. Schooled to expect closeness with people regardless of their roles, women may take personally the exclusion and impersonality of business friendships. Ultimately, they discover that many of their work relationships are peculiarly unsatisfying. Men will be less likely to see impersonality at work as a problem, but some of them also discover that the personal meaning they thought they would find in their work or in their friendships at work is not really there for them.

Our gender roles undoubtedly constrain women and men in their ability to cope with loneliness. Researchers have confirmed that dropping the extremes of these roles is helpful. In one study that explored the impact of gender-role conditioning on loneliness, a research team separated people into three categories—those who exhibit primarily "masculine" traits, such as assertiveness and independence; those who exhibited primarily "feminine" traits, such as kindness and sensitivity to others; and those "androgynous" individuals who exhibited both sets of traits. They learned that people who exhibit the androgynous traits are significantly less likely to be lonely. Such people are assertive and take the initiative in relating to others. They also are willing to be open about themselves in conversations with others. They are willing to help others by providing guidance and advice—in short, they are good at establishing intimate relationships.[11]

Accounting for Gender Differences

Though their styles differ, both women and men can achieve positive solitude. Both can fill the feedback gap creatively and thoroughly and lead satisfying, meaningful lives alone. Positive solitude is a balanced style of living. It is not only having fun or finding solace or developing a philosophy. It is *all* these things. It means not missing any of life's satisfactions. When it comes to developing the skills of positive solitude, women and men should assess their strengths and weaknesses with special sensitivity to their own gender-role socialization. It will be necessary for men and women who are alone to understand and to consider how their coping styles will differ because of their gender. Each should be sensitive to the influence of society and should value his or her uniqueness.

If you are a women and strongly skilled in building friendships, consider how much you rely on your relationships to the exclusion of positive solitude. Be careful to recognize the opportunities for growth in positive solitude. Give yourself the time and the space to experience these opportunities. When alone, draw on your ability to find solace and on your willingness to be emotionally open with yourself. Ferret out any weaknesses in your decision-making processes, whether the weaknesses are in professional contacts or in analytic skills. In therapy, a major theme for you is likely to be solitude and self-sufficiency. In the realm of sensuality, explore opportunities beyond the sexual. Having been socialized to focus on sexuality and attracting the opposite sex, involve yourself more fully in other sensualities, such as nature, art, and sports. At work, recognize the differences between your emotional goals and the probable goals of your co-workers. While you may wish to help your co-workers be less callous and more intimate, you should also avoid taking their indifference personally.

There are analogous issues if you are a man. Socialized to be emotionally tough and independent, you may assume that you already *do* positive solitude. Recognize what you are missing emotionally when you are alone, including the emotional deepening of solace and the delights of sensualities other than sex and sports. Admit that your decision-making abilities are less than perfect. Acknowledge that, in fact, you may love some of the people with whom you work. In therapy, a major theme for you is likely to be the experiencing of emotions, both alone and in relationships.

Of course, these are caricatures of the sexes. Many men will surely seek fully human relationships at work. Many women will be excellent decision makers. Some men will create solace quite well for themselves. Some women will need to get in touch with their emotions.

Common Problems

We should remember that in their pursuit of positive solitude, women and men also have many problems in common. One is age stereotyping. It is socially acceptable to revel in, say, the sensuality of hard rock when you are twenty, but less acceptable when you are forty. Though in reality solace is important to all people from childhood onward, society may dictate that it is more acceptable to think about solace when you are old.

Another problem that both men and women who are alone will continue to face is social prejudice. As long as he does not let his loneliness show, the single man will feel affirmed by those around him. If he admits to feeling depressed about his status, he may be shunned. He may cope by avoiding his feelings and doing what society expects of him—leading the seemingly carefree bachelor existence. He will "take charge" of his life, but the cost to him will be a reduced capacity for real intimacy, both within himself and within his relationships.

The single woman will face pity and put-downs, and she may feel angry and powerless. People may be willing to accept a woman who says that she is unhappy alone, but at the same time they will think stereotypically about how she should get out of her predicament. She may be led to feel guilty about being alone and either to accept her situation as inevitable or to accept substandard relationships. She may not feel empowered to change her situation.

People who are alone need to recognize these attitudes. When they do socialize, they should choose people, other single men and women and enlightened couples, who will affirm their full personhood. They must associate with people who affirm their positive solitude. It is also important that they develop a philosophy of solitude. Only the development of and unshaking belief in a personal philosophy of solitude can adequately defend you against the negative stereotypes you will so frequently face. You must define your self before society does it for you.

Whether you are a man or a woman, one thing is clear. In your pursuit of positive solitude, you should be cautious about using members of the opposite sex as role models. The circumstances of women's and men's lives differ in important ways, and in pursuing positive solitude you will be wise to keep these circumstances in mind.

Notes

1. Meryl Gordon, "Rough Times," *New York Woman* 2 (March 1988): 80–83.

2. Claude S. Fischer and Susan L. Phillips, "Who Is Alone? Social Characteristics of People with Small Networks," in Letitia Anne Peplau and Daniel Perlman, eds., *Loneliness, A Sourcebook of Current Theory, Research and Therapy* (New York: John Wiley & Sons, 1982), 21–39.

3. Ibid.

4. Letitia Anne Peplau, *et al.*, "Being Old and Living Alone," in Peplau and Perlman, eds., *Loneliness,* 327–47.

5. Ibid.

6. Louise Bernikow, *Alone in America: The Search for Companionship* (Boston: Faber and Faber, 1987), 61.

7. Fischer and Phillips, "Who Is Alone?"

8. Norman R. Schultz, Jr., and DeWayne Moore, "The Loneliness Experience of College Students: Sex Differences," *Personality and Social Psychology Bulletin* 12 (March 1986): 111–19.

9. Suzanne McNear, "Crazy with Loneliness," *Cosmopolitan,* October 1987: 264.

10. Peplau, et al., "Being Old and Living Alone."

11. Mitchell T. Wittenberg and Harry T. Reis, "Loneliness, Social Skills, and Social Perception," *Personality and Social Psychology Bulletin* 12 (March 1986): 121–30.

III
Developing
a Philosophy
of Solitude

13
Finding Meaning
in a Life Alone

And Wisdom's self
Oft seeks to sweet retired solitude
Where, with her best nurse Contemplation,
She plumes her feathers, and lets grow her wings.
—JOHN MILTON, *Paradise Lost*

The message of positive solitude is that when you are alone, it is possible to lead a highly satisfying life, that although your beliefs about being alone may pull you into loneliness traps, by careful thought and action you can overcome your social conditioning and learn to practice a personal positive solitude. When you are alone, you yourself can provide the feedback you need to survive. You can provide feedback for yourself that is highly rewarding, loving, and exciting. You can be self-sufficient economically and psychologically.

Yet, given the prevalent attitudes in our society, you may continue to be skeptical. You may realistically ask, "Is this enough? Can the person alone really lead a fulfilling life?"

These questions suggest another, more basic one: By whose standards are we to decide what a fulfilling life is? The answer is, of course, that only the individual human being can decide. Only the person who is responsible for running his or her life can judge what is fulfilling. Ultimately, each of us needs to develop beliefs and goals that make sense of who we are in our aloneness. No one else can allay our doubts about the meaningfulness of our lives. Our answers will be found in the development of a personal philosophy for being alone.

Exploring our basic beliefs and goals is essential to the successful experience of aloneness, and holding a personal philosophy for being alone is the ultimate antidote to loneliness. Dealing with these beliefs and goals is even more important to your well-being than is dealing with the more mundane issue of daily loneliness because the belief system is the basis from which all other approaches to your aloneness derive. Your ability to deal with the bad times, to overcome pressures to "meet people," and to deal with all the other separate issues that face the person alone will be enhanced if you have a perspective on them that comes from a personal philosophy of solitude.

Individuals who do not see themselves as primarily alone also need a philosophy, a kind of life plan, of course, but while leading their busy lives they are less likely to recognize its importance. Furthermore, society conveniently defines for them many molds that fit their lives. It recognizes distinct norms for married life and for family life. For the person who is alone, however, norms are relatively unformed, and to maintain a psychological equilibrium, it is crucial to develop a philosophy.

If you don't build a coherent philosophy, you are more likely to fall back into the loneliness traps. You will be more susceptible to society's mistaken notions of the ideal life. As a counterbalance, you need to articulate why you are alone, what is positive about it, and what is negative about it.

The development of a personal philosophy of solitude is rooted in the awareness phase of positive solitude. When you begin to understand the "problem" of loneliness, you often gain your first inkling that adopting a new attitude toward being alone may change your life. As you then start to alter some of your counterproductive behaviors, you are rewarded by seeing the loneliness fade and your new understanding strengthened.

As you spend more of your time alone, you begin deliberately to explore positive solitude. Having achieved a large measure of personal contentment, even happiness, in this stage, you will naturally begin to ask broader questions—to contemplate what is unique about yourself and to explore the meaning of your life. Developing a new life philosophy that includes positive solitude becomes a dominant task.

In its earliest form the philosophy of solitude is mainly a belief that positive solitude makes you happier. This elementary belief is necessary to achieve positive solitude, and it sustains you as you work to build new habits for being alone. At this early point, however, you are testing the idea of positive solitude, rather than really developing it. Your philosophy of solitude is, in a way, borrowed, because you simply have not had enough experience in positive solitude to build something more. Gradually, however, creating your own philosophy of solitude becomes a major interest, truly an exploration that you embark upon as a major source of deep personal satisfaction. Your philosophy will emerge from your own experience.

Though developing a personal philosophy of positive solitude includes understanding the feedback gap and changing your behavior accordingly, it also goes well beyond them. For one thing, it means that you will address the basic issue of why one type of feedback is meaningful to you while another is not. Why, for example, is reading a book better than watching television (if it is for you)? Why is seeking emotional independence better than looking for love? How important to you are the kinds of feedback that you get from your work? How much contact do you want with others? What type of contact do you want?

Your manner of deciding is just as personal as the contents of your decision. Do you like to be spontaneous in your decision making or do you relish structure and planning? What time perspectives make sense to you? Developing a philosophy for solitude is not merely the one-time act of establishing your beliefs. It is also a process of understanding and developing your preferred, continuing ways of making decisions about beliefs. It is a highly individualized, creative exploration in which people design their own unique processes and by which people select the content that seems important to them.

During your exploration, three themes will emerge. The first theme is your search for meaning. You will begin to ask yourself such questions as, "What is really meaningful to me?" and "What is important to my life?" One of my favorite questions to explore is, "Were I to project myself into the last hours of my life, looking back, what would my regrets and satisfactions be?"

A second theme will be your relationship with others. You will begin to ask yourself, "Now that I understand and live positive solitude, what is to be my relationship with other people? What does love mean in my life? What is the role of responsibility? What do others contribute to me, and what do I give to them?"

The third theme is your potential for self-fulfillment. You will begin to ask yourself, "In a life lived alone, how can I become yet more creative and self-actualized? What new avenues are open to me?"

This chapter is the first of three that are devoted to these basic themes.

Finding Your Personal Meanings

To achieve positive solitude, you must figure out how to fill the feedback gap with activities and ideas that are personally meaningful. Without meaning in life, we actually feel lonely for our *selves*. To demonstrate this point, let us look closely at a quotation from a letter to Clark Moustakas in response to his book *Loneliness*. In the letter, a reader describes his own realization of the need for meaning. I have italicized the more relevant ideas:

> *The vacuum of "being,"* if not filled with the substance of *life-realized in depth* . . . will gain so much power that our people will collapse inwardly in the clutter of their own psychic debris. The loneliness each man feels is his hunger for life itself, not only life in his being, but *life in the being of creation, past, present and future.* [1]

Not only does this writer recognize the feedback gap—the vacuum of being—and its great importance to his happiness, he understands that filling it requires more than merely keeping busy. Filling it requires living life deeply rather than superficially. It requires an active search—"life in the being of creation."

Modern life has made it easy for us to acquire meaningless habits; it has addicted us to the quick fix. Instead of devoting ourselves to deepening human relationships, for example, we are likely to busy ourselves with clubs and other activities. Instead of finding a vocation, we take the highest-paying job. Instead of taking the time to find something good to read, we flip on the tube. It is not that we necessarily enjoy the fast life or the television programs or the less-than-satisfying work any more than we would enjoy their more meaningful alternatives. But they do reward us immediately, and they are highly convenient. We often find, however, that we become bored with them after a time, and they leave us curiously unfulfilled.

Unfortunately, realizing the lure of the quick fix does not itself change our behavior. Often we know what is meaningful, yet we cannot do what is meaningful. The problem of finding meaning is analogous to losing weight or augmenting our physical exercise. Wanting to change—exerting will power—is not enough to cause change. We will continue doing the less meaningful things because they have become reinforcing to us. Perhaps our friends are doing them or the routine of doing them has itself become comfortable. Initially, the more meaningful alternatives are not practiced enough to become reinforcing in themselves. Sadly, when we know what is meaningful and then do meaningless things anyway, we get discouraged about our ability to change. We learn to mistrust our own judgment.

The journey to meaning requires not only that we recognize what is good for us, whether physically, mentally, or spiritually, but that we pursue it with a definite plan. A person decides what is truly important to him or her and then actively plans a life around these meanings. In a life that is well planned, eventually healthy and meaningful pursuits will seem to come naturally.

Setting and pursuing meaningful goals requires understanding our lives in context. We must each become students of ourselves and our environments. An important piece of this learning is understanding the culture in which we live. In his role as social critic, psychologist B. F. Skinner pointed out that modern cultures are more often punishing than rewarding. In today's societies people do things primarily to escape that punishment. We study not so much to get ahead or to learn as to avoid the failure of low grades or of flunking out.

People work not for the love of what they are doing but to avoid losing their income. Similarly, we may find ourselves "loving" other people because we are afraid that they will leave us.

In contrast, the goals in a rewarding culture are clear and predictable. People can actually look forward to their rewards—a vacation, the completion of a project, an anniversary. In rewarding systems, individuals can decide what they want and then go for it. Having satisfied one desire, they can happily and confidently move on to satisfying another. They feel in control of their lives. One of the most pleasant aspects of committed relationships, whether one to one or in groups and communities, is this ability to look ahead toward mutual rewards. One goal of a positive solitude philosophy is to establish this kind of affirmative control in our lives.

In the punishing environments in which we live, people do not usually know exactly where and how the punishments will be administered. They do not know when they might lose their jobs or if their spouses will leave them. We Americans spend a lot of energy worrying about where the next punishment is likely to come from and defending ourselves. In the short term, we worry about keeping our jobs or our partners. In the long term, we worry about how to support our parents or ourselves. Escaping punishments becomes a major goal in our lives.

What happens to people who live in this kind of society? Psychologists have done extensive studies on the effects of punishing environments on rats. When the animals are trained by being punished for doing wrong, rather than being rewarded for doing right, they become incessantly, anxiously active. In a real sense, they are constantly trying to avoid the inevitable. Since they do not know exactly when a punishment will be administered, they never cease their neurotic vigilance. Similarly, human beings who live in punishing environments become stressed and anxious. They are hyperactively vigilant. When people are in the habit of trying to avoid punishment in such important areas of their lives as work, they carry the habit over into other parts of their lives as well. They take their anxiety home with them, acting as though they are constantly trying to protect themselves. Often they are afraid to do nothing. They cannot relax. They are afraid to be alone.

When people do not study what they want to learn; when they do not work at what they really want to spend their life doing; when they need others, rather than want others, then they eventually lose touch with their own needs and dreams. This is one way of saying that life becomes meaningless to them.

So we too often study and work and even love to avoid punishment, not primarily because we like what we are studying or because we believe in our work or because we have found people who fascinate us. Society compensates us for living in this meaningless way. We are "rewarded" for studying what we do not want to study and for performing tasks that we do not wish to perform by such inducements as career advancement and money. Then, on weekends or, if we survive, in retirement, society encourages us to use our position or our money to acquire for ourselves things that are interesting, tasty, sexy, or beautiful. Instant gratifications are substituted for the truly meaningful in our lives.

Ultimately, whether instinctively or consciously, we do not find the constant diet of instant gratification to be satisfying. As Skinner pointed out:

> It may not seem that one could fail to enjoy a life spent looking at beautiful things, eating delicious foods, watching entertaining performances, and playing roulette, but it would be a life in which almost nothing else was done, and few of those who have been able to try it have been notably happy. What is wrong with life in the West is not that it has too many reinforcers, but that they are not contingent on *the kinds of behavior that sustain the individual.* [2]

Existentialist psychologist Rollo May reached a similar conclusion, albeit by way of a different theoretical approach. As May put the issue:

> We in the Western world are the heirs of four centuries of technical achievement in power over nature and now over ourselves; this is our greatness and, at the same time, it is also our greatest peril. We are not in danger of denying the technical emphasis. . . . But rather we repress the opposite, the *awareness of being.* . . . One consequence of this repression of the sense of being is that modern man's image of

himself and his experience and concept of himself as a responsible individual have likewise disintegrated.[3]

Meaninglessness is what we are left with when we let others fill the feedback gap with their threats of punishment and their trivial entertainments. It characterizes the life we lead when we do not face our selves, alone, when we do not find our own meanings and when we do not set our own goals and find true rewards. Alienation is the guilt we feel when we fail to be who we are.

Our goal, then, must be to make productive decisions that will lead us toward the discovery of our own meaning. Finding such personal meaning has been a major theme in Western literature, from Joseph Conrad to William Styron.[4] Novelist Herman Hesse, whom Moustakas quotes frequently as an expert on loneliness, put the issue most eloquently:

> Each man has only one genuine vocation—to find the way to himself. He might end up as poet or madman, as prophet or criminal—that [is] not his affair, ultimately it [is] of no concern. His task [is] to discover his own destiny—not an arbitrary one—and live it out wholly and resolutely within himself. Everything else [is] only a would-be existence, an attempt at evasion, a flight back to the ideals of the masses, conformity and fear of one's own inwardness. The new vision rose up before me, glimpsed a hundred times, possibly even expressed before but now experienced for the first time by me. I was an experiment on the part of Nature, a gamble within the unknown, perhaps for a new purpose, perhaps for nothing, and my only task was to allow this game on the part of primeval depths to take its course, to feel its will within me and make it wholly mine. That or nothing![5]

I will not here presume to describe what meanings, or even what types of meanings, you will discover in your personal exploration. To do so would violate the very notion of this exploration. But let me give you an example.

For me, as I write this, the major lines of meaning in my life are clear. Usually, I find that there is more meaning in activities that have significant long-term, rather than short-term, payoffs in self-satisfaction, in intimacy, and in contributions to the well-being of others. In short and long bursts, over a period of four years, I chose to work on this book, rather than write more articles or do more consulting. You will not be surprised to learn that I prefer to minimize my dependence on entertainments, though I do tend to fall back on them and really enjoy them when I am tired out by other activities. I believe that the kinds of behaviors that are healthy and meaningful involve learning, personal growth, providing security for myself or others, helping, and solving problems. Fortunately, I am able to pursue these goals through a career that includes a great deal of teaching and writing. In addition, I am interested in understanding character, both my own and that of others. To this end, I read widely in the psychological literature. I often focus on making and finding peace in my life.

You can see that in my life there are many ways to meaning. I relish this variety. Another person might opt for only one major pursuit or perhaps for even more variety than I have chosen.

Solitude as a Path to Meaning

I get in touch with my own meanings through solitude. Probably the most important aspect of gaining control over one's life is simply making decisions—and making them alone. Make decisions that matter about who you are and what you are going to pursue. Decide how your time will be structured. Make your decisions and then implement them. As the existentialist philosopher Jean Paul Sartre put it, "We *are* our choices."[6] And Moustakas wrote:

> The self cannot develop unless there is freedom, choice, and responsibility, unless each person experiences his own senses and becomes an active force in life, free to choose and select, free to feel and express openly and honestly the nature of these feelings, free to identify with living forces, with alive persons who encourage growth in individual identity, who value being for itself, and who can enable the person to engage himself and be committed to meaningful inquiry and activity.[7]

Having decided to embark upon this exploration to meaning, what path should you take? There are as many paths as individuals, yet with some commonality among them. First, avoid meaningless activities—however you choose to define them—in all aspects of your life. Second, be aware of the process itself—how you have decided to pursue meaning in your life. Whatever your personal idea of what is meaningful, the journey to meaning itself is crucial to your personal sense of well-being, and the path begins with spending a significant amount of time alone. Remember, too, that our modern society inundates us with more stimulation, and more intense stimulation, than any other society in history. The world is shrinking, and there is less and less space in which we can be alone.[8] Solitude, deliberately pursued, can help you to overcome this feedback overload.

Reduce your external stimulation so you can experience inner feelings and voices, memories and interpretations. As research psychologist Suedfeld pointed out:

> We are at last coming to realize the aversiveness of the social and sensory overload that bombards us almost constantly. It has taken a long time. The fish is not aware of the water, as a general rule. But when the water becomes first dirty and then poisonous, and the fish gets sick, it will—if it is a thinking and self-aware fish—eventually recognize the existence of a problem. And picine psychologists will start teaching their schools the facts, as human psychologists are beginning to pass the word about the effects of crowding, noise, information overload, future shock, lack of privacy, and the rest. The antidote is solitude, stillness, and time out. In an environment with fewer frantic distractions, we can learn once again to appreciate the important things that we have been driven to ignore.[9]

Once environmental overload is reduced, energy is released in the individual for pursuit of more personally relevant interests. There is more air time for your own thoughts and feelings. An additional reward is that you will experience the environmental inputs that still exist, be they sensory experiences or appreciation of other human beings, with increased freshness and intensity.

Withdrawal from everyday stimulations must be coupled with enough patience to listen to yourself. Moustakas has had many experiences in which he entered into his private thoughts in search of new truth and meaning:

> At times, life is empty and meaningless and ugly and terribly, terribly denying and isolating. I walk for hours, talking to myself, trying to make sense out of the senselessness and shock. Then I find an isolated spot, I sit under a tree, and waves of feeling assault me, cover me intensely, until I am shattered and my mind is empty of all thought. I wait, mindlessly, for some new hope to emerge, for some sign in the universe to make a new beginning. In a trance, I remain simply present, rooted in nature, and, by some very gradual, mysterious process, I return to a consciousness of my own existence. "Does the way I live really matter?"[10]

Author-philosopher Alice Koller wrote a careful autobiographical account of a personal exploration that occupied several months.[11] Distanced from her family and friends and even from her self, Koller had contemplated suicide. She felt she had no reason to live. Emotionally stretched and with few financial resources, she decided to spend the last of her money to rent a house on Nantucket for the winter. Her life felt meaningless, yet instinctively she knew she had to be "really alone."[12] Early in her book, she describes a positive solitude high during which she trembles in wonder: "I have a goal." She adopts a puppy and names him *Logos,* the Greek word for meaning. She spends all her time alone on the island in a quest for personal meaning.

Near the end of her stay, Koller expresses a fear of people's influence on her: "Will I be free, back among people again? Will I be able to guard against trying to please them at all costs?"[13] She does not want her new equilibrium, a crucial part of her positive solitude, to be disturbed. Ultimately, too, we learn that Koller finds personal meaning in a new sense of time in her life. She realizes as she is leaving the island that, "I don't need to condense this into one parting memory: I have three months of days to remember."[14]

What meanings will you discover when you are alone? The meanings will be inseparable from your own experience of solitude.

When we are spending too much of our psychic time in abstractions and conversations, solitude helps us to recapture a more primitive and profound mode of living, and in this mode we may find new meanings. William James suggested that modern man has forgotten that he has the ability to be alone, but that with some deliberation this ability can be recovered:

> The savages and children of nature, to whom we deem ourselves so much superior, certainly are alive where we often are dead, along these lines . . . "Ah! my brother," said a chieftain to his . . . guest, "thou wilt never know the happiness of both thinking of nothing and doing nothing. This, next to sleep, is the most enchanting of all things."[15]

James also captured one man's experience of a particularly marvelous solitude that I have included here. While reading, note that the speaker loosely but actively structures his long periods of solitude; he establishes a routine within which being alone is one theme. This structuring is a factor in many personal explorations. The speaker describes a winter he spent in the Rio Negro, a province in Patagonia, seventy or eighty miles from the sea:

> It was my custom to go out every morning on horseback with my gun, and, followed by one dog, to ride away from the valley; and no sooner would I climb the terrace, and plunge into the gray, universal thicket, than I would find myself as completely alone as if five hundred instead of only five miles separated me from the valley and river. So wild and solitary and remote seemed that gray waste, stretching away into infinitude, a waste untrodden by man, and where the wild animals are so few that they have made no discoverable path in the wilderness of thorns. . . . Not once nor twice nor thrice, but day after day I returned to this solitude, going to it in the morning as if to attend a festival, and leaving it only when hunger and thirst and the westering sun compelled me. And yet I had no object in going,—no motive which could be put into words; for, although I carried a gun, there was nothing to shoot,—the shooting was all left behind in the valley. . . . Sometimes I would pass a whole day without seeing one mammal, and perhaps not more than a dozen birds of any size. The weather at that time was cheerless, generally with a gray film of cloud spread over the sky, and a bleak wind,

often cold enough to make my bridle-hand quite numb.... At a slow pace, which would have seemed intolerable under other circumstances, I would ride about for hours together at a stretch. On arriving at a hill, I would slowly ride to its summit, and stand there to survey the prospect. On every side it stretched away in great undulations, wild and irregular. How gray it all was! Hardly less so near at hand than on the haze-wrapped horizon where the hills were dim and the outline obscured by distance. Descending from my outlook, I would take up my aimless wanderings again, and visit other elevations to gaze on the same land-scape from another point; and so on for hours. And at noon I would dismount, and sit or lie on my folded poncho for an hour or longer. One day in these rambles I discovered a small grove composed of twenty or thirty trees, growing at a convenient distance apart, that had evidently been resorted to by a herd of deer or other wild animals. This grove was on a hill differing in shape from other hills in its neighborhood; and, after a time, I made a point of finding and using it as a resting-place every day at noon. I did not ask myself why I made [the] choice of that one spot, sometimes going out of my way to sit there, instead of sitting down under any one of the millions of trees and bushes on any other hillside. I thought nothing about it, but acted unconsciously. Only afterward it seemed to me that, after having rested there once, each time I wished to rest again, the wish came associated with the image of that particular clump of trees, with polished stems and clean bed of sand beneath; and in a short time I formed a habit of returning, animal like, to repose at that same spot.

It was, perhaps, a mistake to say that I would sit down and rest, since I was never tired; and yet, without being tired, that noon-day pause, during which I sat for an hour without moving, was strangely grateful. All day there would be no sound, not even the rustling of a leaf. One day, while listening to the silence, it occurred to my mind to wonder what the effect would be if I were to shout aloud. This seemed at the time a horrible suggestion, which almost made me shudder. But during those solitary days it was a rare thing for any thought to cross my mind. In the state of mind I was in, thought had become impossible. My state was one of suspense and watchfulness; yet I had no expecta-tion of meeting an adventure, and felt as free from apprehension as I feel now while sitting in a room in London. The state seemed familiar rather than strange, and accompanied by a strong feeling of elation; and I did not know that something had come between me and my intellect until I returned to my former self,—to thinking, and the old insipid existence [again].[16]

This man puts a simple structure in his days. He is not merely lying around in revery. Nor—as is often the case when a person is physically and mentally inactive for long periods—is he experiencing a depression. He is moving and observing. He is deliberate in his exploration of the unknown. The resulting reflections are on a plane of consciousness not familiar to most of us, and the result for him has obviously been profound. Of course, we do not know whether, given the same circumstances, most of us would have a similar experience. We can only guess at what is beyond the primitive feeling he describes. Once it has been experienced, does one continually seek it? Does one get bored with it? What happens when it is desired, but cannot be obtained? We can only say for certain that for this man the experience had meaning, and we can imagine that for all of us who are bound by modern society, similar experiences may be worth trying.

Finding Guidance in Models and Counseling

Finding models who exemplify meaning in their lives is another way of finding avenues to our own personal meanings. I once found such a model in a character in the film *Ikiru,* by the Japanese director Akira Kurosawa. In English *Ikiru* means simply "to live." In the film a man searching for meaning in his life tries to understand why a naive girl whom he meets seems important to him. The central character, Watanabe, is a solitary and grumpy old man who is a minor clerk in a city-government bureaucracy. We first see him sitting at his desk, hiding behind two-foot stacks of paperwork. Watanabe learns that he has stomach cancer and knowing that he has less than a year to live, despairs that his life has been wasted. In the time left to him, he is determined to find out how to live. By chance he meets an ordinary young woman, Toyo, who makes toys in a manufacturing plant, and realizes that he wants to spend time just being with her. She is reluctant:

TOYO: You make me nervous. Why do you pay so much attention
to me?

WATANABE: It's because. . . .

TOYO: Because why?

WATANABE: Well, I just enjoy being with you.

TOYO: I hope it isn't love.

WATANABE: No, it's not. . . .

TOYO: Why don't you speak more clearly—say what you mean! . . .

WATANABE: . . . I don't know myself . . . why I like being with you.
All I know is that . . . is that I'm going to die soon. I have
gastric cancer . . . In here. You understand? I have less than a
year to live. And when I found that out . . . then, somehow, I
was drawn to you. Once when I was a little boy I nearly
drowned. It is just that feeling. Darkness is everywhere and
there is nothing for me to hold on to, no matter how I try.
There is only you.

TOYO: What about your son?

WATANABE: Don't even talk about him. I have no son; I'm all alone.

TOYO: Don't talk like that.

WATANABE: You don't understand. My son is somewhere far away,
just as my parents were far away when I was drowning. I can't
bear to think about it.

Thus, Watanabe, with an unimaginably sad face, describes his profound loneliness. The dialogue continues:

TOYO: But what help am I?

WATANABE: You . . . well, just to look at you makes me feel better.
It . . . it warms this . . . *(He looks down). . .* this mummy heart
of mine. And you are kind to me. No, that's not it. It's because
you are so young and healthy. No, it isn't that either. *(He rises,
comes to her side of the table, sits down; she is repelled, and tries
to move farther away.)* You are so full of life and . . . and I'm
envious of that. If only I could be like you for one day before I
die. I won't be able to die unless I can be. Oh, I want to do
something. Only you can show me. I don't know what to do. I
don't know how to do it. Maybe you don't either, but, please, if
you can, show me how to be like you.

TOYO: I don't know.

WATANABE: How can I be like you?

TOYO: But all I do is work and eat—that's all.

WATANABE: Really?

TOYO: Really. That and make toys like this one. *(She has a toy rabbit in her pocket. She takes it out, winds it up, puts it on the table in front of them; it hops toward him; she picks it up, starts it over again.)* That's all I do, but it's fun. I feel as if I were friends with all the children in Japan now. Mr. Watanabe, why don't you do something like that, too?

WATANABE: What can I do at the office?

TOYO: That's true. Well then, resign and find some other work.

WATANABE: It's too late. *(Cut to her looking at him; then cut to both of them with the mechanical rabbit between them.)*

WATANABE: No, it's not. It isn't impossible. *(A shot of him, with tears in his eyes. She is afraid; she moves back. He suddenly turns to her, smiling; she shrinks back.)*

WATANABE: I can do something if I really want to!

With new insight into the potential for meaning in his life, Watanabe returns to his office. He takes the first document from one of the huge stacks on his desk and reads it. It is a petition from some women in a slum district who want to turn a vacant city lot into a park for their children. These women have been continually rebuffed by the system. The rest of the film describes Watanabe's quest to help them. For months he does anything he can to create the park. He cuts through the bureaucracy. He humbles himself. In the end we see him sitting alone on a swing in the park he has created. It is snowing. He is singing to himself; he knows he will die there alone and happy.

Watanabe observed the life around him and discovered that the girl's simple pleasure in doing meaningful work, making toys to delight children, could be his as well. The girl did not recognize her own meaning for what it was, for its importance or centrality in her life, but the fictional Watanabe, like the real person Alice Koller, had come to a crossroads. Facing his own death, he forced himself to face his life.

Less dramatic scenarios are played out around us daily, as people try to build meaning into their lives. Here is a modern widow, quoted by the noted researcher Helena Znaniecki Lopata:

If I haven't got anything else to do, I'll make a pie for somebody, one of the neighbors that I hear is going to have company—get busy and do something, no matter what it is—just keep busy. Even if you can't do anything else but sit down and make paper flowers—make them. If you don't know how to do it—then throw them away and make some more. Make cookies, give them away; gee, there's always places where you can take pounds of cookies—orphanages . . . Lake Bluff. I often go up there during the wintertime. I'll make cookies, then hope for a good day and take them up there, and those kids love them, you know, and it's wonderful. You come home and you think, "Gee, I did something," you know. The space you're occupying counts for something.[17]

One systematic way to search for your personal meaning is through guided counseling. Victor Frankl's logotherapy, which I described in chapter 11, emphasizes that meaning in life is to be found in the process of achieving a goal, the exploration itself, more than in any particular end goal. Frankl was so convinced that the path to meaning is central to life adjustment that he would actually provide goals for clients who could not discover them for themselves. Though criticized by other professional colleagues for interfering in the lives of his clients, Frankl believed that as long as clients had goals, they could focus happily on the process of achieving them.

Creating a Life Myth

In the search for meaning, it can be valuable to have what may be called a *life myth* or *life map*—a general plan and philosophy about how to live. Thoreau created such a life map in *Walden,* which was as much a plan for his life as a description of the beautiful environment in which the plan was created. Obviously, most of us do not have Thoreau's literary talent and would not wish to publish our written work. Still, most of us could write a simple diary that would collect what we have learned about ourselves and our meanings and that would, in the midst of a confusing and distracting world, remind us of our personally meaningful paths. One of Thoreau's biographers pointed out that after Thoreau left Walden Pond, his life myth became increasingly important to him.[18] In the drawn-out process of revising

Walden, Thoreau kept alive and elaborated upon the myth of personality and experience that helped to give meaning to his existence.

Once Thoreau was back in society, the life mode that *Walden* represented for him began to change. The day before the book was published, he wrote, "Methinks I have spent a rather unprofitable summer thus far. I have been too much with the world, as the poet might say."[19] Having spent more time with other people, Thoreau felt himself more susceptible to their influence, as is revealed in his remark, "My companion tempts me to certain licenses of speech, i.e. to reckless and sweeping expressions."[20] Having worked so hard in the preceding years to distance himself from the opinions and expectations of his townsmen, Thoreau for a time found himself becoming more vulnerable and defensive and less serene. Of course, later his serenity was to return. A visitor to Thoreau shortly before he died remarked that he had never seen anyone die with such peace. It seems clear from his subsequent writings that Thoreau journeyed beyond the ideas of *Walden* as he grew older. Nevertheless, the map guided him wonderfully for a time. Today we are fortunate to have it because it has provided the basis for a life myth for many other people as well.

Of Meaning and Aloneness

Humankind is destined to search for meaning, and there are many paths to it. I cannot here define the spectrum of possible meanings that may be experienced in modern times. We are only at the beginning of understanding such possibilities.

Yet some may still doubt that the discovery of "true" meaning is possible in solitude. Individuals who are alone may doubt their ability to find meaning alone. They may doubt the legitimacy of living for meaning that is discovered primarily in themselves. Are such meanings legitimate that would be found only in the exploration of your own creativity, the development of your sensuality, the expansion of your intellectual capabilities, or the development of your physical capabilities? If you believe that meanings discovered in the self are less worthwhile than are meanings discovered among other human beings and if you then cannot connect with others, then it follows that your experience, indeed your life, will feel trivial and meaningless.

We need to challenge the beliefs that life is meaningful only when it is lived in the context of others and that it is most meaningful when one is contributing to the well-being of others. Rather than accept these beliefs as fact, we should consider the view that, with respect to involvement of self and others, there are probably many different approaches to meaning. Adopting this view is an important part of the positive-solitude experience. You can discover meaning in the interests you pursue for yourself alone, in the interests you pursue with others you know only casually, in the interests you pursue with others you know intimately, and in the interests you pursue for or with the larger society. Most people will pursue each of these types of meaning at some time in their lives; the "proper" mix of these components is unknown, however. It is highly dependent on individual circumstances, and it is the individual's right to explore the possibilities. In the next chapter we will investigate more fully this important question of meaning in contexts that include other people.

Notes

1. Clark Moustakas, *Individuality and Encounter* (Cambridge, Mass.: Howard A. Doyle Publishing Co., 1968), 115.

2. B. F. Skinner, "What Is Wrong with Daily Life in the Western World?" *American Psychologist* 41 (May 1986): 568–74.

3. Rollo May, "The Emergence of Existential Psychology," in Rollo May, *Existential Psychology* (New York: Random House, 1960), 3.

4. Carin M. Rubenstein and Phillip Shaver, "The Experience of Loneliness," in Letitia Anne Peplau and Daniel Perlman, eds., *Loneliness: A Sourcebook of Current Theory, Research and Therapy* (New York: John Wiley & Sons, 1982), 208.

5. Quoted in Moustakas, *Individuality and Encounter,* 30.

6. Quoted in May, *"The Emergence of Existential Psychology,"* 13.

7. Moustakas, *Individuality and Encounter,* 10.

8. Thomas Merton, *Love and Living* (San Diego, Calif.: Harcourt Brace Jovanovich, 1979), 16.

9. Peter Suedfeld, "Aloneness as a Healing Experience," in Peplau and Perlman, eds., *Loneliness,* 65.

10. Moustakas, *Individuality and Encounter,* 30–31.

11. Alice Koller, *An Unknown Woman* (New York: Bantam Books, 1981).

12. Ibid., 2.

13. Ibid., 253.

14. Ibid., 256.

15. William James, "On a Certain Blindness in Human Beings," in Josephine Miles, ed., *Classic Essays in English* (Boston: Little, Brown & Co., 1961), 236–37.

16. *Ibid.* 237–38.

17. Helen Znaniecki Lopata, "Loneliness: Forms and Components," in Robert S. Weiss, ed., *Loneliness, the Experience of Emotional Isolation* (Cambridge, Mass.: MIT Press, 1975), 111.

18. Richard Lebeaux, *Thoreau's Seasons* (Amherst, Mass.: University of Massachusetts Press, 1984).

19. Quoted in ibid., 201.

20. Ibid.

14
And Who Are All These Others?

*Though I am surrounded by people, I am beginning to realize
how lonely I am. I feel as if I live in two houses. In one I am
huddled together with my family. In the other I am all alone,
looking for someone to talk to.*

—ANNE LASOFF, "Writing in the Real World"

In developing a personal philosophy of solitude, at some point
you will consider issues that concern your self in your relation to
others. Can individuals really nurture themselves alone? Is togetherness necessary in some way? *If* togetherness is necessary, how much
is needed? What type is needed? If it is not necessary, then how much
togetherness may be preferred? What types of togetherness may be
preferred? All these questions and more must be considered when
you are creating a personal philosophy of solitude. The only rule is
that as students of positive solitude, we no longer assume that togetherness is the ultimate answer. Instead, in the context of positive
solitude, we assume that togetherness is one important question.

Do People Need Each Other?

Certainly, children need their parents, but what is really true of adults? Do we really need others? Information available on this issue is mixed. At one extreme are studies of individuals who have lived almost totally alone. The hermits of antiquity, monks of ancient and modern times, and individual ancient and modern explorers are all examples. If togetherness is innate, then these people have success- fully fought their instincts. They often feel complete peace and con- tentment in their aloneness, and they seldom feel an overpowering or enduring drive to return to the company of others. Their moments of loneliness for others are often short-lived, as was this experience described by Henry David Thoreau at Walden Pond:

> I have never felt lonesome, or in the least oppressed by a sense of solitude, but once, and that was a few weeks after I came to the woods, when, for an hour, I doubted if the near neighborhood of man was not essential to a serene and healthy life. To be alone was something unpleasant. But I was at the same time conscious of a slight insanity in my mood, and seemed to foresee my recovery. In the midst of a gentle rain while these thoughts prevailed, I was suddenly sensible of such sweet and beneficent society in Nature, in the very pattering of the drops, and in every sound and sight around my house, an infinite and unaccountable friendliness all at once like an atmosphere sustaining me, as made the fancied advantages of human neighborhood insignifi- cant, and I have never thought of them since.[1]

In spite of such examples, however, the belief that people need other people continues to be strong in our culture. No doubt this belief originates in the experiences of childhood, when we really do need the protection of others. Somewhere near the time that they discover their own separateness and self, infants begin to form a question in their minds, "If this is my self, then who are all these others?" To the child, the others are mother, father, siblings, the extended family, and selected outsiders. The child experiences the others in various ways. Others are alternatively hurtful, loving, good for me, bad for me, people I am dependent upon, or people I am not dependent upon, or people I am superior to or equal to or inferior to.

Early in life children create their very identities by taking their cues from others. The issues we have been exploring in this book so far are related to the infant's earliest internal question, "Who am I and what does it mean to be here alone?" But as life progresses, it is inevitable that we will also ask the question, "What does it mean to be here alone—with all these others?" Certainly, as adults, when we want to understand our own solitude, our need to understand our relationships also deepens. Because of their childhood habit, and to meet their needs as they grow older, adults also ask themselves, "Who are all these others? Do I like them? Can I trust them?"

Much of philosophy, literature, and social science has been devoted to this question of relationships, and I will not presume even to encapsulate the discussion here. But let us focus on the issue of relationships in one special case, the case of the person who is seeking positive solitude. What place do others have in the lives of people who believe in positive solitude? For them, what does togetherness, or otherness, really mean?

In all societies there is a tension between togetherness and solitude. In the United States this tension is resolved more toward the pole of togetherness. The predominant belief in American society is that positive solitude is impossible. This belief has been called "the impossibility of individuality."[2]

In our culture it is often argued that we require significant people in our lives to validate our own existence. Anthropologist Yehudi Cohen asserted that we must have feedback from others:

> Everyone has the experience of periodically asking in one way or other, "You're O.K., how am I?" assuming that the question elicits the response that one seeks, one experiences a sense of good fellowship and of being welcome in the world; one feels at home with oneself and others. But there are times when the plea for reassurance goes unanswered. Then there follows a void, a feeling of personal meaninglessness, a lack of self-definition, because it drains one of personal identity. It results from a lack of feedback.
>
> Loneliness in this sense connotes longing; we always long for others when the lack of reassuring feedback threatens the integrity of the personal self. This is not the loneliness we experience when we

long for a particular person who is absent or when we are homesick while on a trip. It is rather the loneliness that signifies a longing for people in the abstract whose feedback is personally meaningful and who can validate our sense of worth and being.[3]

Cohen further stated that no one is able to subsist emotionally on inner feedback alone. He believes that feedback from other human beings is essential for life itself and that external feedback should come from more than one source. People "who have only one self-defined place in the scheme of things . . . are among the most fragile members of the species."[4] People whose identity is tied up in only one aspect of their lives—in their financial achievement; their children; or their literary, scientific, or artistic creativity alone—are especially vulnerable to emotional loss.

To what extent are Cohen's views valid in the context of positive solitude? It is true that people do need social validation at crucial times in their lives. Social scientists who have studied what is called "the motivation for validation" suggest that whenever objective criteria about an important issue are not available to them, people will actively seek information from others. By obtaining confirmation from other people, the individual's feelings of ambiguity in such a situation are reduced. The need for validation occurs especially when a person is trying to find his or her place in society, as in adolescence. Validation is much less important to the fully formed adult. In fact, there is little evidence that validation is a necessity, though it may be a preference, in adult life. Clearly, there are some single-minded individuals, such as some inventors and intellectuals, who care not a whit for what others say. The self-actualized among us have made their peace both with their solitude and with their place in society.

Even if some self-validating feedback was a necessity for adults, the question must be asked, "How *much* is necessary?" And the answer is—probably not very much. For some of us, only one or a few significant validations may be needed during our entire lifespan. The validating words of a parent, a special teacher, a respected person in our line of work, or a valued friend may sustain us over many years. We learn that we really are good at math or that we really can become a good manager. Once reassured and directed, we can proceed happily and independently from that point. Many profession-als rarely receive feedback from others about their jobs. After their training—after their validation by teachers and mentors—their own knowledge, ability to learn, and subsequent successes are feedback enough. Indeed, this is why we often associate the word *independent* with the word *professional.*

Also we should realize that the notion of having one's existence "validated" is actually vague. We cannot with any intellectual honesty extrapolate an infant's need for touch into an adult's supposed need for cognitive feedback. If by validation we mean having the rightness of one's choices in life confirmed by others, whether emotionally or intellectually, the idea of validation is closely related to the discovery of meaning in life. Discovering meaning is largely a personal issue. For the mature individual, the discovery of one's meaning is far more important than is the discovery of the meanings held by others. In adulthood, continuing to seek validation is a way of copping out on one's individual responsibility to find meaning.

But the hypothetical need for personal validation is only one argument that is made for the necessity of togetherness. A second argument, which achieved special prominence in the sixties, focuses on the supposed need for deep emotional experience with others.

Authenticity in Relationships

Clark Moustakas was a popular voice among the many advocates of the human need for what was termed the "encounter" experience. Moustakas believed that people need a significant amount of togeth-erness in their lives. He taught that a full human experience requires the fulfillment of three desires—the desire for solitude, the desire to be with others, and the desire to be a part of groups. By his reasoning, both solitude and togetherness are necessary because each "serves different human capacities and enables different human meanings to be actualized."[5] Moustakas thought that the group contributes to self-fulfillment in a particular way, by providing a type of encounter that cannot be achieved by the person alone or by the person in one-to-one meetings. His extensive experience with encounter groups led him to believe that the concrete encounter with others is basic to actualizing one's potential as an individual and as a member of a community: Group encounter provides "an incomparable experience of human meaning."[6]

We cannot fully evaluate Moustakas's point of view without understanding authentic group encounter as he saw it. Fortunately, in his extensive writings, Moustakas has provided us with an example. During a conference of human-relations professionals who worked together in the same institution, an encounter group was formed and initially was congenial, but not "real": No open, intimate encounter occurred. As a member of the group, Moustakas fought continually for a day and a half to encourage the group to attain intimacy. Eventually, one group member agreed with him, saying, "The only time I feel accepted is when I discuss safe, academic topics. None of you really know of the way I live or what I want in life but I guess none of you care. After weeks of futile effort, I decided to put on my professional mask and keep it there."

Pat, a prominent professor and supervisor of the group spoke in a choked voice, struggling with his feelings. He had not uttered one word until this moment:

> Right now I'm just so mad at all of you and so hurt I don't know where to begin. . . . I want to shake you up, and . . . it . . . Oh God . . . it hurts. . . . (Pat began weeping and covered his face momentarily; then he looked straight at Jim with tears streaming down his face.) It's so painful to want to reach you . . . I really want to reach you . . . and it's so hard . . . because . . . because, Jim, *I love you.*

As this revelation of people's feelings continued, Moustakas felt that:

> We all shared in this moment of human encounter, in this dialogue of love, and we were no longer strangers. With each new struggle and confrontation, with each sharing, a new level of community developed. Though we were separate, we were one, and we kept this rich human meaning alive and moving until the final moment came, when none of us wanted to leave what we had created together. But we also knew that it had to end, so we let go, each in his own way, and we took with

us a new dimension of individual identity and a feeling of communal richness.[7]

Certainly, this sort of sharing is beautiful. It is unique because of its human context, its pursuit of honesty, and its love. But, we may reasonably ask, what is it that a person takes away from such an experience? What *is* the "new dimension of individual identity and communal richness" of which Moustakas speaks? Even if this encounter is lovely and memorable, its existence does not argue convincingly that it is a new and unique experience that is *necessary* for a happy life. Nor is it convincing evidence that encounter is a unique experience emotionally. Any of the many beautiful solitude experiences that I have noted in this book may have similar effects. Sometimes for the person who is alone the community experienced is the community of nature or the community, in the abstract, of humankind. But the feelings experienced by the person in solitude are arguably analogous, and possibly identical, to those experienced in encounter: feelings of contentment and peace, the sense of being together with something beyond oneself, and the contentedness of knowing continuity.

Yet though we may conclude that the encounter experience is not a necessary part of a good life, it may nevertheless be something that we desire. Is it something that every self-actualized individual will eventually seek? Togetherness has dominated our thinking so much that at this point we cannot answer this question definitively. We simply do not yet know enough about the potential for positive solitude in our modern society. Certainly, there have been people who have happily eschewed others' company, but certainly, too, there have been many more who sought to understand "man with man," what philosopher Martin Buber averred is "the fundamental fact of human existence."[8] I agree with Buber that this relationship with others is what makes humankind unique. But I am not yet ready to agree that it is what makes us happy.

For difficult as solitude is, togetherness may be even more so. The moment of authenticity between two people that Moustakas described is but that—a moment, a unique event in human encounters. It is a rare event, and it is an event that obviously has to be nurtured, even demanded. For the self-aware individual, moments of authenticity with the self must be more frequent than most moments of authenticity with others if for no other reason than that one spends more time with oneself. Who can judge the intensity of these moments or their importance to the human experience? Who is to say that connection with others is more important than, or as important as, connection with the self?

I believe that, at the least, the assertion of the impossibility of individuality needs to be balanced with the assertion of the impossibility of togetherness. The assertion of the impossibility of individuality originates in the belief system that is most common in our culture, while the assertion of the impossibility of togetherness follows from the newer philosophy of solitude.

Understanding Love

Much of what is positive in our relationships with others—friends, lovers, children, parents—falls into the category "love." Philosophical, psychological, and even physiological arguments have been made about the human need for love. Let us try to see this "need" in light of the two poles of togetherness and solitude—the impossibility of individuality and the impossibility of togetherness.

In the early 1970s a number of noted psychologists and psychiatrists, spurred by an article entitled "This Thing Called Love Is Pathological" in *Psychology Today,* organized a conference, the Symposium on Love, to discuss what is actually known about love. They observed that in the twenty-three annual volumes in the indexes of the prestigious *Annual Review of Psychology,* love was not mentioned once.[9] They also pointed out that although many emotions are characterized by specific and separate biochemical reactions in the human body and can be activated by operations performed on fairly circumscribed portions of the anatomy (for example, anger derives from adrenal and other secretions and is controlled by the hypothalamus), no such discrete physiological indexes have been discovered for love.[10] Much as the research on loneliness has discounted its validity as a discrete emotion, so such findings have discounted the common belief in the emotion of love.

What, then, is love? Why does it seem so powerful? One interpretation of the psychologists' inability to "find" symptoms of love
is the possibility that love is a composite of several emotional states
that, at times, cancel each other out. For example, happiness is often
associated with relaxation, yet love reactions often produce arousal
and excitement. Perhaps in situations described as "love," the relaxation that one usually gets from having one's needs satisfied is balanced and neutralized by such tension-producing emotions as sexual
arousal, fear, and anger. The relationship of sexual arousal to love is
obvious. But why are fear and anger related to love? The person who
is loved becomes the actual or potential gratifier of more and more
needs, and the lover may come to *fear* the loss of this gratifier. When
fear exists, anger is seldom far behind. Lovers sometimes resent the
power their loved ones have over them.

One definition of love that has emerged from this line of research
is that "love is the fear of losing an important source of need gratification. . . . The fear increases as a function of the importance and the
number of needs that are involved in the relationship."[11] This practical line of reasoning is different from a more conventional definition
of love as a state in which you are not happy if the other person is
not happy. But the conventional definition tells only part of the story.
Why, precisely, is the other person's happiness essential to yours?
It may be essential because when the other person is unhappy, he or
she is more likely to leave you.

Although this modern definition of love lacks the touch of the
poet (perhaps the touch of the poet is our cultural masque on this
harsher reality), it is especially useful for people who are developing
a philosophy of positive solitude. In our words, when one is in love,
the loved one is seen as essential to filling the feedback gap.

In more recent scientific research, the dark side of love is widely
discussed. One study noted five major components of love. Four of
the components are positive: communicative intimacy, physical
arousal, respect, and romantic capability.[12] But one is romantic *dependence*. In a similar study, three major components were identified:
lust, affection, and *longing*. [13] For the person in love, loneliness occurs
when the primary source of the gratification of needs is threatened
or lost. Such loneliness occurs particularly when only one person has

been meeting most of the individual's needs. Dependence and longing are the downside of love. In such cases, the romantic idea, "I can't live without you," expresses a paralyzing fear of facing an unusually large feedback gap. The feared loss of the loved one can even become equated with the feared loss of self.

If one can fill the feedback gap by oneself, one eliminates the fear of the loss of others. It follows that the choice of being alone may be essentially, profoundly, rational. It is also rational to avoid investing one outside person with all or even most of one's sources of gratification—given the tenuous nature of relationships in life overall, especially in busy, transient America.

Americans are beginning to get this message. While our modern day-care system has been criticized for breaking down the emotional bonds between parent and child, a more positive view is possible: Modern day care may be helping children to feel loved not only by the members of their nuclear family, but by caring adults in the larger society. We may actually be teaching our children the emotional skills they need to survive the weakening of the nuclear family. The increased strength of peer groups for adolescents and the rise of many kinds of social groups for adults are our response to the weakness of significant others in filling the feedback gap.

Is love—having a loving relationship—necessary? Many people believe that it is not, that it is quite possible to be a healthy, love-free adult. A major conclusion from the Symposium on Love is that "there is no evidence that love is either necessary or sufficient for psychological maturity. Indeed, to the extent that love fosters dependency, it may well be a deterrent to maturity."[14] A love-free and contented person, a person without a current intimate relationship, lives in positive solitude. For such a person, a loving relationship may be a pleasure, but it is not a necessity. For her or him, intimate love is a set of feelings to remember with fondness and a fine experience to anticipate.

Loving Alone

A person who is alone can experience the positive side of love at any time. For one thing, even though a love object, in the traditional, narrow sense, is not immediately available, the positive feelings of love can be reexperienced as a vivid memory. These feelings can also be experienced as a current love of life, or self, or nature, or humankind. They can be felt as a closeness with an admired stranger. People in positive solitude may not be in love in the traditional sense, but if they so choose, they can live with love.

Of course, not all relationship-free people are able to experience loving feelings when they are alone. Sometimes we are angry or frightened or withdrawn. Achieving a psychologically comfortable maturity while conforming to societal beliefs and expectations about togetherness is difficult enough. Achieving maturity through a nonconforming positive solitude creates an additional challenge.

Living alone without feeling insecure, without conforming to social pressures, and without needing romantic love is difficult. The process of changing your beliefs requires an investment of time and energy in your self that is difficult to make for the many reasons I have already talked about. Yet today, this challenge is becoming more possible to meet. As more people understand positive solitude, unattached adults will not feel incomplete. Instead, they will love themselves. Each will be, as psychologist Lawrence Casler said, "a person who does not find his own company boring—a person whose inner resources are such that other people, while providing pleasure and stimulation, cease to be absolutely necessary."[15] We have often been told to love others as we love ourselves. But sometimes we seek love relationships with others when we do not love ourselves enough.

Therapists Mildred Newman and Bernard Berkowitz, in their best-selling book *How to Be Your Own Best Friend*, take a practical approach to being alone. When one of their clients laments that "I wouldn't want a life without love in it," they answer: "Who would? Everything you do is richer and fuller when love is there. But love is not always there, and how you feel about yourself the times there isn't someone around to receive and return your love has a lot to do with how rewarding the experience of love is when you have it."[16] To the extent that positive solitude encourages self-love and independence, rather than love, neediness, and dependence, it helps a person to be more effective. Wise words on this subject come from a surprising corner: Ralph Nader says of his Nader's Raiders, a premier citizen activist group of our time, that many fail because they want to *be* loved. They develop personal relationships with the agencies they are monitoring and then find that they cannot criticize them. As Nader puts it, "It is better to love, than to need to be loved. If you need to be loved, you can't do this kind of work."[17] This is a truly mature perspective on love.

Unfortunately, in spite of all these arguments, most Americans still believe that for human beings love is a necessity. It is certainly true that we Americans are raised to want love. In particular, we want the love of a significant other. The first significant other is our mother, followed later by our father and then by our romantic lovers. In those societies that are built around extended families, children grow up with many love objects and learn much earlier that when one love object fails or disappoints, another can fill their need. In a society that is built around the nuclear family, the child experiences primarily two sources of attention—the father and the mother. Thus, the child learns that love is relatively scarce. These primary relationships assume monumental importance, and logically and naturally, the child is afraid of losing them.

In our society, too, children have relatively few outlets for expressing their own caring. They learn little about how to manage their love for others—to understand their love, to set limits on it, to give it appropriately.

While it may be true that the need for love in adulthood is not innate, we Americans do "need" others in this sense. We have been raised, both at home and in school, to feel dependent on others and insecure in ourselves. We believe, especially, that we "need" to find that one special person. Sadly, we raise our children to feel the same way. As adults they will continue their desperate searching.

Is love necessary? Are we to think of it primarily as a drug that prevents suffering? Drug addicts who are deprived of drugs also suffer, yet we do not say that drugs are a necessity in their lives. The existence of withdrawal symptoms does not prove that love is a need.[18]

Choices: Being Alone/Being Together

The issues around solitude and togetherness are complicated and extensive. One way of gaining a clear perspective on them is to study the lives of people who have made obvious choices, people like Henry David Thoreau and Ralph Waldo Emerson. Both Thoreau and Emerson made deliberate philosophical choices about their lives. Each developed and lived by a personal philosophy that carefully considered the tension between self and other. The results, as seen during the full course of their lives, were distinct.

It is especially interesting to compare these two men because their different philosophies were lived out in the same town, during the same era (the mid-nineteenth century), among the same people. Thoreau and Emerson were friends who spent most of their adult years in and around Concord, Massachusetts. Today their respective family homesteads, and Thoreau's cabin site at Walden Pond, can still be seen there. Their philosophies have also endured.

First consider Thoreau. Thoreau's view on solitude as expressed in *Walden* was, "Why should I feel lonely? is not our planet in the Milky Way? . . . What do we want most to dwell near to? Not to many men surely . . . but to the perennial source of our life."[19] Thoreau believed that the source of life is most certainly the self. At the same time, he recognized the power of togetherness. He wrote: "I think that I love society as much as most, and am ready enough to fasten myself like a bloodsucker for the time to any full-blooded man that comes in my way."[20] Thoreau fervently believed, however, that our interest in others should be controlled:

Society is commonly too cheap. We meet at very short intervals, not having had time to acquire any new value for each other. We meet at meals three times a day, and give each other a new taste of that old musty cheese that we are. We have had to agree on a certain set of rules, called etiquette and politeness, to make this frequent meeting tolerable and that we need not come to open war. We meet at the post-office, and at the sociable, and about the fireside every night; we live thick and are in each other's way, and stumble over one another, and I think that we thus lose some respect for one another. Certainly less frequency would suffice for all important and hearty communications.[21]

Living in the woods, Thoreau appreciated that fewer people came his way on trivial business. "My company was winnowed by my mere distance from town. I had withdrawn so far within the great ocean of solitude, into which the rivers of society empty, that for the most part, so far as my needs were concerned, only the finest sediment was deposited around me."[22]

As a corollary of his belief in positive solitude, Thoreau emphasized living in the present through the full experience of one's senses. He advocated the pursuit of purely individual meaning by concentrating on this experience:

> I wish so to live ever as to derive my satisfactions and inspirations from the commonest events, every-day phenomena, so that what my senses hourly perceive, my daily walk, the conversation of my neighbors, may inspire me, and I may dream of no heaven but that which lies about me.[23]

Being with others diluted this experience for Thoreau, and so it diluted the essential spirituality of his life, which he valued above all else:

> Let nothing come between you and the light. Respect men as brothers only. When you travel to the celestial city, carry no letters of introduction. When you knock ask to see God—none of the servants. In what concerns you much do not think that you have companions—know that you are alone in the world.[24]

Thoreau believed that his own mode of living could ultimately improve civilization and thus that he was a good citizen, a participant in the life of the community. But, as has been pointed out by his biographer Joel Porte, a thoughtful analyst of Thoreau's work and life, in his lifetime Thoreau never drew a close philosophical connection between himself and his society. Porte concluded that, for Thoreau, "shared existence was only the unfortunately necessary precondition of his selfhood."[25] If he erred, it was in the direction of positive solitude, rather than in the direction of togetherness.

While he lived at Walden Pond, Thoreau created and wrote his plan for himself—his life myth. Later, while living within society, experiencing his cherished plan became more difficult. Though he often remembered, and sometimes experienced, the kinds of sensual pleasures and spiritual peace that he had found during his two years at Walden, within society Thoreau often felt that he was wasting his time. He believed that he was in danger of sacrificing his true self to the petty demands of everyday society. Although he cared for his family—his parents and siblings, nieces and nephews—soon after leaving Walden, he found living with his family to be confining. That winter he wrote in his diary:

> My attic chamber has compelled me to sit below with the family at evening for a month. I feel the necessity of deepening the stream of my life; I must cultivate privacy. It is very dissipating to be with people too much. . . . I cannot spare my moonlight and my mountains for the best of man I am likely to get in exchange.[26]

Thoreau had chosen to cultivate solitude and to focus on his senses. For him, failure meant being drawn away from his positive solitude.

Thoreau's neighbor and friend Ralph Waldo Emerson lived at the opposite end of the solitude-togetherness spectrum. His philosophy and life provide a revealing counterpoint. A well-to-do writer, lecturer, and minister, Emerson led an active parish in the Unitarian Church in Concord and became famous in his lifetime as a writer. It is not surprising that this family man, preacher, and solid citizen believed that affiliation is central to life. While Thoreau praised solitude, Emerson wrote in his journal, "Do you not see that a man is a bundle of relations, that his entire strength consists not in his properties, but in his innumerable relations?" And in later years he wrote, "It is only as our existence is shared, not as it is selfhood, that it is divine."[27]

Emerson suggested that we must accept a certain tension between solitude and society:

Solitude is impracticable, and society is fatal. We must keep our head in the one and our hands in the other. The conditions are met if we keep our independence, yet do not lose our sympathy.[28]

Still, on balance, he favored finding meaning in life through contact with others. Although he praised solitude, in his writings he constantly returned to asserting the value of a life lived in service to others. Certain extreme individualists, he complained, withdraw "from the labors of the world; they are not good citizens. . . . What right . . . has the man of genius to retreat from work, and indulge himself? . . . Genius is the power to labor better and more availably."[29] Emerson believed that even those who advocate solitude as a "divine" condition (and here he was most probably talking of his friend Thoreau) actually value others and merely wish to communicate with exceptional rather than mundane parts of humanity. Of these independents he believed, "If they tell you their whole thought, they will own that love seems to them the last and highest gift of nature; that there are persons whom in their hearts they daily thank for existing,— persons whose faces are perhaps unknown to them, but whose fame and spirit have penetrated their solitude,—and for whose sake they wish to exist."[30]

In his essay "Solitude and Society," Emerson asserted his belief that most, though not all, people need others:

A man must be clothed with society, or we shall feel a certain bareness and poverty, as of a displaced and unfurnished member. He is to be dressed in arts and institutions, as well as in his body garments. Now and then a man exquisitely made can live alone, and must; but coop up most men and you undo them.[31]

As solitary Thoreau was a sensualist, so Emerson the community man was a model Transcendentalist. Emerson believed that individual reality should be understood through the processes of thought and spiritual intuition. Much of the emphasis in his thinking was on abstractions, rather than on concrete realities. Emerson believed that the highest good was to be experienced in the abstractions developed out of the experience of reality, rather than in the direct sensual experience of reality.

We can draw many contrasts between Thoreau and Emerson. Thoreau believed in solitude, with togetherness as a sometimes pleasant, sometimes disturbing, adjunct. Emerson preached togetherness, the virtue and necessity of living within and for a community; he sought a connection with life through society.

Thoreau experienced life concretely and sensually, especially through his love of nature, while Emerson preached Transcendentalism, the search for meaning in eternal laws that transcend the concrete world.

Thoreau was troubled when threatened with the loss of the solitude that allowed him to experience life fully and sensually; solitude, which was his personal style of self-actualization, was his central life myth. Emerson was troubled by sensuality; he found his spirituality, his life myth, in abstractions, rather than in sensuality.

It is interesting to contemplate the effect that their different life myths had upon these two men. Porte draws a fascinating comparison of Thoreau and Emerson when they were in their forties.[32] By that time, the two men's lifestyles had resulted in different attitudes. At forty, Emerson was a disillusioned spirit, a spectator but not a participator in life. Even five years later, he still felt depressed. He had found some eternal laws in the universe, but he had also found more dross than he preferred. Thoreau in his forties was still in love with his life. He loved his New England earth, and he believed that heaven, if anywhere, is here in this life. The follower of positive solitude was ultimately more content than was the advocate of society.

Of course, it would be an oversimplification to draw the conclusion that as a life plan, solitude is totally preferable. For one thing, it is not fair to suggest that Thoreau's solitude was pure. He had, for example, an emotionally supportive family who lived nearby. Also, although his family was not wealthy, he was not dependent totally on himself for support were he to face times of trouble. Indeed, through his illness until his early death of tuberculosis, his family cared for him lovingly. Thoreau was also connected with society through his work. Although his writing was not well recognized in his own day, he was deeply concerned that its influence be felt; for him, it was a major expression of love. In his later years, Thoreau found some consolation when friends reassured him that his ideas would live beyond him.

Practically speaking, it is important to understand that although Thoreau could have returned to Walden Pond after he left it, he did not. Even this man, the writer who in all of American literature most perfectly advocated solitude, was connected in significant ways with others. If Thoreau was more content than was Emerson, we cannot conclude that his contentment was only because of his solitude. It would be more accurate to conclude that he was content because he found a substantial amount of solitude and because he developed a meaningful solitude in the context of a life lived also with, and in some ways for, others.

Neither was Emerson's life entirely social. He had definite inclinations toward valuing solitude: "The necessity of solitude is deeper than we have said, and is organic. I have seen many a philosopher whose world is large enough for only one person."[33] And, like Thoreau, Emerson was not uncritical of society:

> The people are to be taken in very small doses. If solitude is proud, so is society vulgar. . . . Society we must have; but let it be society, and not exchanging news or eating from the same dish. Is it society to sit in one of your chairs? I cannot go to the houses of my nearest relatives, because I do not wish to be alone. Society exists by chemical affinity, and not otherwise.[34]

Contrasting Thoreau and Emerson enriches our sense of the tension in our lives between solitude and society, but it does not resolve the dilemma of choosing.

No human life can be a pure example of either solitude or affiliation. And while the evidence seems to indicate that Thoreau's life was happier than was Emerson's, who is to say whether it was more successful? Emerson led a spiritual community; raised his family; touched the lives of thousands through his writings; and, all in all, lived a generous life filled with responsibility to others.

Yet, it should be said that many of us today would lean more toward Thoreau's choice if we could realistically make it. Living in a society that is crowded and anxious, we naturally cry "enough," and if we are not eager to live fully alone, we at least recognize the potential of solitude. In this land of frequent mobility, society that is positive and supportive is probably more difficult to discover than it was for the latter-century residents of Concord. Perhaps, too, it is less needed. The physical care Thoreau received from his family we can purchase through health insurance. The financial independence Thoreau achieved by living simply and off the land we achieve through our greater prosperity. As a result, today when we are alone, we can choose many different lifestyles.

Our lives are full of tensions that pull us in opposite directions. Among them, the tension between self and other is paramount. The inner tension between self and other that is embodied in the differences between the two friends Thoreau and Emerson is found throughout our literature, as this sampling of quotations reveals:

> Thrice blessed are our friends: they come, they stay,
> And presently they go away.[35]

> Only solitary men know the full joys of friendship.[36]

> How sweet, how passing sweet, is solitude.
>   But grant me still a friend in my retreat
> Whom I may whisper, Solitude is sweet.[37]

The Trend to Solitude

We live in a society that believes in togetherness but that lives increasingly alone. We will practice more solitude. Throughout recent history the stronger social pressure toward resolving the self-other tension has been in the direction of togetherness; it has been the Emersons, not the Thoreaus, that society has rewarded. But today, a different attitude may be emerging. In a society that understands positive solitude, the resolution of the tension will be more in the tradition of Thoreau. It is interesting to note that in Japan, one of the most crowded societies in the world, the figure of the hero is a solitary, independent man. In that crowded country, mastering, though not banishing, the need for companionship and other human solace is considered to be an important part of character development.[38] As the level of social interactions intensifies in our own society, we may predict that such an increased yearning for and valuing of solitude will result.

It is safe to say that we probably need others a lot less than we think we do. If we do need others, the need is intermittent. About this point there is no argument. The questions that we must ask are, then, If we are to be with others, when? How? Why? These are legitimate questions that must continue to be uppermost in the minds of free-spirited individuals.

Notes

1. Henry David Thoreau, *Walden* (Boston: Houghton Mifflin Co., 1957), 91.

2. Clark Moustakas, *Individuality and Encounter* (Cambridge, Mass.: Howard A. Doyle Publishing Co., 1968), 11.

3. Yehudi A. Cohen, "You're O.K., How Am I?" in Joseph Hartog, J. Ralph Audy, and Yehudi Cohen, eds., *The Anatomy of Loneliness* (New York: International Universities Press, 1980), 457–58.

4. Ibid., 460.

5. Moustakas, *Individuality and Encounter* 41–42.

6. Ibid., 60.

7. Ibid., 61–63.

8. Martin Buber, "Prospect: What Is Man?" in Hartog, Audy, and Cohen, eds., *The Anatomy of Loneliness,* 557.

9. Mary Ellen Curtin, ed., *Symposium on Love* (New York: Behavioral Publications, 1973), ix.

10. Lawrence Casler, "Toward a Re-evaluation of Love," in ibid., 8–9.

11. Ibid., 10.

12. Joseph W. Critelli, Emilie J. Myers, and Victor E. Loos, "The Components of Love: Romantic Attraction and Sex Role Orientation," *Journal of Personality* 54, (June 1986): 354–70.

13. Phillip Shaver et al., "Emotional Knowledge: Further Exploration of a Prototype Approach," *Journal of Personality and Social Psychology* 52, (1987): 1061–86.

14. Casler, "Toward a Re-evaluation of Love," 18.

15. Ibid., 20.

16. Mildred Newman and Bernard Berkowitz, *How to Be Your Own Best Friend* (New York: Random House, 1971), 43.

17. Quoted in Robert F. Buckhorn, *Nader: The People's Lawyer* (Englewood Cliffs, N.J.: Prentice-Hall, 1972), 88.

18. Casler, "Toward a Re-evaluation of Love," 24.

19. Thoreau, *Walden,* 92.

20. Ibid., 96.

21. Ibid., 94.

22. Ibid., 99.

23. Ibid., 204.

24. Henry David Thoreau, "Letter to Harrison G. O. Blake," in August Derleth, *Concord Rebel, A Life of Henry David Thoreau* (Philadelphia: Chilton Co., 1962), 81.

25. Joel Porte, *Emerson and Thoreau: Transcendentalists in Conflict* (Middletown, Conn.: Wesleyan University Press, 1965), 149.

26. Quoted in Derleth, *Concord Rebel, A Life of Henry David Thoreau,* 124.

27. Ralpho Waldo Emerson, "Journals" in Porte, *Emerson and Thoreau,* 149.

28. Ibid., 394.

29. Ralph Waldo Emerson, *"The Transcendentalist,"* in Carl Bode, ed., *The Portable Emerson* (New York: Viking Penguin, 1981), 103.

30. Ibid., 100.

31. Ralph Waldo Emerson, "Society and Solitude," in Bode, ed., *The Portable Emerson,* 391.

32. Porte, *Emerson and Thoreau,* 130–34.

33. Emerson, "Society and Solitude," 391.

34. Ibid., 393.

35. Richard R. Kirk, quoted in *Bartlett's Familiar Quotations* (New York: Pocket Books, 1963), 207.

36. Willa Cather, *Shadows on the Rock,* Book III, Part V, quoted in *Bartlett's Familiar Quotations,* 66.

37. William Cowper, "Conversation," line 740, quoted in *Bartlett's Familiar Quotations,* 88.

38. Christie W. Kiefer, Loneliness and the Japanese. In Hartog, Audy, and Cohen, eds., *The Anatomy of Loneliness,* 434.

15
Solitude and Self-Actualization

The nurse of full-grown souls is solitude.
—JAMES RUSSELL LOWELL, *Columbus*

While positive solitude is the focused process that dwells on recognizing and transcending the problems of being alone, self-actualization is the wider, more complex process of creating and deepening personal life experiences in all spheres. Positive solitude contributes to self-actualization by helping you to face the vicissitudes of life from a self that is centered but realizing that at the same time your self is always changing. When you enter the exploration stage of positive solitude, you begin a lifetime of working and playing toward self-actualization.

Solitude—Essential to Self-Actualization

Popularized in the sixties by humanist psychologist and philosopher Abraham Maslow, today the term *self-actualization* is often used but seldom really understood. I first studied and appreciated

Maslow as a graduate student in the seventies. Fifteen years later, while doing research for this book I reviewed the characteristics of the self-actualized person as Maslow had conceived them and realized that nearly every one of them depends on some measure of solitude.[1]

Though solitude is not sufficient for achieving self-actualization, it is a necessary precursor to it. Maslow says that *self-actualizers experience "fully, vividly, selflessly, with full concentration and total absorption."*[2] They are totally aware of the moment and of their surroundings. Their experience is the opposite of self-consciousness, that intense adolescent desire to please and to fit in. Instead, self-actualizers are grounded in self-confidence and self-knowledge. Obviously, this characteristic of self-actualization is easier to experience in solitude than in company: In solitude your concentration is not disturbed by other people or their expectations. With practice, this focus gained in solitude translates into an ability to stay centered in the self and self-aware in the presence of others.

Maslow also tells us that *the self-actualizer is courageous. In a life that consists largely of a process of choices, such a person chooses growth over fear many times a day.* When you experience a serious loss in your life, you can darken your windows and give up, or you can go out into the world and break new ground—take a job, meet new people, learn to nurture yourself alone for perhaps the first time. There is fear in either alternative, but only the latter alternative leads to growth. Ultimately, what you will do is your choice alone, but you should know that the courage to make such decisions is nurtured in your ability to experience positive solitude. Only by building the secure emotional foundation that comes with knowing how to be alone can you find the courage to take risks.

Self-actualizers listen to their self; they let their self emerge. The self seldom emerges when you are occupied fully with work and other activities. It is usually through your times alone that you experience your true and subtle emotions, test your instincts, and analyze your thoughts. Among other things, self-actualizers work to expose their own psychopathologies. They identify their own psychological defenses and find the courage to give them up. All these processes are an integral part of listening to yourself. People who overintellectualize as a way of ignoring their emotions or who occupy themselves to avoid listening to themselves must recognize these tendencies. Of course, an important way to do so is through solo introspection.

Self-actualizers are honest with themselves; they avoid playing games and posing. Maslow points out that this statement suggests taking responsibility for yourself. Responsibility has been studied very little by social science, but it is a crucial human capacity that is closely related to the process of finding meaning. Taking the responsibility for finding the meanings in your life is a skill that not all of us possess, yet it is one that most of us can gain.

Self-actualizers choose lives that are appropriate to their natures. This choice is based upon their ability to listen to themselves and to form their own judgments about themselves, the world, and their place in the world. Self-actualizers will know what amount of solitude suits them because they will have taken the time to experience their own taste in the matter. They will choose vocations, avocations, and family and friendship patterns that are based on their knowledge of themselves, rather than on the shallow fashions of the time. They use their intelligence to become as effective as possible in seeking their goals. Often they work hard for their achievements. "Self-actualization does not mean doing some far-out thing necessarily, but it may mean going through an arduous and demanding period of preparation to realize one's possibilities. Self-actualization can consist of finger exercises at a piano keyboard. Self-actualization means working to do well the thing that one wants to do."[3]

Self-actualizers have peak experiences—"transient moments of self-actualization . . . moments of ecstasy which cannot be bought, cannot be guaranteed, cannot even be sought."[4] While most people have peak experiences, Maslow suggests that many do not recognize them. Whether people are alone or in the company of others, the peak experience transcends most other moments of thought or perception. It is a moment of joy that is perfectly felt, and it is experienced alone. It is most likely to occur when you are, if not physically alone, then at least fully centered in yourself.

Clearly, self-actualization requires a significant measure of positive solitude. You must have time and aloneness to be able to focus on yourself—on your ideas, sensations, emotions, dreams, choices, and defenses. As Maslow describes the *process* of self-actualization:

> Self-actualized people . . . go about it in these little ways: *They listen to their own voices;* they take responsibility; they are honest; and they work hard. They find out who they are and what they are, not only in terms of their mission in life, but also in terms of the way their feet hurt when they wear such and such a pair of shoes and whether they do or do not like eggplant. . . . All this is what the real self means. [Italics added.][5]

Although there are many paths to self-actualization, all wend their way through this discovered self. The journey requires time, introspection, and concentration.

Clark Moustakas emphasized the contribution solitude makes to self-actualization:

> In real solitude we are expansive, limitless, free. We do not disguise our feelings from ourselves, but rather we renew contact with ourselves and discover who we are. At other times we are pulled into the collective stream that surrounds us. We experience the collective sense that we have incorporated in order to achieve recognition, security, and comfort. In solitude, one breaks through the dead, static patterns and has an opportunity to see life as it really is and to become aware of a desire for new meaning, excitement, and vitality, of a desire to be whole and to live more fully and completely.[6]

Solitude for Creativity

Maslow believed that self-actualization and creativity are probably the same process.[7] Although his view has been disputed, it is well known that to be creative, people must have periods of being alone, away from distraction. This time alone allows you to concentrate, to reflect, to generate ideas. As Maslow noted, "[the] ability to become lost in the present seems to be a *sine qua non* for creativeness of any kind."[8] When you are alone, you drop your mask, your efforts to please or to flatter or to impress others. Without an audience, you stop being an actor and can be yourself, with your unique visions. Anthony Storr's fine book *Solitude* is a thorough investigation of solitude and the creative process.

Social interactions distract us from this solitude. We are forever enticed by the immediate gratifications to be found in our social surroundings; we are continually tempted to say and do the socially desirable thing and even to feel the socially desirable emotion. Independence is nurtured in solitude. As Ralph Waldo Emerson so eloquently put it: "[The] voices which we hear in solitude . . . grow faint and inaudible as we enter into the world. Society everywhere is in conspiracy against the manhood of every one of its members."[9]

Creativity requires resisting these temptations and preserving a strong measure of independence. When we are with others, it is expedient to conform; when we are with ourselves, it is more natural to be independent. Of course, the clever among us can do both. "It is easy in the world to live after the world's opinion; it is easy in solitude to live after our own; but the great man is he who in the midst of the crowd keeps with perfect sweetness the independence of solitude."[10]

It is not surprising that many artists have chosen to spend extensive periods alone. To defend their solitude and independence, some have chosen, for example, not to have families. As was asserted centuries ago by Francis Bacon, "he that hath wife and children hath given hostages to fortune, for they are impediments to great enterprises. . . . Certainly the best works, and of greatest merit for the public, have proceeded from the unmarried or childless men, which both in affection and means have married and endowed the public."[11] For many artists being alone may simply be essential to their creative process.

Vincent Van Gogh certainly believed that his self-isolation was essential: "If at present I am worth something, it is because I am alone, and I hate fools, the impotent, cynics, idiotic and stupid scoffers."[12] Van Gogh asserted that his shocking appearance, poverty, and neglect were "a good way to assure the solitude necessary for concentrating on whatever study preoccupies one."[13] We may suspect that this statement was partly a rationalization. It is difficult for us at this time to tell which came first for Van Gogh, the solitude or the antisocial behaviors. Yet Van Gogh believed that his art was essential to his mental health—it was the only thing that allowed him to work through his periodic deep depressions. And if solitude was necessary for his art, it was necessary for his life: "I feel inexpressibly melancholic without my work to distract me. . . . *I must forget myself in my work,* otherwise it will crush me."[14] Van Gogh also appreciated the heightening effects that solitude could have on him: "It is true that there may be moments when one becomes absent-minded, somewhat visionary; some become too absent-minded, too visionary. This is perhaps the case with me, but it is my own fault . . . but one overcomes this. The dreamer sometimes falls into the well, but is said to get out of it afterward."[15]

Other artists have had less dramatic, but nevertheless central, experiences with solitude. Some have learned early in life what most of us learn only later: that they are comfortable alone. As a boy entering private school, novelist Louis Auchincloss faced a difficult period of hazing. This period of suffering taught him to appreciate the peace of being alone. In his autobiography, he wrote: "My persecution ebbed at last, and I experienced the bliss of simple neglect. Even today I find it a bit difficult to comprehend the modern terror of loneliness."[16] Artist Georgia O'Keeffe also knew the value of solitude quite early. As a young woman, O'Keeffe spent a year alone painting. In later years she expressed the opinion that if she were not able to spend such a period alone doing her own work, "I wouldn't be worth very much, would I?"[17]

It is important to point out that though it is creative, such solitude is not necessarily joyful and "happy." Hard work, even if it is self-actualizing work, can be fatiguing. It can be emotionally draining and sometimes tedious. Working through the solitude, sticking with the task, may be one of life's most difficult achievements. Novelist Thomas Wolfe's description of the loneliness of creativity is compelling, chastening, and awe inspiring. But, as here excerpted from Jeremy Seabrook's book *Loneliness,* it is also wonderfully alive:

Hideous doubt, despair, and dark confusion of the soul a lonely man must know, for he is united to no image save that which he creates himself, he is bolstered by no other knowledge save that which he can gather for himself with the vision of his own eyes and brain. He is sustained and cheered and aided by no party, he is given comfort by no creed, he has no faith in him except his own. And often that faith deserts him, leaving him shaken and filled with impotence. And then it seems to him that his life has come to nothing, that he is ruined, lost, and broken past redemption, and that morning—bright, shining morning, with its promise of new beginnings—will never come upon the earth again as it did once.

He knows that dark time is flowing by him like a river. The huge, dark wall of loneliness is around him now. It encloses and presses in upon him, and he cannot escape. And the cancerous plant of memory is feeding at his entrails, recalling hundreds of forgotten faces and ten thousand vanished days, until all life seems as strange and insubstantial as a dream. Time flows by him like a river, and he waits in his little room like a creature held captive by an evil spell. And he will hear, far off, the murmurous drone of the great earth, and feel that he has been forgotten, that his powers are wasting from him while the river flows, and that all his life has come to nothing. He feels that his strength is gone, his power withered, while he sits there drugged and fettered in the prison of his loneliness.

Then suddenly, one day, for no apparent reason, his faith and his belief in life will come back to him in a tidal flood. It will rise up in him with a jubilant and invincible power, bursting a window in the world's great wall and restoring everything to shapes of deathless brightness. Made miraculously whole and secure in himself, he will plunge once more into the triumphant labor of creation. All his old strength is his again; he knows what he knows, he is what he is, he has found what he has found. And he will say the truth that is in him, speak it even though the whole world deny it, affirm it though a million men cry out that it is false.[18]

To remove oneself from life—from easy laughter and festivity and some kinds of love—is for some a true sacrifice. But it is in this time away and alone that a person finds truth and possibly, if he or she is blessed, even new truth for humanity. It is also in this time away that the person discovers the conviction to speak the truth. Artists understand this sort of necessary intensity. Nobel prize-winning novelist Herman Hesse described his own agonies in self-exploration:

> I have been and still am a seeker, but I have ceased to question stars and books; I have begun to listen to the teachings my blood whispers to me. My story is not a pleasant one; it is neither sweet nor harmonious as invented stories are; it has the taste of nonsense and chaos, of madness and dreams—like the lives of all men who stop deceiving themselves.[19]

The experience of we mere ordinary self-actualizers is similar to the experience of the fine artists and the literary geniuses, if less articulately expressed. The joy and the pain of creativity are valuable for us all. We all need to provide for ourselves time away from distractions, time away from the influences of others, time to allow ourselves to escape our impulse to conform. We all need to understand that this experience will be difficult, though perhaps not as painful as the creative writers would have us believe, and that it will be worthwhile.

It is in this way that you can be maximally self-actualizing. In your daily life, pursuing your creativity will help you to recapture the spirit of your childhood—the curiosity, wonderment, and playfulness—that through your years of education, work, and adjustment to society have been forgotten. Indulging in your own creativity can be an antidote to the alienation that you experience in the institutions in which you work. Creativity is also the key to personal effectiveness in anything that you do: People who are in touch with their own creativity become increasingly centered, whole, and purposeful. They discover their own meanings; they know what they want; they can pursue their goals with focus and abandon.

Poets are often said to be less alienated than are others, including other artists, in our modern world. Writing alone, they are compelled to face their loneliness and their selves. More essentially, though, their tool of human self-expression is unique. Language is a soothing symbolic connection with one's own experience and with humanity. No other tool—not shapes or forms or mathematics—has the human essence that language contains. No doubt, the large amount of creativity expressed in ordinary lives, especially through poetry, is linked to our need to discover meaning. For many of us, our poems represent our life myths, our intellectual and emotional structuring of experience. Though relatively few Americans publish poetry, millions write it. In our solitude, we find the words that connect us with ourselves and with the contexts of our lives and that allow us to find solace and joy in our continual self-actualizing.

Americans particularly need the solace that is found in creativity. Yehudi A. Cohen, co-editor of an excellent collection of writings on loneliness that I have often cited here, argues that American society is a creative society, in part, because of people's freedom to choose solitude. Although we Americans practice a great deal of togetherness, togetherness is even more extreme in some other societies, where people are never alone. Our privilege in being alone, however, also creates the need to make sense of that solitude.

No society has gone as far as our own in breaking down the barriers among different ethnic, religious, and other groups. Whereas this phenomenon is often viewed as negative—as a "breakdown" of ties with kin and other groups—it can also be viewed as positive: It is true that we have been enormously creative as a society. "Relative to the total span of time during which ideas have been recorded, the intellectual ferment of American society has been staggering."[20] Our ideas come not only from scientists, but from businesspeople, historians, inventors, lawyers, clergymen, and dissidents who fit no categories. On the one hand, these ideas have been possible *because of* a political climate in which new ideas may be expressed without fear of political reprisals. Just as important, these ideas have been possible because of "a strong measure of alienation, anomie, a sense of isolation, of loneliness."[21] It seems that along with our independence, we have taken on the responsibility to develop our own creativity.

Out of our independence must also spring the responsibility to develop a philosophy of solitude. The belief that tight communal forms, such as kinship, religious, and ethnic ties, are entirely positive forces in a society is sentimental. People in such groups tend to watch each other constantly for aberrations; pressure to conform in both thought and deed are high. Innovators remove themselves and deliberately alienate themselves from such groupthink. They commit themselves to being alone and to thinking independently. Such a mode of individuality has historically been possible in this country, beginning with the Puritan dissidents who left their religiously based communities and continuing into modern times. In the United States, diversity is tolerated as nowhere else in the world. While the cost to the individual is often an increased sense of social alienation, for many the trade-off is worthwhile. Self-actualizers balance the ideal of community with their own personhood and creativity.

In giving up our traditional communal structures, we may be opting for anomie. Yet it is also possible that feelings like anomie, despair, and loneliness are not necessary accompaniments to our individual freedom. Though these negative feelings certainly occur during the creative process, they need not be overwhelming or even enormously influential in the life of a self-actualizing person. Through positive solitude, individuals may be able to create a new social structure, a community of self-actualizing individuals that reduces the negatives and instead soothes and connects and satisfies. Perhaps we do not require the strictures of communal life and perhaps the loneliness can also be avoided. Perhaps we can structure the creativity— the living—by ourselves. We are a culture searching for meaning, and we may yet have time to find it.

Solitude, Self-Actualization, and Society

So self-actualization is an individual process, but, importantly, it is one that exists in the context of society. Your own attitude toward solitude and your ability to achieve positive solitude are basic to self-actualization. But also basic are the structures and values of the society in which we all live.

America has been described as a consumer, capitalist, and transient society, but it has not achieved a reputation as a self-actualizing
society. To the contrary, the pervasive, discomforting effects of our
society affect us every day. These influences are portrayed in the
concluding scene of the film *My Dinner with André.* In this scene, the
main character, André, describes his meeting with an unusual man
who has devoted his life to lobbying for saving trees. This eighty-four
year-old man always travels with a backpack because he never knows
where he's going to be the next day. When André tells the man he
is from New York City, the following exchange occurs. The old man
speaks first:

> "Ah, New York, yes, that's a very interesting place. Do you know a lot
> of New Yorkers who keep talking about the fact that they want to leave,
> but never do?" And I [André] said, "Oh, yes." And he said, "Why do
> you think they don't leave?" And I gave him different banal theories.
> And he said, "Oh, I don't think it's that way at all." He said, "I think
> that New York is the new model for the new concentration camp,
> where the camp has been built by the inmates themselves, and the
> inmates are the guards, and they have this pride in this thing that
> they've built—they've built their own prison—and so they exist in a
> state of schizophrenia where they are both guards and prisoners. And
> as a result they no longer have—having been lobotomized—the capac-
> ity to leave the prison they've made or even to see it as a prison." And
> then he went into his pocket, and he took out a seed for a tree, and
> he said, "This is a pine tree." And he put it in my hand. And he said,
> "Escape before it is too late."[22]

It may be that the real societies in which we live—the real New
Yorks, at any rate—constrain our positive solitude and our self-
actualization. Our society changes quickly. It changes literally incredibly fast, faster than we can understand, faster than we as individuals
can analyze and adapt to. And yet, not to analyze our society as it
changes and not to evaluate it critically as an environment that affects
our self-actualization are also impossible. To fail to analyze is to fail
to be free. We need to know where we are going. We do well to heed
the inimitable vision of David Byrne and the Talking Heads when they

warn, "Watch out, you might get what you're after." Our American society gives us individual freedom of many kinds and it fosters our creativity, but it is also a large, complicated, and chaotic place in which to exist. In our lifetimes it will become larger, more complicated, and more chaotic. If the society, and ourselves, are to remain viable, we must find within it the emotional and physical settings for positive solitude and self-fulfillment.

Notes

1. Abraham H. Maslow, *The Farther Reaches of Human Nature* (New York: Penguin Books, 1971), 44–47.

2. Ibid.

3. Ibid., 46.

4. Ibid.

5. Ibid., 49.

6. Clark Moustakas, *Individuality and Encounter* (Cambridge, Mass.: Howard A. Doyle Publishing Co., 1968) 20.

7. Maslow, *The Farther Reaches of Human Nature,* 55.

8. Ibid., 59.

9. Ralph Waldo Emerson. "Self-Reliance," in Carl Bode and Malcolm Cowley, eds., *The Portable Emerson* (New York: Viking Press, 1981), 141.

10. Ibid., 143.

11. Francis Bacon, "Of Marriage and Single Life" (1625), in M. H. Abrams, ed., *The Norton Anthology of English Literature.* (New York: W. W. Norton & Co., 1962), vol. 1, p. 1040.

12. Albert J. Lubin, "Loneliness, Creativity and Van Gogh," in Joseph Hartog, J. Ralph Audy, and Yehudi Cohen, eds., *The Anatomy of Loneliness* (New York: International Universities Press, 1980), 506–36.

13. Ibid., 509.

14. Ibid.

15. Ibid., 509–10.

16. Louis Auchincloss, *A Writer's Capital* (Boston: Houghton Mifflin Co., 1979), 45–46.

17. Georgia O'Keeffe, quoted on "Lumina: A Video Report on the Arts" Hartford, Conn., Public Television, 1988.

18. Thomas Wolfe, "The Anatomy of Loneliness," in Jeremy Seabrook, *Loneliness* (New York: Universe Books, 1975), 7–8.

19. Hermann Hesse, quoted in Moustakas, *Individuality and Encounter,* 29.

20. Yehudi A. Cohen, "You're O.K., How Am I?" in Hartog, Audy, and Cohen, eds., *The Anatomy of Loneliness,* 455.

21. Ibid.

22. Wallace Shawn and Andre Gregory, *My Dinner with André* (New York: Grove Press, 1981), 93.

16
The Positive Solitude Persona

There is a mystery of mutual distance, what the poet Rilke called "the circumspection of human gesture," which is just as humanly important as the mystery of intimacy.

—W. TURNER, *The Ritual Process: Structure and Anti-Structure*

For most of us, there comes a time when we leave solitude. Henry David Thoreau left Walden and lived among his family and the people of Concord. Alice Koller left Nantucket and pursued a career as a professor of philosophy. You, too, will go into society. At times you will choose to mix it up, to get involved with humanity, to love specific people. You will let their lives enter yours, enrich yours, bedevil yours.

Even those of us who have been raised in the latter half of the twentieth century have learned to want each other. We live in a complex, interdependent society that has strong family values, an infusion of romantic love, and an ethic of loving one's neighbor. We are always alone, yet we are never alone. Do we need others? The question is moot. We have learned to want to belong.

How do you maintain the essence of positive solitude within the context of a life lived among others? How do you nurture your beloved self, deepened through solitude, that has been treasured and secreted away from the world?

Your positive solitude persona is much more than a positive self-image. It is an experience of a whole being, of a completed character that you have created. The persona is something that, once gained, you will always have. You may neglect it, you may forget about it for a while, yet it is one of those sets of skills and feelings that will always be in your repertoire.

When it is with you, you will show it in the way you live. If you are single, you are clearly your own person. You are the one among your friends who has your own sense of style. You radiate joy, or concentration, or intensity, or relaxation, or purpose. If you have an intimate partner, you still exude confidence and self-love. You are a partner in one of those couples who admire each other, rather than become each other. Your relationships are built on mutual respect, rather than on dependence. When the world around you is busied by work and play, relationships, and responsibilities, you still hold dear the positive self gained through solitude. Within your relationships, amid complexity and turbulence and distraction, you nurture this self.

This positive solitude persona is a wonderful friend. It is a reservoir of pleasure for those times you spend alone, allowing you to return to relationships refreshed. It is a psychological energizer. In your time alone, you examine and sort through your life, indeed making it more worth living. You become more centered, focused, and knowing.

The positive solitude persona includes a set of skills that are useful whether you are alone or in a relationship. It includes the abilities to manage the loneliness crises in your life, to understand the psychological dynamics of decision-making, and to be aware of loneliness traps in your work. These skills enhance your emotional well-being—your sensuality, contentedness, and happiness. Having created a positive solitude persona for yourself, you know from experience that love is something you feel and do much more than something you receive. You know that many people lack security, confusing it with love, and that security is either something you currently have or it is something you can get.

Once you have developed the persona, you can draw on it to enrich your experience of others. You bring your unique understanding of your own character, creativity, and personality to relationships. Your joy and centeredness will make you a pleasure to be around. Because you have your persona to depend upon, you will be less afraid of losing a relationship. You will be less dependent and less willing to take part in weak relationships.

Also, you can use your own positive solitude as a model for others, particularly your children. As society becomes more crowded, as people seek but are repelled by community, the need to teach others positive solitude will increase.

When you choose to be in relationships, the persona will help you to face the challenges you find in them—the crises that you face on the death of cherished friends and family or, for example, the day-to-day challenges of parenthood.

The Importance of the Positive Solitude Persona: Two Cases

Consider Ann, a woman in her late twenties. Ann has a steady marriage, two young children, and a reasonably interesting part-time job that occupies a dozen hours a week. Ann doesn't plan to seek a full-time job any time soon. She can afford to be a homemaker, and she wants to stay home while the children are young. To many women, her life would seem ideal, yet Ann is dissatisfied. She says she is bored with the routine parts of homemaking and she is worried that her job skills are getting stale. Perhaps, she thinks, she should find a new part-time job that is more interesting, maybe in a different field.

What is Ann's problem really? Is it homemaking? Is it insecurity? Perhaps. But a compelling explanation can be found in Ann's past life—a life in which she failed to learn positive solitude.

Ann had a great time at college. She studied enough to get a B average, but she partied a lot, too. As a freshman and sophomore, she lived in the dorms and had many friends, both female and male; she was always seen with them. Later she lived with three other girls in an apartment, but she also became involved with Alan and his fraternity life. Of course, Ann's parents were delighted with their popular daughter.

During the summers Ann worked a variety of jobs to help with college expenses. A history major, after graduation she worked three years in retail while seeing Alan steadily. When Alan was asked by his company to transfer to another city, they decided to get married. In the new city, she took a job in a real estate office, and after little more than a year she became pregnant and quit. A few years later she would find herself with all the trappings of contentedness, but deeply dissatisfied.

Ann is a young person who has never had to face herself. She has no positive solitude persona. If pressed, she will tell us that she is frightened of loneliness. She has not completed one of the great psychological tasks of youth and adolescence—separating from her parents and creating her own emotional stability. Perhaps she has lacked the courage to face her aloneness. Certainly, she has gone through all the motions of growing up without becoming independent emotionally, intellectually, or economically.

Contrast Ann with Charlotte.

Charlotte is also a young homemaker with preschool children. Charlotte's parents could not fully afford to pay for her college, so Charlotte went to a cooperative school where she would, throughout the year, work three months and then attend school for three months. Charlotte dated and partied in college, but she also put in many hours alone—studying and writing, deciding on how to make a secure future for herself. Her high grades reflected her concentration. Often her jobs took her to new cities where she knew only her co-workers. She spent many nights at home alone and many weekends alone exploring new places.

You can guess the rest of the story. Early in life Charlotte was thrust by circumstances into solitude and contemplation, while Ann spent all her time with others. Of the two, only Charlotte came to define her self. She instinctively learned how to be alone well, and in her times alone she reflects on who she is and what pleases her. Ann, on the other hand, knows herself only in the context of relationships, and she allows herself to be defined by them. When the relationships are not sufficient to boost her ego or to keep her intellectually stimulated—as in her relationship with her young children—Ann feels powerless.

Charlotte, too, has a relationship with her young children and her husband, but she also has one with herself: She creates time during the day to do things she wants to do alone, and she finds part-time work that fulfills long-term goals for her. On a daily basis she lives with a confidence that eludes Ann. Sensing that all relationships are temporary, Charlotte values them—indeed revels in them—for what they are right now, while knowing that she values her time with herself. She is less torn by having to choose between herself and her family. In a profound, confident way she knows that when relationships with others end—as when her children go to school or finally leave home—she can look forward to more time to enrich the relationship she has with herself.

The Charlottes of the world are a lot more fun to live with. They are more relaxed, and they are more able to defer their own gratifications for the sake of those around them. People like Ann are worried about how to find themselves, and they show their worry in a dozen small ways—like whining about getting time alone, but then not taking it, or taking time alone and then not knowing what to do with it. Paradoxically, within relationships it is selfish Charlotte who gives more of herself. Not only does she want to give more, she has more to give. She is an interesting, centered person, with developed, informed opinions and goals.

Yet Charlotte's accomplishment has not been easy. When you live within a relationship or multiple relationships, drawing on the positive solitude persona requires deliberate strategies. You must make a significant effort to maintain the persona, keeping your interest in skiing when your partner hates the snow or pursuing your education when your family would rather spend the money on something else. You want to be together, but you also want and need to be alone.

Vulnerability of the Persona in Relationships

In a positive solitude relationship, you maintain your individuality. You hold your self a bit apart from your relationships, while you continue to develop your positive solitude persona. A positive solitude relationship is the antithesis of romantic love in which two partners seem to become one. Instead, partners are indeed partners, and family members remain distinct individuals. The positive solitude relationship is the hallmark of enduring, respectful love. You continue to build your friendship with yourself, that trusted and amusing friend that you have come to know well. You understand your self, remember it, value it, refresh it. Within your relationships you will gain a new appreciation of its preciousness, and so will your partners, friends, and family.

Yet the positive solitude persona is vulnerable during transitions in relationships. Suppose you have spent many months or several years learning and enjoying positive solitude. What happens when you decide to enter an important relationship—take a lover, deepen a friendship, or have a baby? Just as though you had been in a relationship and lost it, there will be trade-offs. The experience will be something like saying goodbye to a friend, except, of course, that if you take the time to look, this friend will always be there for you. Having had positive solitude, you will find it costly to give up. You will have to learn new modes of living and new ways to fill the feedback gap. Remember that the persona includes a set of attitudes and skills that, once learned, can be tapped relatively easily.

When you enter a relationship after a time of positive solitude, it is natural to feel some relief. After all, you fit the cultural norms now. Whether you find an intimate relationship, make new friends, or have children, society will applaud. You will be tempted at such times to forget about positive solitude, even to downgrade it as a less important experience.

What you should do instead is to take time to reflect on your new situation and to mourn the loss of time spent with yourself. In a way you are saying goodbye to a friend. You will lose time alone to reflect, to appreciate, to be. You will lose precious time for deciding what is important in life. We toss away thinking time as though it were unimportant, but the fact is that in modern times frequent reflection on our lives is more important than ever. Time spent reflecting helps you to establish clear goals and strategies for your life. It helps you to feel settled in life and at peace with yourself. Historically people have had more structure in their lives than we have today. Whereas the feedback gap was once filled with survival needs, social repression, social mores, or common enemies, today few of these compel our behavior. With our modern freedoms comes the responsibility for deciding what to do with our lives. Self-generated values must fill the gap, else we fall into ennui or plain busyness. As social pressures fall, responsibility for life decisions rests with the individual, and it takes time to make such decisions. Within relationships it is much harder to find this time.

By choosing relationships, you may compromise some goals. You choose to raise children instead of becoming an artist. You choose to get married instead of becoming a globe-trotting journalist. There are real losses in these decisions.

By choosing relationships, you also take on some clear hardships—the complications of balancing other people's needs with your own, the demands of others on your time and energy, a loss of control over your environment. Having known positive solitude, you will be especially sensitive to these problems in relationships.

Because of our total conditioning toward relationships, it often takes a major crisis for us to recognize positive solitude in the first place. For the same reason, it will require a special effort to keep it alive when we are no longer alone. Yet when you are in relationships, you will still want to draw on and nurture your solitude persona.

Using the persona requires that you believe in your own healthy selfishness. Your own goals are just as important as the goals of those around you—even those, like your spouse and children, whom you choose to nurture.

You can let yourself become the flotsam tossed around on the waves of others' lives, or you can choose to be the current of your own. We need to hold ourselves apart from others, no matter how much we cherish them. The self can be violated in a relationship when the other person's needs are taken care of and ours are not.

The self is also violated when one person reveals himself or herself fully and the other holds back. As Americans, we are prone to being too self-disclosing in relationships. If one person really opens up and the other does not, the former risks feeling isolated and alienated. In dating situations, being open and personally revealing is one way to sell ourselves. Yet when we have told another person many of the intimate details of our lives and still no intimacy develops with him or her, we feel more isolated than ever.[1] In our search for mutual disclosure and commitment, we need to keep our integrity. Intimacies should be allowed to develop slowly, with trust built in on both sides. The persona is thus protected, and we maintain a sense of dignity.

In relationships you must also avoid the trap of losing yourself among couples. When you are in a relationship, it is important to find friends who understand positive solitude and individualism. In her fine book *Changes,* Liv Ullman asserts that she simply will not attend functions that are primarily oriented toward couples. The dynamics of such groups do not support a strong sense of self.

It is often suggested that singles should avoid couples because couples will only remind them of what they do not have. This suggestion is valid if the couple does not share their love with the single person. If the couple invite a single person to dinner and then talk to each other about each other and are not interested in discussing the single's personal life, as though it were too dull, or unloving, or risqué, then indeed they should be avoided. Cultivate couples who have enough love and sensitivity for three.

Fortunately, as we grow older, being coupled is naturally deemphasized. The heightened romance and sexuality of the teenage years and young adulthood is eventually put behind us. Individuality emerges ever stronger as we mature in our twenties and thirties. In the middle years, people, even those with children, are increasingly expected to stand on their own and to build identities of their own, and this emerging social expectation is healthy.

Valuing Time for Your Self

Whatever your relationships, you must make time for your self. You require time for your persona to be known and enjoyed and developed. It helps to find a place that nurtures solitude. I have found it helpful to go on a retreat at a particular yoga center that is the spiritual home for several hundred people. The men and women who live there and their guests practice a lifestyle based on personal health and growth. Part of their philosophy is to reduce the stimulations of the everyday world through practicing meditation, preparing simple vegetarian meals, eating meals in silence, and reducing socializing with the opposite sex. Before experiencing their lifestyle, I scoffed at the idea of eating my meals in silence ("What are meals for," I protested, "except conversations!"), and I thought that the separation of the sexes was certainly a religious anachronism. But I had a few things to learn!

Mealtimes at the center are a pleasure. Eating in silence does not exclude people, does not make you feel uncomfortable; instead it includes and helps you to relax. To sit in a large cafeteria filled with people who are eating thoughtfully and thankfully is peaceful. There are no social games, no conversations designed to impress or attract, no boring small talk. In the cafeteria men and women mostly sit on opposite sides so as not to distract each other; this practice is observed most strictly by the brothers and sisters who live there, and less strictly by visitors. There are no sexual overtones. We are alone—together.

The same sort of separation is a theme throughout the center. Men and women have separate saunas; they work in separate teams. The retreat is designed to help individuals meet themselves; it is not primarily a place for meeting others.

Until I had this experience of being alone in an environment that supports positive solitude, I had not realized how laden our everyday experience is with relationships, especially sexual ones. We live constantly with the self-consciousness of being attractive to the opposite sex. I was used to being looked at and sized up, first in terms of my sexual attractiveness and only later in terms of my personhood, and I realized how often I do the same. At the center I began to see people in a different light: not in terms of our relationship, but in terms of their health, composure, love, posture, and pleasantness. I learned to see individuals, rather than couples. I came to feel accepted as myself in these terms, too. Even professional roles can be dropped. After spending a couple of days at the retreat, it was actually shocking to be asked what I do for a living. From my centeredness and wholeness, it was an effort to respond to someone who would define me merely in terms of one factor in my life.

At the retreat I feel wonderful—peaceful—centered—alone and ready and open. As I drive home, I can feel the waves of stimulation begin to wash over me. Still, I have been able to carry many of these positive feelings over into my everyday existence.

Sharing Positive Solitude

We must communicate our need for positive solitude to our partners. Ideally, your partners will know or will soon come to understand the importance of positive solitude in your life. I have enjoyed showing a particular wry poem to friends who want to get a fast, though by know means complete, idea of what I mean. Here is "The Voice":

Safe in the magic of my woods
I lay, and watched the dying light.
Faint in the pale high solitudes,
And washed with rain and veiled by night,
Silver and blue and green were showing.
And the dark woods grew darker still;
And birds were hushed; and peace was growing
And quietness crept up the hill;
And no wind was blowing.

And I knew
That this was the hour of knowing
And the night and the woods and you
Were one together, and I should find
Soon in the silence the hidden key
Of all that had hurt and puzzled me—
Why you were you, and the night was kind,
And the woods were part of the heart of me.

And there I waited breathlessly,
Alone; and slowly the holy three,

The three that I loved, together grew
One, in the hour of knowing,
Night, and the woods, and you—
And suddenly
There was an uproar in my woods.

The noise of a fool in mock distress,
Crashing and laughing and blindly going,
Of ignorant feet and a swishing dress,
And a Voice profaning the solitudes.

The spell was broken, the key denied me
And at length your flat clear voice beside me
Mouthed cheerful clear flat platitudes.

You came and quacked beside me in the wood.
You said, "The view from here is very good!"
You said, "It's nice to be alone a bit!"
And, "How the days are drawing out!" you said.
You said, "The sunset's pretty, isn't it?"
. . . . .
By God! I wish—I wish that you were dead.[2]

Transitions

When you join and then leave important relationships to live
primarily by yourself, the positive solitude persona is once again
vulnerable. Once again you will mourn. You will be asked to look into
your heart, and seeing people stripped away from you, you will be
afraid. You will face pressures from friends, family, and society to live
your life according to the way others have lived theirs. You will be
asked to justify their choices by making similar ones in your life. Yet
you wouldn't choose your career because it was your parent's career,
and you should not make your decisions about solitude and relationships for that reason either.

That being alone is an acceptable way to live is an idea that has
gained popularity only in the past twenty years. That being alone is
a joyful, powerful way to live is still a new idea. Though more people

are living alone than at any time in history, society's attitudes toward these people are slow to change. "The singles scene" is now a recognized segment of American life, but it is not as prestigious as the society of conventional relationships. Most people still harbor within themselves the belief that the ideal state of living is being part of a couple. People alone still find in society's attitudes a tyranny of togetherness.

While feminists have succeeded in adopting "Ms." as a way of avoiding being identified primarily in terms of their relationships, all of us, women and men, single or coupled, are still filling out forms that ask us to identify our status as "single, married, or divorced." In many cases, our status as coupled or uncoupled, and certainly the reasons why we are uncoupled, is irrelevant. Most often an inquiry about our relationship status is merely a vestige of a time when being coupled was essential and being uncoupled had revealing, mostly negative, connotations. Yet filling out the form without protesting is the socially acceptable thing to do—and we think nothing of it.

As a society, including even our most innovative thinkers, we are still hung up on the simplistic belief that people need people, as though we are primitive folk who can survive only within the tribe. Change in the collective consciousness is slow, and we can also regress. An increasingly positive climate towards singles—what some have too soon called a revolution—is now threatened by the increased incidence of venereal diseases and AIDS. Homosexuals are increasingly ostracized from society. As AIDS enters the heterosexual population, will single people also be suspect? Already marriage has become more fashionable. Will we also revert to yet more conventional ideas about being alone?

We can be independent persons without denying that we *recognize the pleasures of being together with others;* we can be independent persons without denying that *there are benefits in working together with others;* and we can be independent persons without denying the fact that *society, in order to function, requires individuals to feel some responsibility for others.*

You will recognize your positive solitude persona in your ability to face the fear of being alone. You will know it by your mature knowledge of the problems and prejudices that people alone face. You will experience it in the thoughtful, nondefensive, approach that you take to being alone. Having experienced positive solitude, you will know how central it is to your own personhood.

If we who have thus strengthened our selves can recognize each other in the shared phrase "I have known positive solitude," it will give us great joy.

Notes

1. Helen L. Wintrob, "Self Disclosure as a Marketable Commodity," in Mohammadreza Hojat and Rick Crandall, eds., *Loneliness: Theory, Research, and Applications,* special issue of the *Journal of Social Behavior and Personality* 2, no. 2, Part 2 (1987): 77–88.

2. Rupert Brooke, "The Voice," in *The Collected Poems of Rupert Brooke* (New York: Dodd, Mead & Co., 1915), 88.

Selected Bibliography

Bernikow, Louise. *Alone in America.* Boston: Faber and Faber, 1986.

Curtin, Mary Ellen, ed. *Symposium on Love.* New York: Behavioral Publications, 1973.

Ehrlich, Gretel. *The Solace of Open Spaces.* New York: Viking Penguin, 1985.

Emerson, Ralph Waldo. "Society and Solitude." In Carl Bode, ed. *The Portable Emerson.* New York: Viking Penguin, 1981.

Frankl, Victor. *Man's Search for Meaning.* New York: Simon & Schuster, 1959.

Hartog, Joseph, J. Ralph Audy, and Yehudi Cohen. *The Anatomy of Loneliness.* New York: International Universities Press, 1980.

Hojat, Mohammadreza, and Rick Crandall. *Loneliness: Theory, Research, and Applications.* San Raphael, CA: Select Press, 1987.

Horton, Paul C. *Solace, the Missing Dimension in Psychiatry.* Chicago: University of Chicago Press, 1981.

Koller, Alice. *An Unknown Woman.* New York: Bantam Books, 1981.

Koller, Alice. *The Stations of Solitude.* New York: William Morrow and Company, Inc., 1990.

Lebeaux, Richard. *Thoreau's Seasons.* Amherst, MA: University of Massachusetts Press, 1984.

Maslow, Abraham H. *The Farther Reaches of Human Nature.* New York: Penguin Books, 1971.

May, Rollo. *Existential Psychology.* New York: Random House, 1960.

Merton, Thomas. *Love and Living.* San Diego: Harcourt Brace Jovanovich, 1979.

Moustakas, Clark E. *Individuality and Encounter.* Cambridge, MA: Howard A. Doyle Publishing Company, 1968.

Moustakas, Clark E. *Loneliness and Love.* Englewood Cliffs, NJ: Prentice-Hall, 1972.

Peplau, Letitia Anne, and Daniel Perlman, eds. *Loneliness: A Sourcebook of Current Theory, Research and Therapy.* New York: John Wiley & Sons, 1982.

Porte, Joel. *Emerson and Thoreau: Transcendentalists in Conflict.* Middletown, CT: Wesleyan University Press, 1965.

Reynolds, David K. *The Quiet Therapies: Japanese Pathways to Personal Growth.* Honolulu: University Press of Hawaii, 1980.

Riesman, David. *The Lonely Crowd.* New Haven, CT, and London: Yale University Press, 1950.

Sarton, May. *Journal of a Solitude.* New York: W. W. Norton, 1973.

Seabrook, Jeremy. *Loneliness.* New York: Universe Books, 1975.

Slater, Philip E. *The Pursuit of Loneliness.* Boston: Beacon Press, 1970.

Storr, Anthony. *Solitude: A Return to the Self.* New York: The Free Press, 1988.

Suedfeld, Peter. *Restricted Environmental Stimulation.* New York: John Wiley & Sons, 1980.

Thoreau, Henry David. *Walden.* Boston: Houghton Mifflin Company, 1960.

Weiss, Robert S. *Loneliness, the Experience of Emotion and Social Isolation.* Cambridge, MA: MIT Press, 1975.

Index